# CHICAGO

## FODOR'S TRAVEL PUBLICATIONS

are compiled, researched, and edited by an international team of travel writers, field correspondents, and editors. The series, which now almost covers the globe, was founded by Eugene Fodor in 1936.

### OFFICES
New York & London

*Fodor's Chicago:*

**Editor:** Audrey Liounis
**Area Editors:** Alfred S. Borcover, Shirley Rose Higgins, Allen and Carla Kelson, Dan Kening, Katherine Rodeghier
**Illustrations:** Ted Burwell, Michael Kaplan, Sandra Lang
**Maps and Plans:** Pictograph

# FODOR'S
# CHICAGO
# 1988

FODOR'S TRAVEL PUBLICATIONS, INC.
New York & London

ISBN 0-679-01495-0
ISBN 0-340-41837-0 (Hodder & Stoughton)

MANUFACTURED IN THE UNITED STATES OF AMERICA
10 9 8 7 6 5 4 3 2 1

# CONTENTS

# FOREWORD

While every care has been taken to ensure the accuracy of the information contained in this guide, the publishers cannot accept responsibility for any errors that may appear.

All prices quoted in this guide are based on those available to us at the time of writing. In a world of rapid change, however, the possibility of inaccurate or out-of-date information can never be totally eliminated. We trust, therefore, that you will take prices quoted as indicators only, and will double-check to be sure of the latest figures.

Similarly, be sure to check all opening times of museums and galleries. We have found that such times are liable to change without notice, and you could easily make a trip only to find a locked door.

When a hotel closes or a restaurant produces a disappointing meal, let us know, and we will investigate the establishment and the complaint. We are always ready to revise our entries for the following year's edition should the facts warrant it.

Send your letters to the editors of Fodor's Travel Publications, 201 E. 50th Street, New York, NY 10022. Continental or British Commonwealth readers may prefer to write to Fodor's Travel Guides, 9-10 Market Place, London W1N 7AG, England.

# INTRODUCTION

*The Ultimate American City*

by
**ALFRED S. BORCOVER**

*Alfred S. Borcover is travel editor of the* Chicago Tribune *and a past president of the Society of American Travel Writers.*

Chicago is the heartland of America and the ultimate American city. Almost any Chicagoan will tell you that. Not because Chicagoans are chauvinistic, mind you, but just because it is so. What you see is what you get in this matter-of-fact city.

Wherever you look, from the glorious lakefront to the sprawling neighborhoods, from the soaring skyscrapers to the screeching elevated trains, you see the fabric of America and the forces that built this city of 3 million that is the ultimate melting pot. Beyond it lies the all-American dream, the suburbs with another 4 million.

You name it and Chicago has it or has been an integral part of it. Architecture. The skyscraper took its form here. Atomic energy. The first sustained nuclear chain reaction was achieved here. Art. Just wander through the Art Institute of Chicago, the Museum of Contemporary Art, the new Terra Museum of American Art, or view the city's collection of plaza art. Music. The Chicago Symphony is world renowned. Business. Education. Finance. Ballet. Opera. Industry. Theater. Publishing. It's all here. Chicago has given the world great writers, Nobel laureates, social reformers, and a saint, as well as a goodly share of sinners.

Chicago owes much of its greatness to its crossroads position. Jets roar in and out of Chicago's O'Hare International Airport by the minute, making it the world's busiest. O'Hare is in the midst of expansion and its new look is best exemplified by United Airlines' "Terminal for Tomorrow."Midway Airport also continues to undergo renewal as a convenient-to-downtown domestic hub. On Lake Michigan, ships still carry ore to the steel mills in nearby Gary and East Chicago and imports from distant lands via the St. Lawrence Seaway to Chicago. And Chicago in turn sends machinery and grain from the Midwest to destinations around the world. As it has been for decades, Chicago also remains the nation's rail hub, not only for freight but for Amtrak passenger service to the East and West coasts and the South.

Chicago, always on the move, changes as quickly as its fickle weather. Some old buildings disappear, for example, and new ones sprout, making Chicago a collection of architectural styles. Few things stay the same, although old perceptions of the city linger. They are difficult to dispel. In 1916 Carl Sandburg succinctly captured Chicago when he wrote about "Hog Butcher for the World . . . City of the Big Shoulders." But the stockyards and the hogs are long gone. The shoulders are still big, but not in the sense of pure brawn that Chicago used to display. Later, Nelson Algren wrote "Chicago: City on the Make." The city still hustles, but in a more refined way.

### Class Takes Over

Chicago acknowledges its global greatness, but it is unpretentious about it. It doesn't display the lofty airs of a New York or Paris, just a resoluteness to be Chicago and succeed with its own style, from crass to world-class.

In appearance, class wills out at Chicago's unmatched lakefront, 29 miles of verdant parkland backed by spectacular high-rise condominiums and apartments as well as the downtown skyline. Not just a stretch of green, the lakefront embraces yacht and sailboat harbors, tennis courts, a golf course, bicycle and jogging trails, beaches, picnic facilities, the Lincoln Park Zoo, even a chess pavilion. During the summer, the lakefront serves as a metropolitan resort. During the winter, the lake, white with ice floes, takes on an Arctic mood. Throughout the year Lake Michigan acts as a thermostat that can cool the lakeshore in the summer and warm it in the winter. It also adds to the air the moisture for monumental snowstorms.

Class takes other forms along Michigan Avenue's ever-expanding Magnificent Mile and the Loop, the city's two main commercial areas. The glamorous stretch of North Michigan Avenue between the Chicago River and Oak Street Beach is lined with such landmarks as the 100-story John Hancock Center, Water Tower Place, Olympia Centre, Tribune Tower, the Wrigley Building, and the old Water Tower, a survivor of the Great Chicago Fire of 1871. Interspersed between the new One Magnificent Mile shopping and residential tower and the river are great hotels, superb stores, fine restaurants, innovative architecture, luxury condominiums—all expressions of an elegant standard of living.

A new Cityfront Center of office high rises, a plaza, a hotel, and a rehabbed warehouse adds a dramatic addition to the skyline east of Michigan Avenue and Tribune Tower.

Chicago's Loop, the central downtown with a slightly less affluent shopping appeal, nevertheless is dotted with new dramatic glass and steel skyscrapers and plazas decorated with outdoor sculpture by Pablo Picasso, Marc Chagall, Alexander Calder, and Joan Miró. The modern towers include the Civic Center, the First Chicago complex, State of Illinois Building, Xerox, and the Federal Center, all guarded by the 110-story Sears Tower, tallest building in the world. Shoppers flock to State Street, that great street, now a pedestrian mall that's getting a new look. Chicago's financial hub throbs on La Salle Street in the brokerage houses, the big banks, the Midwest Stock Exchange, and the Board of Trade. Yet another commercial center lies along Wacker Drive and the west side of downtown, marked by Presidential Towers and the shimmering glass Northwestern Center.

The old steel elevated train structure that frames the five-by-seven-block Loop is anything but delicate no matter how many coats of paint it wears. Even the bridges that span the Chicago River wear their rivets like badges of honor. It's all part of the Loop's masculine environment. The plazas, however, with splashing fountains, shady trees, and seasonal flowers add human touches to a city where form usually follows function. None of this diminishes the fact that Chicago always seems to say, "I'm tough and don't forget it."

## Ethnic Pockets

As if to prove the point, a mile beyond Chicago's pretty face lie declining areas and the projects such as Cabrini-Green, where the people are poor and the gangs prevail. Farther west the skyline flattens out, punctuated only by smokestacks, water tanks atop buildings, and church steeples. Tucked in between are the shot-and-a-beer neighborhoods, rows of bungalows, three-flats, and gingersnap brick homes. That view to the west seems to go on and on as the endless prairie unfolds.

As one observer described Chicago, "It's the town with a Queen Anne front and a Mary Ann back."

The neighborhoods, the city's ethnic pockets, keep changing, but you can identify many by the signs and grocery store merchandise. Chicago's hearty Midwest stock is derived from the early waves of Poles, Germans, Irish, Italians, Greeks, Scandinavians, Bohemians, Lithuanians, Ukrainians, and Czechs and joined by blacks, Hispanics, and Orientals. And thus there are several Greektowns, enclaves of Italians around the University of Illinois-Chicago Campus, Latinos in Pilsen, Scandinavians in Andersonville, Irish in Bridgeport, and blacks on the south and west sides. Even a Chinatown. Add to this the University of Chicago crowd in Hyde Park, lakefront liberals in Lincoln Park and Streeterville, and a mix of everything in New Town and Rogers Park. New neighborhoods, born of gentrification, include River North, Printer's Row, West Loop, and Lincoln Square.

While Chicagoans cling to their neighborhoods, they, along with visitors share a common playground—that marvelous lakefront with its diverse activities, athletic as well as cultural. On a summer evening, downtown Grant Park attracts tennis players, softball teams, cyclists, and joggers while the Grant Park Symphony lures its own audience to the James C. Petrillo Music Shell. On a flawless July night, 750,000 people jammed the park for a triple-header: *A Taste of Chicago* (a week-long food celebration with some 80 restaurants serving their specialties), a free concert, and spectacular fireworks set off to Tchaikovksy's "1812 Overture."

A gentle breeze off the lake drifted across the eight-lane OuterDrive and through the park's tree line, caressing the listeners fanned out from the bandshell in the vast expanse of green. Another cultural treasure, the modern wing of the Art Institute and the adjoining Goodman Theater, formed a pleasant wall across the street to the west of Grant Park. Farther west along Michigan Avenue stood a mix of grandiose architectural styles from decades ago.

The sterile 80-story Standard Oil Building and the glass facade and sloped roof of the 41-story Associates Center monopolized the view to the north, along with the 41-story Prudential Building, the city's tallest in the mid-1950s, and farther north, the Illinois Center complex.

Evident at the concert was a mix of young picnickers, elderly groups on an outing, politicians, the stylishly affluent, and down-at-the-heels residents representing Chicago's rich ethnic mix. Every walk of Chicago life was enjoying the cultural evening and the dramatic setting, both products of a city driven by achievement.

## Over 150 Years of Greatness

In 1983, Chicago marked the 150th anniversary of its incorporation as a town and in 1987 celebrated its 150th birthday as a city. Chicago has managed to thrive and survive on adversity from its earliest swampy days. It rebuilt with abandon and verve after the Great Chicago Fire of 1871 left most of the city in rubble. By 1893 Chicago was hosting the Columbian Exposition, a great world's fair. Today, the glorious building that houses the Museum of Science and Industry stands as a lasting reminder that Chicago did things in big ways, even then.

It was the farsightedness of city fathers that made the lake a treasure. In the late 1800s, the Chicago River carried the city's waste into Lake Michigan, polluting the water supply and creating typhoid epidemics. Engineers devised an ingenious scheme to reverse the flow of the river, which, in turn, preserved the lake for the people.

While engineers were reversing the course of the Chicago River, a remarkable feat, Chicago's architects were producing buildings that reached for and scraped the sky. William Le Baron Jenney started the style, and the greats that followed are legend—Louis Sullivan, Dankmar Adler, Frank Lloyd Wright, Ludwig Mies van der Rohe, Bertrand Goldberg, Harry Weese, Helmut Jahn, and Bruce Graham. And let's not forget Daniel Burnham, whose grand design shaped much of today's Chicago.

Over the years, Chicago also has provided the environment for Jane Addams, Carl Sandburg, Nelson Algren, Saul Bellow, Studs Turkel, and such institutions as the Art Institute, Lyric Opera, and the Chicago Symphony, oft described as the finest orchestra in the world. With equal fervor, Chicagoans support their sports teams, once perennial losers, but now sometime contenders. The darlings, of course, are the Chicago Bears, the National Football League's 1986 Super Bowl XX champions. Both the Cubs and White Sox have won baseball division championships in the 1980s. The Bulls have made it to the playoffs in basketball; so have the Black Hawks in hockey. The Sting won a championship in soccer. For every fan, though, it's usually "wait until next year."

For several years Chicago moved tentatively toward a 1992 World's Fair, but soaring costs, dwindling civic support, and city and state politics scuttled the effort. Now efforts are afoot to build new stadiums for the Chicago Bears and Chicago White Sox. Chicago continues to struggle to overcome its past and come to grips with its contradictions. Those who seek to make Chicago a world-class city have lost sight of the fact that it is. Politically, the city has been groping for leadership since the death in 1976 of Richard J. Daley, the mayor who ruled Chicago for 21 years. A snowstorm did in Mayor Michael Bilandic and Mayor Jane Byrne did in Mayor Jane Byrne. Today, Harold Washington, Chicago's first black mayor and first mayor to be reelected to a second term since Daley, still struggles to reform a classic political city that sometimes is and sometimes is not ready for reform.

A *New York Times Magazine* article summed up Chicago's extremes:

"Chicago is a blunt, quid-pro-quo, punch-in-the-nose city that could in all its tumult harbor Al Capone and Mother Cabrini, the first American saint; Eugene Debs, the Socialist, and Milton Friedman, the conservative economist; the first sustained chain reaction, which launched the nuclear age, and a nuclear-freeze advocate named Joseph Cardinal Bernardin, the city's archbishop."

The beat goes on and on in the city that some people love to hate, but most simply forgive and love. Every day in Chicago is a new chapter, a new day of drama.

# PLANNING YOUR TRIP

# PLANNING YOUR TRIP

**WHEN TO GO.** Guidelines once dictated by school schedules and rigidly set vacation times are no longer true in this changing world. When you go is pretty much determined by what you want to do when you get there.

City-bound types really have their choice—Chicago with its wealth of museums, entertainment, and excellent shopping possibilities is a special delight just before Christmas, when State Street stores welcome Santa with eye-opening window displays and tempting gifts. January with its bountiful discount sales offers unexpected fringe benefits. There is so much going on in the city at any time that it is up to travelers to decide whether they prefer a summer sightseeing boat trip on the lake or a winter view of that snowy shore from the comfort of a cozy rooftop dining room.

Yes, it can get brisk in this region in midwinter and Chicago has recently been buried under several newsmaking blizzards. So do bring the woolies. Temperatures in the teens are not uncommon, but neither are those in the 30s. Weather patterns seem to be changing and there have been a number of very mild winters. Windchill factors often tend to make it all sound rather more ominous than it is. There is no disputing it can be quite raw and damp in winter, then equally humid in summer when temperatures climb into the 90s during hot spells. But there is plenty of glorious weather too and there are so many worthwhile indoor attractions that weather need not be a factor.

A word about that wind and the lake effect. Lake Michigan has a marvelous cooling effect in summer and a moderating effect in winter. Areas on the shore can be many degrees cooler in summer and many degrees warmer in winter than places farther inland. It may come as a surprise to learn that in terms of wind velocity Chicago ranks seventeenth among major American cities.

There are a few interesting stories on how Chicago got nicknamed "The Windy City," and none of them has anything to do with the weather. It seems that way back in one of those whoop-and-holler elections the city seems to prefer, one candidate generated so much hot air during the campaign that eastern papers began to label Chicago the Windy City. The term stuck and is now part of the vernacular. However, there are admittedly places downtown on a brisk day where the combination of open plazas, tall buildings, and wind currents will make you inclined to believe otherwise.

**PACKING.** *What to take, what to wear.* Where you are staying and what you plan to do will determine the kind of clothes you need. Obviously a super deluxe hotel, dinner at posh restaurants, and evenings at the theater call for a dressier wardrobe than staying at a motel, frequenting museums and moderate-priced restaurants. Men will want a jacket for dining out. Also keep

9

in mind the city's changeable climate and always be prepared by bringing something to get through a weather emergency, whatever the season.

 **CLIMATE.** There are almost always breezes off the Lake. This is more desirable in the summer—and remember that downtown Chicago has a beachfront—than in the winter, when gales can knock you off your feet. Below is a table of weather by month, but "rainfall" in wintertime (mid-November to mid-March) will most likely mean snow, and more snow, which is measured as melted down.

*Daily Average Temperature (F)*

| | | | |
|---|---|---|---|
| January | 25 | July | 74 |
| February | 27 | August | 73 |
| March | 36 | September | 66 |
| April | 48 | October | 55 |
| May | 58 | November | 40 |
| June | 68 | December | 29 |

 **TIPS FOR BRITISH VISITORS. Passports.** You will need a valid passport and a U.S. Visa (which can only be put in a passport of the 10-year kind). You can obtain the visa either through your travel agent or directly from the *United States Embassy,* Visa and Immigration Department, 5 Upper Grosvenor St., London W1A 2JB (01–499 3443).

No vaccinations are required for entry into the U.S.

**Customs.** If you are 21 or over, you can take into the U.S.: 200 cigarettes, 50 cigars, or 3 lbs. of tobacco; 1 U.S. quart of alcohol; duty-free gifts to a value of $100. No alcohol or cigarettes may be included in this gift exemption, but up to 100 cigars may be. Be careful not even to try to take in meat or meat products, seeds, plants, fruits, etc. And avoid narcotics like the plague.

**Insurance.** We heartily recommend that you insure yourself to cover health and motoring mishaps with *Europ Assistance,* 252 High St., Croydon CR0 1NF (tel. 01–680–1234). Their excellent service is all the more valuable when you consider the possible costs of health care in the U.S.

**Air Fares.** We suggest that you explore the current scene for budget flight possibilities, including *Virgin Atlantic Airways.* Be warned, however, that these cut-rate flights are fiendishly hard to come by, so be sure to book well in advance. Check, also, on APEX and other money-saving fares, as quite frankly, only business travelers who don't have to watch the price of their tickets fly full price these days—and find themselves sitting right beside an APEX passenger!

**Tour Operators.** Among the many tour operators who offer packages to Chicago, you may like to consider some of these as you plan your trip:

*American Airplan,* Marlborough House, Churchfield Rd., Walton-on-Thames, Surrey KT12 2TJ (0932–246166).

*Premier Holidays America,* 10 Rose Crescent, Cambridge, Cambs. CB2 3LL (0223–355977).

*Trekamerica,* Trek House, The Bullring, Deddington, Oxford OX5 4TT (0869–38777).

**Information.** For more information on Chicago, you can contact, in **England:** *United States Travel and Tourism Administration,* 22 Sackville St., London W1 (tel. 01–439–7433).

 **WHAT IT WILL COST.** This is a crucial question and one of the most difficult to answer. Even within Chicago there are some startling price differentials. A fairly well-located family-oriented motel could be as low as $60 double, with children free. One of the older but well-maintained big name hotels pretty much in the center of things might charge you $60 a night for a single and $70 for a double. Yet just down the street, gilt-edged prestige establishments on Michigan Avenue could easily cost twice that. Breakfast in one of those posh establishments might run to $10, while the budget conscious could eat in a coffee shop around the corner for $2.50. It is not uncommon to see a coffeeshop or fast-food-chain breakfast "to go" being carried across the lobby of one of those hotels.

For the above reasons, any talk of cost can be only a broad estimate. Two people who watch their spending carefully can travel in Chicago for $110 to $125 a day (not counting gasoline or other transportation costs, but considering lodging, meals, at least one museum admission, and even an evening drink). More typical expenses for two people for a day including a moderately priced room, three meals, a sightseeing tour, museum admission, and an evening drink range from $150 to $170.

The budget-minded traveler can also find bargain accommodations at Bed & Breakfast establishments covered in the Practical Information section. Many colleges and universities offer inexpensive accommodations to tourists during the summer vacations (some year-round) at single room rates of $7.00 to $16.00 per night, doubles from $6.00 to $10.00 per person, with meals around $3.50. A directory of 200 such opportunities all over the U.S. is *Mort's Guide to Low-Cost Vacations and Lodgings on College Campuses, USA–Canada,* from CMG Publishing Co., P.O. Box 630, Princeton, NJ 08540 ($5.00 postpaid). Included are such surprises as Barat College in Lake Forest, Evanston's National College of Education (both just outside Chicago), and Chicago's Roosevelt College.

A word of explanation. A 2 1/2-hour sightseeing bus tour of Chicago costs $10.00 per person, a 6-hour tour can cost $27.00 per person. Although many of the major museums have a $2.00 admission charge per person, they also have days when admission is free.

If you are budgeting your trip, don't forget to set aside a realistic amount for the possible rental of sports equipment, entrance fees to amusement and historical sites, etc. Allow for tolls for superhighways, extra film for cameras, and souvenirs.

After lodging, your next biggest expense will be food, and here it is possible to cut costs if you are willing to eat just one major restaurant meal a day. Lunch can vary between economical fast-food chains and some outdoor picnics as weather permits. Settling down at a park or rest area can add a more relaxing dimension to any trip and is especially good for those traveling with restless youngsters. Many travelers find it far more enjoyable to be out lunching at a picnic table surrounded by beautiful scenery than crowded into a restaurant at midday. Those so inclined will find it helpful to put together a picnic kit and be ready to enjoy the bountiful Midwest crop of melons, farm-grown tomatoes, fresh berries, and other seasonal favorites.

 **HOW TO GET THERE. By car:** I–80 in the northern part of Illinois comes in from neighboring Iowa and Indiana, and I–70 in the south crosses the Mississippi River from Missouri as the 2 major east-west highways. I–90 and I–94 approach Chicago from Wisconsin to the north and I–57 slices across the state from the Kentucky border on the south.

**By train:** *Amtrak* serves Chicago from major cities throughout the United States and cities on the Canadian rail systems. Check for schedules and costs with your travel agent or nearest Amtrak passenger station. Call 800–USA RAIL toll free from anywhere or 558–1075 from Chicago.

**By air:** Chicago currently has 3 airports. O'Hare is about 18 miles west of the downtown area, accessible by I–90, 294, and Ill.–53, and has long been rated the world's busiest airport. Midway Airport is off the Stevenson Expressway (I–55) bounded by 55th and 63rd streets about 1/2 hr. from downtown. Meigs Field is at 15th St. and the lakefront, less than 15 min. from downtown. Chicago's O'Hare Airport is served by numerous major airlines, including *Delta, Eastern, Northwest, United, American, Trans World, Piedmont, U.S. Air, Pan Am, Continental,* and *America West. Midstate Air Commuter United Express,* and *American Eagle* are other feeder airlines. There are also direct overseas flights via *Alitalia, Air France, British Airways, Lufthansa, K.L.M., Sabena, S.A.S., Icelandair, Swissair, Air Canada, Japan Airlines, Iberia, Yugoslav Airlines, El Al, Mexicana, Condor, LOT Polish, Philippine, Royal Jordanian, Cayman,* and *Ecuatoriana. Midway, Southwest, United, Continental, America West, Iowa Airways, Midstate,* and some *Northwest* flights fly into Midway Airport and private planes still use Miegs Field along the lakefront, although its future is always the subject of discussion. Allow plenty of airport time. O'Hare is under perpetual construction, resulting in confusion and delays; Midway is generally unkempt.

**By bus:** *Greyhound* and *Trailways* both serve Illinois from around the country. Consult a travel agent or the carriers directly: Greyhound at 74 W. Randolph; 781–2900, covers 48 states and Canada. Trailways at 20 E. Randolph; 726–9500, also has nationwide service.

**HOTELS AND MOTELS.** Don't take pot luck for lodgings. You'll waste a lot of time hunting for a place and often won't be happy with what you finally get. If you don't have reservations, begin looking early in the afternoon. If you have reservations, but expect to arrive later than 5:00 or 6:00 P.M., advise the hotel or motel in advance. Some places will not, unless advised, hold reservations after 6:00 P.M. And if you hope to get a room at the hotel's *minimum* rate, be sure to reserve ahead or arrive very early.

In addition to the hundreds of excellent independent motels and hotels throughout the country, there are also many that belong to national or regional chains. The insistence on uniform standards of comfort, cleanliness, and amenities is more common in motel than in hotel chains. Some travelers, however, prefer independent hotels because they are more likely to reflect the genuine character of the surrounding area.

Since the single biggest expense of your whole trip is lodging, you may well be discouraged and angry at the prices of some hotel and motel rooms, particularly when you know you are paying for things you neither need nor want, such as a heated swimming pool, wall-to-wall carpeting, a huge color TV set, two huge double beds for only two people, meeting rooms, a cocktail lounge, etc.

Prices in the budget chains are fairly uniform, but this is not the case in chains such as Ramada, Quality, Holiday Inn, Howard Johnson's, and TraveLodge. Their prices vary widely by location and season. Thus, in Illinois alone, two adults in one bed may pay $55.00 in a Springfield Holiday Inn and $117 at one in Chicago. Among the national nonbudget motel chains, the upper price range is occupied by Hilton, Marriott, and Sheraton; the middle range includes Holiday Inns, Howard Johnson, Quality Inns, and TraveLodge; and the least expensive are usually Best Western and Ramada. In the budget category, Days Inns, Royal 6, and Regal 8 Inn are in the Chicago area.

Hotels and motels in the Fodor's guidebooks are divided into five categories *(Super Deluxe, Deluxe, Expensive, Moderate, and Inexpensive),* arranged by price, and taking into consideration the degree of comfort you can expect to enjoy, the amount of service you can anticipate, and the atmosphere that will surround you in the establishment of your choice.

Limitations of space make it impossible to include every establishment. We have, therefore, listed those that we recommend as the best within each price range. Our ratings are flexible and subject to change.

Senior citizens may in some cases receive special discounts on lodgings. The *Days Inn* chain offers various discounts to anyone 55 or older. *Holiday Inns* give a discount to members of the NRTA (write to National Retired Teachers Association, Membership Division, 401 Grand Ave., Ojai, CA 93023). *Howard Johnson's Motor Lodges, Marriott, Quality Inns, Ramada Inns,* and *Sheraton* have all offered varying discounts to members of the AARP, the NRTA, the National Association of Retired Persons, the Catholic Golden Age of the United Societies of U.S.A., and the Old Age Security Pensioners of Canada. However, the amounts and availability of these discounts vary, so check their latest status.

*The National Council of Senior Citizens,* 925 15th St. NW, Washington, D.C. 20005, works especially to develop low-cost travel possibilities for its members.

**DINING OUT.** For evening dining, the best advice is to make reservations whenever possible. Most hotels have set dining hours.

Some restaurants are relatively fussy about customers' dress, particularly in the evening so it's wise to check ahead. But, standards of dress are generally becoming more relaxed, so a neatly dressed customer will usually experience no problem. If in doubt about accepted dress at a particular establishment, call ahead.

If you're traveling with children, you may want to find out if a restaurant has a children's menu and commensurate prices (many do).

When figuring the tip on your check, base it on the total charges for the meal, not on the grand total. Don't tip on tax.

The restaurants mentioned in this volume that are located in large metropolitan areas are categorized by type of cuisine: French, Chinese, Armenian, etc., with restaurants of a general nature listed as American-International. Restaurants are further divided into price categories as follows: *Super Deluxe, Deluxe, Expensive, Moderate,* and *Inexpensive.* As a general rule, expect restaurants in Chicago to be higher in price than what you may be used to, although many restaurants that feature foreign cuisine are surprisingly inexpensive. We should also point out that limitations of space make it impossible to include every establishment. We have, therefore, listed those we recommend as the best within each price range. Prices do not include alcoholic beverages, cover or table charges, tip, or extravagant house specialties.

**Chains:** There are now several chains of restaurants, some regional, some nationwide, that offer reliable eating at budget prices. Look for them as you travel and check local telephone directories in towns and cities where you stop. Chains that operate in the Chicago area are: *Arby's* (noted for roast beef); *Arthur Treacher's Fish and Chips* (low prices, Tuesday-night special); *Big Mac* (sit-down restaurants along with drive-in facilities); *Bob Evans Farm Restaurants* (good dollar value); *Brown's* (specializes in chicken); *Burger King; Church's* and *Kentucky Fried Chicken* (dish up all kinds of chicken); Holiday Inns (many have all-you-can-eat buffets and special days; nationwide); *Long John Silver* (nautical theme, specializes in seafood); *Marc's Big Boy* (burgers, but lots of other specials); *Mr. Steak* (children's portions, Senior Citizen discounts; entire Midwest); *Pizza Hut* (try their salads, too; nationwide); *Bakers Square* (regular menu, noted for variety of pies); *Ponderosa Steak House* (excellent all-you-can-eat salad bar, lots of specials); *Red Barn Restaurants* (all Midwestern states); *Red Lobster Inns of America; Popeye's* (fried chicken); *Taco Bell* (Mexican); *Chi Chi's* (Mexican); *White Castle* (good for budget breakfast, moderate meals). Even *McDonald's,* the granddaddy of them all, is changing its image. They range from highway drive-ins to two rather posh locations on Chicago's Michigan Avenue. One is in Water Tower Place, the other on the avenue.

**TIPPING.** Tipping is supposed to be a personal thing, your way of expressing your appreciation to someone who has taken pleasure and pride in giving you attentive, efficient, and personal service. Because standards of personal service in the United States are highly uneven, you should, when you get genuinely good service, feel secure in rewarding it, and when you feel that the service you got was slovenly, indifferent, or surly, don't hesitate to show this by the size, or withholding, of your tip. Remember that in many places the help are paid very little and depend on tips for the better part of their income. This is supposed to give them incentive to serve you well. These days, the going rate for tipping on restaurant service is 15% on the amount before taxes or 20% if service has been exceptional; and 15% for most other services as well.

If you check in with one or two bags in a top hotel, it is assumed you will give the bellboy $1.00. For one-night stays in most hotels and motels, you leave nothing. But if you stay longer, at the end of your stay leave the maid $1.00–$1.25 per day.

When taking a taxi 15% of the fare is an appropriate tip.

 **BUSINESS HOURS AND LOCAL TIME.** Illinois is on central time. Central Standard Time is six hours earlier than Greenwich Time, one hour earlier than Eastern Standard Time, and two hours later than Pacific Time. Most businesses keep about the same hours as do those in your own community. However, you will find that some stores stay open later than the usual 5:00, 5:30 or 6:00 P.M. closing, although hours do fluctuate considerably. It is the custom for many shops in suburban areas to close on Wednesday afternoon during the summer. Some gas stations also close on Sunday, so it is wise to fill your gas tank on Saturday.

Clocks "spring ahead" early in April when Standard Time changes to Daylight Saving Time, and "fall back" the last Sunday in October.

 **HOLIDAYS.** Most businesses, banks and many restaurants will be closed the following holidays (the dates are for 1988): New Year's Day, January 1; Washington's Birthday (observance), February 15; Easter Sunday, April 3; Memorial Day (observance), May 30; Independence Day, July 4; Labor Day, September 5; Thanksgiving Day, November 24; and Christmas Day, December 25.

In addition, banks and some businesses may be closed on Martin Luther King's Birthday, January 18; Lincoln's Birthday, February 12; Good Friday (from noon), April 1; Columbus Day (observance), October 10; Election Day (partially), November 8; Veterans Day, November 11.

**INFORMATION FOR DISABLED TRAVELERS.** One of the newest, and largest, groups to enter the travel scene is the handicapped, literally millions of people who are in fact physically able to travel and who do so enthusiastically when they know that they can move about in safety and comfort. Generally their tours parallel those of the non-handicapped traveler, but move at a more leisurely pace, and all the logistics are carefully checked out in advance. Important sources of information in this field are: 1) the book, *Access to the World: A Travel Guide for the Handicapped* by Louise Weiss, published by Henry Holt & Co. and available upon order from your local bookstore; 2) the *Travel Information Center,* Moss Rehabilitation Hospital, 12th Street and Tabor Road, Philadelphia, PA 19141; 3) *Easter Seal Society for Crippled Children and Adults,* Director of Education and Information Service, 2023 West Ogden Avenue, Chicago IL 60612 (tel. 243–8400). For a list of tour operators who arrange travel for the handicapped, write to: *Society for the Advancement of Travel for the Handicapped,* 26 Court Street, Brooklyn, NY 11242.

You can arrange tours for four or more through *Access Tours* (Suite 1801, 123–33 83rd Ave., Kew Gardens, NY 11415; 212–828–8334 or 800–533–5343) which specializes in tours and travel arrangements for the disabled.

Chicago's various private and public agencies offer art, culture, and a helping hand to the disabled visitor. Silent Sounds is a nonprofit arts organization that brings arts to all people through sign language. Obtain their schedule from Box 8205, Chicago, IL 60680 or (tel. 778–0910) or teletype 381–1640. Rehabilitation Institute of Chicago, 345 E. Superior St., Chicago, IL 60611 (tel. 908–6071), can offer helpful information. So can Access Living (tel. 226–5900), a private nonprofit agency with knowledge of everything from transportation to emergency wheelchair repair. The City of Chicago sponsors a referral service through their Information and Referral Service For Persons With Disability, 121 N. LaSalle, Room 703, Chicago, 60602 (City Hall). It maintains an access directory of Chicago (tel. 744–4016), T.D.D. number 744–6777. The Chicago Hearing Society also maintains a teletype line at 427–2166.

CAST, Chicagoland Advocates for Signed Theatre, 22 W. Monroe, Suite 806, Chicago, 60603 (tel. 341–6823) advises travelers where to find theatre interpreted in sign language for hearing impaired. T.D.D. number 341–6823.

Chicago Transit Authority's Special Service Department (tel. 664–7200) can arrange pickup in special vehicles at airports and train stations. Minimum cost. Several days notice required.

 **SECURITY.** To its great embarrassment, Chicago seems to be remembered worldwide for its infamous gangsters. And so-called gangland slayings still continue to generate national news. Yes, bodies do still turn up stuffed in trunks with some regularity, but these are strictly very professional, interorganizational killings and certainly not something a tourist has to worry about. But, like most major cities, Chicago does have a crime problem and the wise traveler takes the same precautions reasonable anywhere. Except for the

Magnificent Mile along Michigan Blvd., it is wise to be cautious about roaming around on foot at night. Don't stroll through parks after dark, keep your hotel door securely locked, don't carelessly leave valuables in your room, and ask at the desk about the safety of that particular neighborhood. Districts can go from ultra posh to poverty in blocks, and it's safe to walk in one direction, but not another. Use common sense in all things, particularly at night when muggers and purse snatchers lurk in even the best neighborhoods.

**SIGHTSEEING CHECKLIST.** Chicago of the 1980s is undergoing a building renaissance that has lasted over 25 years. Every day, construction is underway on one new skyscraper or another as the Loop and Near North Side literally transform themselves into modern-day wonders. But there's far more to Chicago than these two areas, and so we've compiled a checklist of "must see" places not only in the city, but in outlying areas as well. You may not get to see all of them in one visit, but Chicago's the kind of place that always welcomes the visitor for a second and different look. The following are the places to plan a first- or second-time visit around, but allocate your time carefully, virtually all of them can keep you longer than you anticipate.

**Sears Tower.** Now the tallest building in the United States, the Sears Tower, in the Loop at Wacker Drive between Adams and Jackson, is the place to go for an overview of downtown Chicago, the city's gorgeous lakefront, and the fascinating North Side. Just picking out the tops of distinctive buildings in and around the Loop can take a half hour or more.

**The Art Institute of Chicago** stands out as one of the city's (and the nation's) great repositories of European paintings (especially French). It also has an outstanding oriental collection, and you can usually count on at least one temporary exhibit of national or international stature.

**The Chicago Board of Trade.** Now in larger quarters at the foot of La Salle Street in the heart of the Financial District, the Board of Trade is a block-size building that is great to look at from the outside and better still to browse in on any business day. Try to witness the exciting close of trading on two great trading floors around 1:00 P.M.

**State Street, That Great Street.** Parts of the northern section are under renewal, but the street that made Chicago famous still stands as a major attraction, especially for daytime browsing along the mall-like walkways dotted with popcorn, nut, and snack stands. Here you'll find the home base of Marshall Field & Co., Carson, Pirie, Scott & Co., the Palmer House with its great lobby, and the city's Hot Tix Booth, a bonanza for theatergoers on a budget.

**The Chicago Public Library Cultural Center.** Don't let the somber facade at Michigan and Randolph turn you off: walk inside to a wonderland of Tiffany glass domes, modern comfortable reading areas, and a truly delightful room in Preston Bradley Hall, third floor south.

**Daley Center and the City Hall-County Building.** This complex of city and county offices plus a distinguished courthouse includes the Chicago Picasso, a lovely fountain, and a great cross section of the city. The new State of Illinois Building at the corner of Randolph and Clark is also worthwhile.

**Dearborn Street in the Loop.** From Madison to Jackson. Walking here is truly a great experience of seeing architecture blend the old with the new: First National Bank and its lower-level plaza; the ultramodern Xerox Building; the old Marquette Building with its colorful interior murals; and the Federal Center with the stunning sculpture *Flamingo*.

**Water Tower Place and Magnificent Mile.** This is a great area to begin or end a visit to Chicago. Water Tower Place is a throbbing vertical center of department stores, boutiques, restaurants, theaters, and even a world-class hotel, the Ritz-Carlton. And it's all within steps of Chicago's most distinctive landmark, the original Water Tower, which survived the great Chicago Fire of 1871. Buildings and shops along the Magnificent Mile, extending north and south of Water Tower, include the John Hancock Center, a Neiman-Marcus in Olympia Center, I. Magnin, Tiffany's, Elizabeth Arden, Saks Fifth Avenue, plus any number of art galleries, jewelry stores, etc.

**The Chicago Lakefront.** Seeing the city from Lake Michigan is truly a joy, and you can do so best by taking one of the boat rides from the Michigan Avenue Bridge over the Chicago River. Best time is toward the end of the day when the setting sun gives the whole city a soft, golden glow.

**Lincoln Park and Lincoln Park Zoo.** Animals freely roaming in large natural confines: apes and gorillas, lions and tigers, polar bears and giraffes. There's also a delightful Children's Zoo, an intriguing animal-filled Farm-in-the-Zoo, and one of the city's outstanding flora collections in the nearby Lincoln Park Conservatory. And it's all free.

**Grant Park Museums.** Located at Roosevelt Road and Lake Shore Drive south and east of the Loop, Field Museum of Natural History, John G. Shedd Aquarium, and Adler Planetarium always rank among the city's top attractions. The Field Museum especially is not to be missed, with its fantastically high entrance hall and labyrinth of lifelike exhibits depicting man and mammal from over the world since the beginnings of time.

**Museum of Science and Industry.** Located in Jackson Park on the city's South Side, this is a veritable wonderland of technology and nostalgia: exhibits touch on virtually all things scientific, mathematic, medical, and technological —from coal mining to agriculture, railroading, and nuclear energy, with a great exhibit on outer space.

**OUTLYING AREAS. Baha'i House** of Worship, on Sheridan Road at Linden Avenue in Wilmette. One of the area's outstanding architectural sights, a photographer's delight.

**Frank Lloyd Wright Prairie School of Architecture Historic District.** Dedicated to Wright and his colleagues, who literally changed the face of American homebuilding architecture early in the twentieth century. Most of it began right here in the western suburb of Oak Park in an area bounded by Harlem Avenue, Division, Clyde and Lake Streets.

**Brookfield Zoo,** in the suburb of Brookfield. Always well regarded, the zoo now has an added feature in its great dolphin show and Tropic World, an indoor rain-forest structure with all sorts of mammals and birds seemingly close enough to reach out and touch.

**O'Hare International Airport.** Just in volume of travelers and size alone, this is worth looking at, but there are other features too: an intriguing underground series of shops and restaurants, and a great cocktail lounge and dining room between two major terminals with great views of planes taking off and landing at a rate of one or more every minute.

**Fort Sheridan, Highwood.** This historic fort was established in 1887 and its 695 acres contain an impressive collection of buildings dating from the 1890s. Forty percent of the post has been designated a national historic landmark and is open to daytime visitors. Its vast property borders Lake Michigan and many special events are open to the public.

# CHICAGO

# CHICAGO FOR THE BUSINESS TRAVELER

by
**KATHERINE RODEGHIER**

If the Midwest is the Heartland, then Chicago is the heart of the nation—a hub of commerce and transportation.

The nation's largest convention and exhibition facility, McCormick Place, sprawls along the lakefront drawing more than half of the nation's largest trade shows and conventions. O'Hare International Airport, which vies with Atlanta's Hartsfield International for top billing as the world's busiest, continues to add terminals northwest of the central city. Most east-west Amtrak routes converge here at Union

Station and half a dozen interstate highways pass through the metropolitan area.

Business travel naturally gravitates to the midsection of the nation in spite of the rise of the Sun Belt and Chicago's loss to Los Angeles as the nation's second city.

## Getting Oriented

Getting your bearings in Chicago is easy once you recognize a few geographic landmarks. Lake Michigan is the eastern boundary, and from it flows the Chicago River, which divides downtown into two sections. North of the river lies Upper Michigan Avenue, the Magnificent Mile. This is the city's premier shopping and dining district. Many ad agencies and public-relations firms are located in this neighborhood. South of the river lies Chicago's Loop, a commercial district named for the elevated train tracks that surround it. The Loop contains Chicago's financial district—LaSalle Street—and most of its government buildings. Its concrete canyons are a den of lawyers, brokers, bankers, and bureaucrats.

As in most major metropolitan areas, Chicago's suburbs continue to grow as business districts. Business travelers heading in this direction may never see the central city. The western suburbs, from the village of Oak Brook west to the city of Aurora, are home to a handful of Fortune 500 companies scattered along the Illinois Research and Development Corridor, I-88. O'Hare International Airport draws business to the northwest suburbs, including the village of Rosemont, which has a convention and exposition center larger than that of many mid-size cities. The tollway that runs through the northern suburbs is lined with major corporations, including leaders in the drug and health-care industry.

Most air travel into Chicago comes to O'Hare International Airport about 20 miles northwest of the Loop, but the number of flights at Midway Airport, 15 miles southwest of the Loop, is increasing. Midway is much less congested and is often more convenient for business travelers bound for downtown Chicago or western suburbs. Both are served by cabs, limos, and motorcoaches that make regular runs to downtown hotels. Only O'Hare has an elevated subway line connecting the terminal with the Loop, and it's an excellent means of transport for anyone traveling in the daytime and carrying light luggage. Passengers board the subway below the baggage claim area and in 35 minutes are at Dearborn Station in the heart of the Loop. The fare is $1. A cab would cost about $30 and would take 45 minutes to more than an hour depending on traffic conditions.

A third airport, Meig's Field, handles a few commuter flights and a helicopter service. Located on the lakefront, it is a five to 10-minute cab ride to most downtown hotels.

Once in downtown Chicago cabs are usually plentiful and easily hailed. Buses and elevated trains are a viable alternative only if you know the city or are willing to study a transit map. Renting a car is impractical unless your business will take you to outlying neighborhoods or suburbs. In the central city, parking can be scarce and expensive. Given good weather conditions and enough time, walking is a good way of getting around downtown. With a few exceptions, streets are laid out in a grid pattern and the street numbering system is logical. Walkers should be able to make it from the Chicago Board of Trade on the south end of the financial district to Water Tower Place near the north end of Michigan Avenue in about half an hour.

For more information about all establishments listed below, see *Practical Information for Chicago,* later in this book.

## Places to Stay

Selecting a hotel, or rather a hotel location, that's close to where you'll be conducting your business can save time and taxi fares. In the Loop, the **Palmer House and Towers** (17 E. Monroe), just east of the State Street Mall, is within seven blocks of most government buildings and banks. If your business is in the financial district, an ideal location is the **Midland Hotel** (172 W. Adams), just off LaSalle. If you're in town to attend a show at McCormick Place, which lies about two miles south of the Chicago River at the lakefront, consider a South Loop location such as the **Essex Inn** (800 S. Michigan) or the **Chicago Hilton and Towers** (720 S. Michigan). The Hilton recently completed a $150-million renovation and added a large business center offering guests a full range of computer and secretarial services. The **McCormick Center Hotel** (23d Street and the Lake) is the only hotel connected to McCormick Place, but the neighborhood is not for walking, so any dining or entertainment outside the hotel would mean a 10- to 15-minute cab ride downtown.

From Illinois Center on the south side of the Chicago River, to Oak Street near the top of the Magnificent Mile, business travelers find a dizzying array of hotels. Choosing among them depends on personal taste and budget. Most of the major hotel chains have properties in this neighborhood, something to consider if you are a member of a frequent-traveler club. Hotels range from the modern skyscraper variety, such as the **Chicago Marriott** (540 N. Michigan), to the grand and elegant— **The Drake** (140 E. Walton). Some, such as the 2,033-room **Hyatt Regency Chicago** (151 E. Wacker), are cities in themselves, while others are small and intimate, such as the 139-room **Tremont** (100 E. Chestnut), which has a program of services and amenities designed specifically for women business travelers. Among the best hotel values near the Magnificent Mile is the **Richmont** (162 E. Ontario), which offers guests a complimentary Continental breakfast. Those on generous expense accounts might choose the understated elegance of the **Park Hyatt** (800 N. Michigan), or the glamor of the **Ritz-Carlton** (160 E. Pearson) in Water Tower Place. All-suite properties downtown include the **Lenox House** (616 N. Rush), and the **Barclay Hotel** (166 E. Superior), known for its exclusive dining club, and properties managed by the **Gold Coast Group** (312–943–0161). Business travelers weary of hotels might give **Bed and Breakfast-Chicago, Inc.** a call (312–951–0085) to arrange a stay in a private condo or town house.

Business travelers heading for the suburbs will find a wide range of chain hotels in both the O'Hare area and the Oak Brook area. The number of hotels near O'Hare has grown rapidly in the last three years with a new Radisson, an Embassy Suites, and a Hotel Sofitel joining Hyatt, Marriott, Sheraton, Hilton, Holiday Inn, Westin, and properties of other major hotel chains.

Because Chicago hosts so many major trade shows, hotel accommodations can be hard to come by when a "super show," such as the Consumer Electronics or the National Hardware Show, is in town. Book accommodations as far in advance as possible. Hotel reservation desks, located in airport baggage claim areas, assist travelers arriving without reservations.

### Dining Out

Chicago is a great restaurant town. Some of the Midwest's most innovative chefs turn out surprising creations in culinary art from kitchens here. Cuisine is as diverse and varied as the city itself, ranging from haute cuisine prepared and served in classic style to hearty pub grub served in back-room saloons with elbows-on-the-table ambience. Chicago's heritage as the melting pot of the Midwest has added flavor to local cuisine. Dozens of ethnic restaurants serve the native foods of Germany, Poland, Greece, China, Mexico, Thailand, Japan, India, Italy, and France—to name but a few. And then there are Chicago's native foods—thick prime steaks, the kind that used to come from the old Chicago stockyards, and thick Chicago-style pizza.

If you want to impress a business associate with your knowledge of the latest culinary trends, take him or her to **Foley's** (211 E. Ohio, 645–1261), where owner-chef Michael Foley redefines American cuisine with innovative combinations of fresh ingredients, such as fish and saffron stew, salmon stuffed with sun-dried tomatoes, and grilled veal medallions served with leeks. The menu emphasizes seafood with few red-meat dishes available. Clients will be impressed with the food and the setting of **La Tour** in the Park Hyatt (800 N. Michigan, 280–2230). Ask for a table or booth facing Chicago's historic water tower, a landmark set in a small park of trees and twinkling lights. Order champagne by the glass. Prix-fixe dinners feature seasonal specialties and are served with superb sauces and garnishes. If you want to go all out, hire a limo and head north to Wheeling, Illinois, and **Le Francais** (269 S. Milwaukee Avenue, 541–7470), which is often ranked by restaurant critics as one of the top five restaurants in the country. Chef-owner Jean Banchet was once asked why he chose a blue-collar suburb to operate a restaurant serving the finest in classical French cuisine. He reportedly replied that if you are good enough, people will seek you out. They do. Tables are reserved weeks, if not a month, in advance. The menu features some 60 items, and there are often another 30 specials made with ingredients that may have been flown in fresh that day. Dinner from pâté to soufflé may last three hours and cost $75 a person plus wine. Your guest departs feeling that he or she has not just had dinner with you, but that together you've achieved a culinary feat.

If your goal in entertaining a guest is not to make his jaw drop, but to simply enjoy a fine meal, you have many choices. If your dining companion enjoys a good steak, try **Morton's** (1050 N. State, 266–4820), which serves prime, dry-aged beef steaks, as well as veal, fish, and lobster. In place of a dinner menu, a waiter pushes a cart of fresh ingredients to your table and points out the raw steaks, the giant baked potato, and the fat tomato as he describes the salads and entrees featured that evening. If you have a taste for seafood, a good lunch or dinner choice is **Shaw's Crab House** (21 E. Hubbard, 527–2722), an old-fashioned seafood house serving raw oysters on the half shell, crab cakes, and lobster salad. Entrees change with availability. They may include fresh stone crab claws, salmon, trout, or lobster. The adjoining **Blue Crab Lounge** has an excellent oyster bar. If you're dining with an out-of-towner, try a room with a view. Request a window seat at the **95th,** located on the 95th floor of the John Hancock Building. Chicagoans might find it passé, but lunch and dinner guests enjoy the spectacular view of the lakefront as well as the well-prepared and expertly served American cuisine. A restaurant with a view of another sort is **The Pump Room** in the Omni Ambassador East Hotel (1301 N. State, 266–0360). People watchers eye Booth One where celebrities have been served since the 1930s when the hotel was the stopping-off point for stage and screen stars making the transcontinental trek between Broadway and Hollywood. It's a good "let's do lunch" spot and a quiet spot for dinner if you're seated away from the teensy dance floor and bar. The menu contains standard fare—steaks and chops.

If you're treating a business associate to breakfast, a stylish spot is the **Ciel Bleu** on the 19th floor of the Mayfair Regent Hotel (181 E. Lake Shore Drive, 787–8500). This fine French restaurant is a good choice for lunch or dinner, but the soft east light of morning over the lake makes it a memorable spot to begin the business day. Croissants come with a spectacular view of Oak Street beach and the Lake Michigan shoreline.

When meeting friends for lunch or an evening of fun and it doesn't matter who's picking up the check, head west of the Loop to Greek Town and the **Greek Islands** (200 S. Halsted, 782–9855). Begin with *saganaki,* a flaming cheese dish, and move on to braised lamb, mousaka, or dolmades. Can't decide? Choose a family-style meal featuring a selection of Greek dishes. If there's a sports fan in your crowd, check out **Ditka's** (223 W. Ontario, 280–1790), owned by Chicago Bears coach Mike Ditka and frequented by sports personalities and fans. Dinner appetizers include Harry Caray's fried calamari and entrees include Tom Lasorda's linguini and clam sauce and Ditka's pork chops. The lunch menu features Jack Brickhouse's chili and cheese chopped steak.

If you are trimming your expense account, try lunch or dinner at **The Berghoff** (17 W. Adams, 427–3170), a German restaurant that has been serving customers in the Loop since the end of the last century. Inside it resembles a Munich beer hall. The restaurant has house brands of beer and root beer and serves moderately priced German dishes, including schnitzel and sauerbraten. Chicago-style pizza, the deep-dish knife-and-fork variety, makes for an economical meal, and an evening spent in a graffiti-covered pizzeria is a true Chicago experience. **Pizzeria Uno** (29 E. Ohio, 321–1000) and the larger **Pizzeria Due** (619 N. Wabash, 943–2400) are operated by Ike Sewell, creator of Chicago pizza. A tough competitor is **Gino's East** (160 E. Superior, 943–1124). Cheap eats are part of the novelty at **Ed Debevic's** (640 N. Wells, 664–1767), a zany knockoff of a 1950s rural roadside diner. Gum-chewing waitresses, booths with built-in juke boxes, and a garish sign that commands, "Eat at Ed's," are just some of the reasons customers stand in line for more than an hour on Friday and Saturday nights for a seat at a formica table. Another reason is the food—good, down-home fare such as meat loaf, chicken, fried steak, and pot roast, all priced around $5.

If you're dining alone, ask for a stool at Ed's lunch counter. The menu is the same but the wait is shorter. A solo diner might also enjoy the all-you-can-eat Chinese buffet luncheon at the **Szechwan House** (600 N. Michigan, 642–3900) or a quiet table where he or she can study the dinner menu containing 112 items. Among the specialties are Szechwan crab claws, governor's chicken, and phoenix and dragon (chicken and lobster). A comfortable spot for dining alone is **Rue St. Clair** in the Richmont Hotel (640 St. Clair, 787–6907). This cozy little bistro has the casual feeling of a Parisian café. Lunch and dinner choices include light entrees as well as meat, fowl, and fish dishes and an array of tempting desserts.

## On the Town

After-dinner diversions in Chicago range from nightclubbing, to theater, to bar hopping.

Chicago has a reputation as a theater town. Its Off-Loop theaters, such as the award-winning **Steppenwolf Theater Company** (2851 N. Halsted), are noted for their innovation, while downtown theaters, such as the **Schubert** (22 W. Monroe), stage Broadway hits. The **Chicago Theater** (175 N. State), which reopened in 1986 after a $4-million renovation restored it to its grandeur of 50 years ago, stages musicals and concerts by big names such as Frank Sinatra. Information on what's playing in Chicago is available by phoning 977–1755 and tickets can be ordered by calling 853–0505. Half-price, day-of-performance tickets to many shows are often available from the Hot Tix booth at 24 S. State Street.

If you enjoy comedy, don't miss **Second City** (1616 N. Wells), which has nurtured the talents of Bill Murray, Valerie Harper, and others. The troop's second-string players of improvisational comedy perform next door at **Second City, Etc.** (1608 N. Wells). **Zanies, Chicago** (1548 N. Wells), a comedy club where it's often standing room only on weekends, books some of the best wits in the Windy City.

If you and the person you are entertaining are music fans, stop by one of Chicago's live entertainment spots for a few sets after dinner. For jazz try **George's** just west of Michigan Avenue (230 W. Kinzie); for blues make it **Blue Chicago** (937 N. State) in the Rush Street neighborhood.

Rush Street has long had a reputation as the place to spend a night on the town in Chicago. The late-night bars and nightclubs along Rush and Division streets have attracted conventioneers, out-of-towners, and suburbanites for years. Recently Rush Street has been overshadowed by Ontario Street, west of Michigan Avenue, as an after-dinner entertainment spot. **City Lights,** which adjoins Ditka's restaurant (223 W. Ontario), draws a sophisticated crowd to its tables and dance floor. Music for dancing alternates with videos and performances by dancing waiters and waitresses auditioned by Coach Ditka himself. A young crowd frequents the **Hard Rock Cafe** (63 W. Ontario) where patrons divide their time between munching on burgers, listening to rock music, and gazing at the rock memorabilia hanging on the walls. Somewhere in between is the **Limelight** (632 N. Dearborn), a dance club that specializes in the bizarre—a mix of artsy avant garde and punk.

## In Your Free Time . . .

If you have an hour or two to spare between business appointments, take in some of the sights that make Chicago unique among cities. Chicago has the world's tallest building, the **Sears Tower** (233 S. Wacker), with an observation deck on the 103d floor. The view, however, is often better from the 94th-floor observation deck of the **John Hancock Center** (875 N. Michigan) because it affords a sweeping panorama of one of the city's biggest assets, the lakefront.

Few cities can claim a more dramatic front yard than Chicago. Thanks to turn-of-the-century preservationists, much of Chicago's 29 miles of Lake Michigan shoreline is undeveloped. In place of high-rise condos and office buildings there are parks, beaches, and museums. During warm weather the marinas are jammed with pleasure boats. Excursion boats docked along the Chicago River and near Navy Pier take patrons up and down the shoreline for a wide-angle view of the Chicago skyline. One vessel, the *Star of Chicago,* has lunch, dinner, and cocktail cruises. The two lakefront parks most accessible to downtown, Lincoln Park and Grant Park, have jogging and bicycle paths. Lincoln Park has an excellent zoo and botanical conservatory, both free. Grant Park has Buckingham Fountain and the Petrillo Music Shell, where free concerts by the Grant Park Symphony Orchestra are held on summer evenings.

Another of Chicago's unique features is its abundance of buildings of architectural renown. The Chicago Fire of 1871 leveled most of downtown and gave architects of that era the chance to create anew. Their efforts resulted in the Chicago School of Architecture—not a school, actually, but a style of commercial architecture followed by architects Dankmar Adler, Daniel Burnham, John Root, Louis Sullivan and his young protegé Frank Lloyd Wright. Some of the buildings they designed, as well as those of later architects such as Ludwig Mies van der Rohe and Helmut Jahn, are studied on daily, two-hour walking tours of the Loop sponsored by the Chicago Architecture Foundation. Information on these tours and a variety of other Chicago tours led by the foundation is available at the **Archicenter** (330 S. Dearborn, 782–1776).

Lovers of Frank Lloyd Wright architecture might want to take half a day to visit suburban Oak Park where Wright spent his Golden Years and designed nearly two dozen buildings. Tours of the **Frank Lloyd Wright Home and Studio** (951 Chicago Avenue) are given daily; self-guided recorded walking tours of the exterior of other homes Wright designed can be arranged at the **Oak Park Visitor Center** (158 N. Forest Avenue). Oak Park is 10 miles west of the Loop and can be reached on the Lake Street elevated train. Disembark at the Harlem-Marion stop, walk a block east to Forest Avenue, then two blocks north to the visitor center or about four blocks north to the home and studio.

If your business or interest is financial, you might want to stop by the visitor centers of the **Chicago Board of Trade** (141 W. Jackson Blvd.) or the **Chicago Mercantile Exchange** (30 S. Wacker), both open until mid-afternoon every business day. Each deals in commodities futures and has viewing galleries overlooking the trading floors.

Chicago is blessed with several fine art museums. The **Terra Museum of American Art** (644 N. Michigan), opened in 1987, houses the work of Daniel J. Terra, appointed by President Reagan as America's first ambassador-at-large for cultural affairs. It is one of the few major museums in the country dedicated solely to American Art. Among the works on exhibit are *The Gallery of the Louvre* by Samuel F. B. Morse, *Lilies* by Frederick Carl Frieseke, and works by American Impressionists John Singer Sargent and Mary Cassatt. Further south on Michigan Avenue is the venerable **Art Institute of Chicago** (Michigan at Adams). The European galleries, where a $6.6-million renovation was completed in 1987, house such well-known works as El Greco's *Assumption of the Virgin* and Rembrandt's *The Artist's Father,* as well as a fine collection of Impressionist and Post-Impressionist paintings including Seurat's *Sunday Afternoon on the Island of La Grande Jatte,* Gauguin's *The Old Women of Arles,* and a Van Gogh self-portrait. The galleries are housed in the original 1893 neoclassical structure built for the World's Columbian Exposition that year in Chicago. The Museum of Contemporary Art (237 E. Ontario St.) has seven galleries devoted to painting, sculpture, photography, architecture, and graphics. It has a growing permanent collection and hosts changing exhibits throughout the year.

### For Shopping

If you can squeeze a shopping spree into your schedule, start at the 600 block of North Michigan Avenue and work your way north along the Magnificent Mile past Burberry's, Gucci, Tiffany & Co., Saks Fifth Avenue, Elizabeth Arden (where you can also get a massage, a manicure, and a facial), Neiman-Marcus, and I. Magnin to Water Tower Place. This atrium mall in the 800 block of North Michigan contains more than 100 stops, including Lord & Taylor, Godiva Chocolatier, Rodier, F.A.O. Schwarz, Talbots, Laura Ashley, and Marshall Field & Co. You'll also find Accent Chicago, Inc., a wonderful little gift shop with some nice Chicago souvenirs. If you still have the strength, continue north to Bonwit Teller and Hermès in the John Hancock Center, then on to Bally of Switzerland. Make a left on Oak Street at the end of the Magnificent Mile and you'll find a handful of New York–style boutiques, most of them in renovated brownstones. **My Sister's Circus-ISIS** (38 E. Oak) features California designs, **Ultimo** (114 E. Oak) is European.

Shopping in the Loop means a walk down the State Street Mall. The shops are not as upscale as those on the Magnificent Mile, but two are worthy of a special trip. **Carson Pirie Scott & Co.** (1 S. State) is a large department store with a wrought-iron art-nouveau facade designed by Louis Sullivan and featured on architecture tours. The flagship **Marshall Field & Co.** store (111 N. State), where Nancy Reagan once worked as a sales girl, is one of the oldest and largest department stores in the Midwest, and contains a warm, skylit central court. Field's Frango mint chocolates are a true taste of Chicago and a nice gift to take home, particularly to a former Chicagoan who feels nostalgic about the Windy City.

# EXPLORING CHICAGO

by
**MICHAEL J. CONNELLY and SHIRLEY ROSE HIGGINS**

*Michael Connelly was editor of* Consumers Digest *magazine and formerly Editorial Director of Signature Publications. Among his many published articles are "Chicago, A Most American City" and "In Search of Abe Lincoln" in addition to a 32-page guide to the United States. Shirley Rose Higgins is a freelance travel writer whose writing has won three Mark Twain Awards and a George Hedman Memorial Award. Her column covering international travel appeared in the* Chicago Tribune *for 14 years and is now syndicated around the country.*

Your first look at Chicago is likely to be from the window of a jet liner headed for the world's busiest airport—O'Hare International. If you fly in from the east, you'll be over water for a while—Lake Michigan. Then, off to the south, you'll suddenly see the impressive skyline of the city. If you fly in from the south or the west, you will see some of the downtown area from the plane's right side. The tallest building you'll be able to spot—even at night—is Sears Tower. Other tall ones are the Standard Oil (of Indiana) building and John Hancock Center, both super-skyscrapers.

After landing, two main areas of interest to the visitor are the Loop and the Near North Side. The Loop is roughly the area bounded by Michigan Avenue on the east, Wacker Drive on the north and west, and Congress on the south. Purists contend that the Loop's borders are smaller than that, but in practical terms, this larger area is what most Chicagoans have in mind when they refer to "the Loop."

What is designated as the Near North side is the area immediately north of the Chicago River, bounded by Lake Shore Drive on the east, North Avenue on the north, and La Salle Street on the west. This and the Loop are where most hotel visitors stay, whether they're well off or on a tight budget.

Michigan Avenue, since it takes you through sections, is a good artery to use as a guide. Beginning at Oak Street on the north (the Drake Hotel and the towering "Magnificent Mile" buildings are located here), you'll encounter these major east-west streets, successively, south to Congress: Chicago Avenue (at the Water Tower), Ohio Street (the Marriott Hotel is nearby), Wacker Drive (immediately south of the Chicago River), Randolph, Madison, Adams (the Art Institute is here), and Congress.

The major streets west of Michigan to look for are Wabash, State (State and Madison form the numerical center of the city), Rush (north of the River only), Dearborn, Clark, La Salle (in the Loop, the city's financial center), Wells, Franklin, and Wacker Drive. (Names of the presidents denote many of the east-west streets in the Loop: Washington, Madison, Monroe, Adams, Jackson, and Van Buren. Lincoln, practically a native son of Chicago, was used for a northwest street that runs on a diagonal beginning around 1800 north and extending into the suburbs.)

If you arrive by car, you're likely to see only the backside of the city along the expressways unless you drive along Lake Shore Drive. To do so, if you're driving in from the east or south, take the Indiana Tollway and Chicago Skyway, to the Indianapolis Boulevard (Route 41) exit and follow the Route 41 signs until you're on Lake Shore Drive. The Drive takes you past Jackson Park and the Museum of Science and Industry, Hyde Park, Soldier Field, the Field Museum of Natural History, John G. Shedd Aquarium, and, off to the right, Adler Planetarium. Turn left at Balbo, just north of the Field Museum, to Michigan Avenue.

To enjoy the lakefront views from the north, take I-94 (the Illinois Tollway) to the Edens Expressway exit and the Edens to Lake Avenue via Skokie Blvd. Then drive directly east to Sheridan Road. From there, stay on Sheridan south through Wilmette and Evanston and into Chicago, where you pick up Lake Shore Drive at Hollywood Avenue, about three miles south of the Evanston-Chicago border at Howard Street. You then drive through Lincoln Park, the city's largest preserve and home of the Lincoln Park Zoo. Exit from Lake Shore Drive at North Michigan Avenue, just before the sharp left turn that takes you around the Gold Coast and into heavy traffic.

Incidentally, driving on Lake Shore Drive at twilight is one of the great joys of the city; the soft light of the setting sun casts golden beams onto the buildings that form Chicago's greatest asset—its lakefront skyline.

## Lake Michigan

Lake Michigan and the city's skyline combine to make Chicago a most attractive place to visit. Photographers delight in standing a few feet north and west of Adler Planetarium to snap pictures of the view that encompasses Monroe Harbor and the skyline extending north as far as the Chicago River. From this location you can easily distinquish most of the city's major skyscrapers: Sears Tower, Standard Oil Building, and three distinctive lakefront apartment buildings: Outer Drive East, Harbor Point, and near Navy Pier, beautiful Lake Point Tower. In summer, the harbor is dotted with luxurious sailboats (in July, it's the starting point of the famous, but grueling, Chicago to Mackinac Boat Race).

Lake Michigan, as one of the Great Lakes, serves Chicago as an outlet to the Atlantic Ocean via the Saint Lawrence Seaway. Lake waters actually flow northward with Chicago at 500 feet above sea level—one of the highest points in the waterway. At one time, Navy Pier was the city's principal commerical dock, but the larger ships in transatlantic commerce required the major port developed at Lake Calumet, some 15 miles south of the Loop. This inland port also serves barge traffic, which transships grain and other local products south through a river waterway that connects Chicago with the Mississippi River.

Lakefront tours are available on the *Wendella, Mercury,* and *Shoreline* sightseeing boats. The first two are docked on the Chicago River at Michigan Avenue. The cruise usually includes a short ride downriver, past the twin "corn cob" towers of Marina City, the imposing Merchandise Mart (at one time the world's largest office building), and the backside of the Civic Opera House. During the rush hour, these

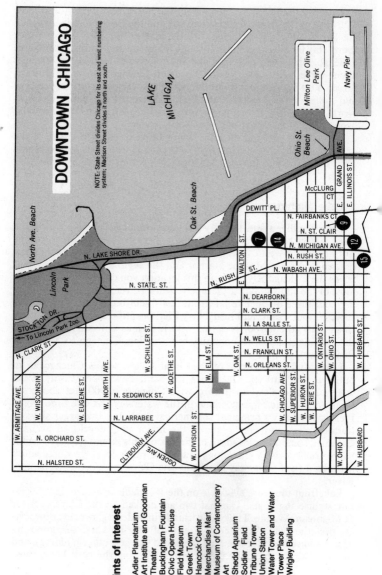

DOWNTOWN CHICAGO

NOTE: State Street divides Chicago for its east and west numbering system; Madison Street divides it north and south.

**Points of Interest**

1) Adler Planetarium
2) Art Institute and Goodman Theater
3) Buckingham Fountain
4) Civic Opera House
5) Field Museum
6) Greek Town
7) Hancock Center
8) Merchandise Mart
9) Museum of Contemporary Art
10) Shedd Aquarium
11) Soldier Field
12) Tribune Tower
13) Union Station
14) Water Tower and Water Tower Place
15) Wrigley Building

boats carry commuters between Madison Avenue at the river and lower Michigan Avenue in a matter of seven minutes.

The boats also take you through the locking system immediately south of Navy Pier. These locks date from the early 1930s, when the flow of the river was reversed, draining (often-polluted) water downstream rather than into the lake.

The city's dependence on the lake for its water supply is abundantly apparent on the cruise: as you leave the locks, you see the Carter Harrison water crib, where some of the lake water enters the city's vast water-processing system. The raw lake water is piped directly to the water-filtration plant, a bit west of Navy Pier, where it is treated and then transshipped to various pumping stations, such as the old one at Chicago and Michigan.

Lake Michigan, of course, is one of the city's great attractions. Generally, the lake has a very positive effect on the climate—keeping lakeside neighborhoods, including the Loop and Near North areas, cooler in summer and warmer in winter. Best times for walking are May, June, September, and October. The very worst is January and early February, when even the lake effect can't guarantee temperatures above zero degrees Fahrenheit.

## Chicago's Pulse

Chicago has a rhythm, what the French call *joie de vivre,* which you can miss completely unless you visit the city on a business day. The Loop and Magnificent Mile (North Michigan Avenue) come alive on summer business days with outpourings of al fresco music, dance, and other mini-entertainments at such locations as the First National Bank Plaza, the Daley Center (adjoining City Hall), and the plazas along Michigan Avenue north of the Chicago River. Programs vary, and it's great fun to mimic Chicagoans by eating a box lunch amid the strains of rock, jazz, or classical music—all free.

The city is far more than the relatively small Loop and Near North sections. Chicago has evolved over the years from a series of neighborhoods that at one time were mostly little towns on their own. As the city grew, from the 1880s on, it gradually took over any number of villages and towns to become what it is today—a major, still highly industrial community of some 3,005,000 residents surrounded by a conglomeration of suburbs in Illinois and northwestern Indiana (encompassing an additional 3.5 million residents). Countless thousands of the suburbanites commute to the city by car and train.

Chicago is one of the nation's major financial centers, with its own stock exchange, several commodities exchanges, a Federal Reserve bank, and two of the nation's leading banks, the Continental and First

National Bank of Chicago. The city has long been a center of graphics and printing; scores of popular magazines—including the *New Yorker* —are printed here, as are three of the nation's major mail-order catalogs: Sears, Montgomery Ward, and Spiegel.

Steel was once the foundation of the industrial belt that borders the city's South Side, but some major plants have closed, causing major unemployment problems in that area. Chicago no longer claims the title, "Hog Butcher for the World," coined by poet Carl Sandburg, once a newspaper reporter here. The old (smelly) stockyards are long gone, leaving in their wake a budding, high-tech industrial park on the South Side.

Being a steel center and centrally located, Chicago at one time was the nation's largest railroad center. It was here that the famous Broadway Limited, linking Chicago with Manhattan, terminated, as did the old Santa Fe Super Chief, running its way from Chicago to glamorous Los Angeles. Amtrak trains still link these cities—and others—with Chicago, but air travel, via O'Hare International Airport, has far outdistanced the old railroad passenger trains. The city remains, however, a major center of rail cargo, with Santa Fe still a major operator of rail transport here. Truck transportation is also important. The Dan Ryan Expressway, the leading artery on the South Side, nearly overflows with truck traffic every day, much of it interstate. And Chicago has developed, too, as an inland port, with ships from throughout the world anchoring in the Port of Chicago at Lake Calumet, especially during the summer months when the Saint Lawrence Seaway route is open to ocean traffic. This combination of water, rail, and truck transport moves thousands of tons of grain and industrial products through the city every year. There's a dramatic alignment of Chicago with Detroit; many of the products that go into the modern car are built in machine shops of Chicago and other Illinois cities.

### Planning Your Tour

Develop a plan to cover as many of the city's diverse attractions as you can with limited time. Fortunately, most of the popular attractions are within walking distance of each other—or at least a short bus or cab ride. Some more distant ones, though, like the Museum of Science and Industry, require some planning. Most visitors begin with the Art Institute of Chicago. It's centrally located, at Adams and Michigan, and you can see the highlights of the permanent and temporary exhibits in a matter of two or three hours.

Then move on to the three Grant Park museums: Field Museum of Natural History, John G. Shedd Aquarium, and the Adler Planetarium, all within walking distance of each other. If you really like to walk,

## CHICAGO NEIGHBORHOODS
North of the River

FOSTER AVE.

LINCOLN SQ.

UPTOWN

N. WESTERN AVE.

LINCOLN

IRVING PK. RD.

LAKE SHORE DR.

N. ASHLAND AVE.

AVE.

LAKEVIEW

BELMONT AVE.

DE PAUL

NEW TOWN

DIVERSEY AVE.

FULLERTON

LINCOLN

PK.

N. LARRABEE

OLD TOWN

NORTH AVE.

DIVISION ST.

GOLD COAST

N. ORLEANS ST.

ST.

AVE.

NEAR NORTH SIDE

N. CLARK

N. MICHIGAN

Chicago R.

STREETERVILLE

## CHICAGO NEIGHBORHOODS
South of the River

Chicago R.

WACKER DR.

LAKE ST.

WACKER DR.

THE LOOP

HALSTED

NEAR W. SIDE

S. MORGAN ST.

U. OF ILL.

CONGRESS PKWY.

MICHIGAN AVE.

LAKE SHORE DR.

ROOSEVELT RD.

HALSTED

CHINATOWN

CERMAK RD.

24TH ST.

STEVENSON EXPWY.

BRIDGEPORT

DAN RYAN EXPWY.

PERSHING RD.

47TH ST.

KENWOOD

56TH ST.

COTTAGE GROVE

63RD ST.

HYDE PK.

## Chicago Neighborhoods

**North of the River**

**Streeterville,** built mostly on landfill, now houses everything from TV stations to great hotels and exclusive condominium apartments. Also located here are the medical-professional campus of Northwestern University and the extremely popular Water Tower Place.

**Near North** is Chicago's renaissance area, gradually undergoing renewal with numerous art galleries at Erie and Wells welcoming visitors. By day the area bustles with office workers. Rush and Division Streets (east of Clark) are focal points of nightlife for singles and conventioneers. However they should be approached with caution. North Michigan Avenue is best known as the Magnificient Mile because of its concentration of exclusive stores, hotels, and galleries catering to a classy clientele.

**Gold Coast** is a three-block-wide strip of high-rise buildings that commands some of the steepest rents and best lake views in the city. The area includes the Astor Street Historic District featuring some great old homes.

**Old Town,** actually Wells Street north to Lincoln Avenue, is undergoing a revival as a nightlife center—although most Chicagoans prefer New Town. Some good shops are here for daytime browsing and area restaurants are competitive in this city where dining is considered one of life's greatest pleasures. Side streets north of North Avenue and west of Wells are remarkable for daytime walking tours of restored 19th-century homes.

**Lincoln Park** is old Chicago at its finest, featuring fine old buildings. The strip along the park itself is particularly beautiful.

**De Paul** area west of Lincoln Park is quiet and neighborly. Renovations during the 1970s and 1980s have improved the small older homes on these tree-lined streets.

**New Town,** primarily Broadway and Clark Street north of Diversey to Belmont, features antique shops, informal bars, and—some say—an occasional Off-Loop theater. Young Chicagoans love this area—especially its nightlife.

**Lakeview** is home to Wrigley Field where the Chicago Cubs play. The Belmont-Lincoln Avenue shopping area retains vestiges of old German-American shops an restaurants.

**Uptown** remains one of Chicago's poorest neighborhoods although it remains hidden behind a façade of lakefront high-rises. It houses a pocket of subsistence level residents—Appalachians, Indians, and Hispanics, primarily, and there is little here for tourists.

**South of the River**

**Jackson Park, Hyde Park,** and **Kenwood** are often referred to as the South Side. This whole area is dominated by the Museum of Science and Industry in Jackson Park—one of the city's leading attractions—and the University of Chicago in Hyde Park. Visits to this area are recommended for daytime only.

**Bridgeport** was home to the late Mayor Richard J. Daley and remains a bastion of Chicago's old-style machine politics based on ethnic interests. The area once housed the Union Stockyards but remains a holdout of Polish, Irish, Lithuanian, and other ethnic groups. Comiskey Park—where the Chicago White Sox play ball—is located here. But a possible new location is being discussed for 1990.

**The University of Illinois** is a combination of low- and high-rise architecture in which many classroom buildings are interconnected by overhead walkways. It is located just south of what was once Chicago's Greek Town.

**Near West Side** is best-known for good restaurants in Greek Town.

**Chinatown** is a four-block area with an Asian accent. Replete with fine restaurants and interesting shops.

**The Loop** is extremely lively any business day and is the city's financial heart—as well as its government center. The shopping areas along State Street and Wabash Avenue are fun on Saturday, as well as on weekdays. Theaters are scattered throughout the city and nightlife has shifted north of Chicago River—so consider the Loop as primarily a daytime attraction.

you can trek from the Art Institute through Grant Park directly to the museums, stopping at Buckingham Fountain for a pleasant rest along the way.

On a business day, you may prefer to head directly into the Loop for a peek at Chicago at work. The important places here would be State Street, the observation deck of the Sears Tower for a great overview, the Chicago Board of Trade at Jackson and La Salle, the Rookery on La Salle, the Federal Plaza at Adams and Dearborn, First National Bank Plaza at Dearborn and Monroe, and Daley Plaza—site of the famed Picasso sculpture—at Dearborn and Washington. Be sure to allow time for Michigan Avenue and the "Magnificent Mile," highlighted by Water Tower Place, one of the nation's great vertical shopping centers. These are but a few of the highlights that you should see in a brief visit to the city by the lake.

One thing you'll notice immediately—just in case you had any fears —is that Chicago is not overrun by gangsters and thugs. The Loop and Near North areas, especially, are made up primarily of office workers, well-tailored business executives, city workers, police officers (some on horseback), and an occasional "blue collar" construction worker engaged in building another skyscraper. When asked what they enjoy most about Chicago, visitors from abroad usually say, "The people; they're so friendly." And, generally, that's true. If you have a question or need directions, don't hesitate to stop a total stranger on the street and ask; you may get a long-winded answer, but an answer—and a friendly one—you will receive.

Like other cities, Chicago has a certain rhythm. Traffic during rush hours can be excruciating, so you're advised to avoid driving between 7:30 and 9 A.M. and 4:30 and 6:30 P.M. on any business day. Rain or snow can stifle traffic too, and for some reason, Fridays in the Loop are always up for grabs, as merchants make their last-minute deposits and many office workers get ready for the weekend. Otherwise, though, traffic moves comfortably, and the pace of pedestrians is relatively slow and easygoing. On a weekend, you practically have the Loop off State Street to yourself.

When you're in Chicago on a Sunday or holiday, take advantage of the CTA (Chicago Transit Authority) super transfer. For $1.75 you can ride on any bus or El train throughout the city. Another 75 cents puts you on the Culture buses, which serve the city's museums and other attractions during the summer from approximately 10:30 A.M. to 4:50 P.M. The Culture bus routes are labeled North, South, and West, and they do get visitors around to the city's major attractions. For instance, if you take the South Culture Bus, you can visit most of the major museums in a day's time: Field Museum, Shedd Aquarium, Adler Planetarium, and in Jackson Park (58th and Lake Shore Drive), the Museum of Science and Industry. Buses operate between the Art Institute and these points at approximately half-hour intervals. The West Culture Bus takes you (from the Art Institute) by the Sears Tower, Merchandise Mart, and into some older, ethnic neighborhoods, while the North route spans Michigan Avenue, Old Town, Lincoln Park, Navy Pier, and Grant Park.

On a weekday, you can easily ride CTA transportation too. Just dial the CTA information number, 836–7000, and ask for the route number of the bus or El that will take you to your destination.

Commuter trains are also available. The old Illinois Central electric trains that depart from below Randolph at Michigan can take you to most South-side destinations such as Hyde Park and the Museum of Science and Industry. Commuter trains from Union Station, at Adams and Canal (just west of the Chicago River) serve the western suburbs and many northern ones, while the Chicago and North Western line will take you north and northwest of the city. All of the commuter trains are now operated by the RTA (Regional Transportation Authority).

Taxis in Chicago are costly. Figure on spending at least $15 or $20 (depending on traffic flow) for a one-way fare from the Loop to O'Hare International Airport. Rides of any distance at all within the city generally cost from $3 to $8 and up, plus tip. When you're in the Loop or Near North areas, don't bother to phone for a cab: just hail one that's passing along the street, or pick one up at your hotel. Limousine services are also available (inquire at your hotel), and if you stay at the Ritz Carlton, you can engage that hotel's Rolls Royce to arrive at your destination in the grand style.

## Touring the Loop

There are few places better than the Art Institute of Chicago at Adams and Michigan Avenue to begin a walking tour of the city. The building is one of the few ever allowed to be erected in Grant Park. With recent additions, it now occupies almost two full city blocks, from Monroe Street on the north to Jackson Boulevard on the south. Among its most distinguished paintings are Rembrandt's *Young Girl at an Open Half-door,* Renoir's *On the Terrace,* Grant Wood's *American Gothic,* the famous painting of a somber farm father and daughter with pitchfork, and Seurat's *Sunday Afternoon on the Island of La Grande Jatte.*

These and countless other art works from the nineteenth and twentieth centuries have been accumulating in Chicago since 1871, when the great Chicago Fire wiped out the old Chicago Academy of Design. The replacement Chicago Academy of Fine Arts, incorporated in 1878, was

## Points of Interest

1) Art Institute
2) Board of Trade
3) Carson Pine Scott and Co
4) Chicago Public Library Cultural Center
5) City Hall—Cook Country Building
6) Civic Opera
7) Daley Plaza
8) Federal Plaza
9) First Nat'l Bank Plaza
10) Fine Arts Bldg.
11) Greyhound Stn.
12) Marshall Field's
13) Chicago Mercantile Exchange
14) Orchestra Hall
15) Palmer House Hotel
16) Rookery and Continental Illinois Nat'l Bank
17) Roosevelt University
18) Sears Tower
19) State of Illinois Center
20) Trailways Stn.
21) Union Station
22) Northwestern Station (RTA)
23) ArchiCenter

renamed the Art Institute of Chicago in 1892, when the main building you see today at Michigan and Adams was occupied. The last major addition, extending the structure eastward to Columbus Drive, was completed in 1977. The institute is one of the nation's leading art schools, with annual enrollment of some 1,800 students, many from abroad.

In addition to the galleries of French Impressionists, Oriental artworks, and the stunning Chicago Stock Exchange Room (salvaged when the old Chicago Stock Exchange building was demolished), the Art Institute contains the renowned collection of miniature Thorne Rooms, a fine children's museum, an excellent gift shop, a film center, and a lovely courtyard for summertime dining.

Orchestra Hall, at 220 South Michigan, diagonally across Michigan Avenue from the Art Institute, is diminutive only in size. Within its walls you can hear great music, with the Chicago Symphony Orchestra reaching extraordinary heights under the baton of music director Sir Georg Solti. From September through May, you can count on some musical event at Orchestra Hall, with seating at Friday afternoon matinees of the Symphony usually available. The Sunday afternoon Allied Arts Series, featuring solo performances by world-famous musicians and singers, is highly popular. Orchestra Hall, itself, has been carefully restored to its original 1904 Georgian design. Intermission cocktails are available in the elegant second-floor ballroom. Call the theater or check local newspapers for program information and schedules.

## South Michigan Avenue

From Orchestra Hall walk south to the Fine Arts Building, 410 South Michigan, one of those vestiges from the past that is a true cultural find. You can have a fine violin repaired (or purchase one) on the tenth floor, or find a comparable quality woodwind on the seventh. The building, itself, is an official city landmark dating from the nineteenth century. It was built for a carriage business in the 1880s, and converted to the Chicago equivalent of Carnegie Hall in 1898. The Romanesque entrance displays the motto: "All passes—ART alone endures." Inside is an ornate marble-and-wood interior that has witnessed much of the city's cultural history. The Fine Arts Theaters now feature a wide variety of films, including foreign films and documentaries. Frank Lloyd Wright had offices here, as did sculptor Lorado Taft, whose works abound in Washington Park on the city's South Side. Other early tenants were Harriet Monroe's *Poetry* magazine (which introduced such writers as Carl Sandburg, T. S. Eliot, and Ezra Pound) and *The Dial* and *Saturday Evening Post*.

Just south Roosevelt University and the Auditorium Theater, at the corner of Michigan and Congress, are both housed in one of Chicago's architectural jewels. Designed by Dankmar Adler and Louis Sullivan in 1889, the structure was originally a grand hotel and theater. The entrance to Roosevelt University still showcases the splendor of the old hotel's lobby. Even more outstanding is the fully restored Auditorium Theater, with entrance around the corner on Congress. The golden, turn-of-the-century lights cast a warm glow over the theater lobby and interior. It was, at the time it opened, one of the largest and most acoustically perfect indoor theaters of its kind, and even today you can practically hear a pin drop on stage from the upper reaches of the top balcony. Virtually every one of the 4000 seats in the theater has an unobstructed view of the stage. Call the theater or check the local listings if you want to see any of its fine concerts or dance programs. Tours are also available.

## State Street That Great Street

Walk west along Congress Street, and you'll come to State Street. State Street is undergoing change, due, no doubt, in part to the overwhelming developments across the river along North Michigan Avenue. While the latter has seen the rise of Water Tower Place and other great centers of shopping, hotels, and modern condominium apartments, State Street has actually gone downhill to some extent. The Sears Roebuck store, a mainstay at the south end of State, has closed, as has Wieboldts and the great old Goldblatts store (under consideration as a permanent site of the main Chicago Public Library).

Still, at least two of State's great buildings survive and prosper. One, Marshall Field's Department Store, occupies the entire block bounded by State, Washington, Wabash, and Randolph. Starting from the day after Thanksgiving through late December, children still ogle some of the city's finest holiday decorations displayed in the store windows—usually themed and highly animated. Inside, at Christmastime, the store takes on a Dickens-like aura—its high, magnificent ceilings reflecting the glitter of thousands of baubles dangling from huge trees, as a department store Santa hears endless requests for those expensive toys advertised on TV. The store at any time of year maintains some 450 separate departments, ranging from fine furs to a bargain basement with direct access to the north-south Howard-Jackson subway of the CTA.

Field's also has an exceptional variety of dining possibilities. Everything from the sophisticated Walnut Room, with its stylish fashion shows, to an assortment of smaller dining areas, all designed with flair and imagination.

A block south of Field's at Madison you encounter the great and grand Carson Pirie Scott & Co., housed since 1904 in a Louis Sullivan-designed building, which is now both a city and national landmark. Windows and a grand rotunda here are accented by Sullivan's iron ornamentation (good photo possibilities). Here you're likely to find the latest in fashion from France and Italy, as well as unusual pieces of furniture and gourmet cooking items from Scandinavia. A favorite stop in the store is the east-wing site of what used to be the Men's Grill and is now a large, wood-paneled room where the luncheon buffet is a true bargain.

You can continue to amble north at will along the relatively new State Street Mall. It is not completely closed to traffic, so be wary of buses and police patrol cars. If you're ready for a night of theater, look for the Hot Tix Booth on the west side of State. Or, if you feel like stopping a while, another grand luncheon spot, the Berghoff, is just west of State on Adams. This nineteenth-century-style German restaurant and stand-up bar has scrumptious food and great beers, served from lunchtime through the moderately early dinner hour. No reservations, though, so be prepared to wait a bit. The room at the east end of the restaurant is extremely popular among Chicagoans because of its great steins of rich German beer and made-on-the-spot sandwiches of beef, corned beef, thuringer, cheese, and ham. This room is strictly stand-up—nary a stool to be seen.

## State and Wabash

In many ways the area of Wabash Avenue (parallel to State one block east) between Congress and Wacker is as good for shopping as is State Street. Field's and Carson's both have entrances off Wabash, but the street is known for smaller, one-of-a-kind stores. Rose Records, at 214 South Wabash, houses a great and comfortably priced collection of records and tapes. You'll also find the city's main Kroch's and Brentano's Bookstore here, a great place for browsing through racks of best sellers, paperbacks (in the basement), and beguiling gifts and magazines.

The old Field's Men's Store at Wabash and Washington has been absorbed into the main building, but Wabash still features two major men's clothiers: Brooks Brothers, just east of Wabash on Madison, and Capper & Capper, at Wabash and Madison. The first and largest Chicago outlet of Eddie Bauer sporting goods and equipment is on the east side of Wabash just south of Randolph. For good food at moderate prices try Mort's Delicatessen on the east side of Wabash between Randolph and Lake.

## Daley Center and Plaza and City Hall

Head west from Wabash on either Randolph or Washington. Every
big city has something of a geographical heart, the place most of the
residents think of as the center of town, or the place where the action
is. Well, Richard J. Daley Center and Plaza seems to fit both criteria.
It's an entire city block bounded by Washington, Dearborn, Randolph,
and Clark.

Daley Plaza, of course, memorializes the late and renowned mayor
Richard J. Daley, who personified the homespun character of Chicago.
He was born, reared, and lived out his life in Bridgeport, a humble
South Side district. The mayor, like many leading Chicago politicians,
was entirely Irish, and rabid about the city and its people, most of
whom were delighted with his somewhat autocratic rule of the "City
that Works." The Daley era (1955–1976) brought to the city not only
the Picasso, which adorns the plaza that bears his name, but countless
skyscrapers that literally transformed the skyline. Since his death, the
construction of skyscrapers has continued unabated under three mayors.

Mayor Daley (and successor mayors) presided over the workings of
the city and the local Democratic Organization from a fifth-floor sanc-
tuary on the Clark Street side of the City Hall-County Building, immediately west of Daley Plaza.

Mayors Row, a restaurant on Dearborn, between Randolph and
Washington, just east of the Plaza, shows pictures of Daley and Chicago's other old-time mayors, including the colorful (but not necessarily
revered) "Big Bill" Thompson, the last Republican mayor. Others,
since the twenties, have included Anton Cermak, who was killed in
Florida by an assassin's bullet intended for Franklin Delano Roosevelt.

Among Daley's other achievements are the new Chicago Campus of
the University of Illinois, immediately south and west of the Loop.

The tall building that overlooks the Daley Plaza is a county courthouse, one the first buildings that used cor-ten, an unpainted, self-
eroding steel, which in its aging years looks pretty good. The Picasso
statue in the southeast quadrant of Daley Plaza is made of the same
metal. Most artistic authorities believe the Chicago Picasso depicts the
head of a woman. However, many local humorists prefer to label it a
political vulture preying on the taxpayers.

The eternal flame on the Washington Street side of the Plaza
memorializes the late President John F. Kennedy, whose 1960 victory
over Richard M. Nixon was decided, they say, by a controversial vote
count under Daley's direction right here in downtown Chicago.

Almost directly across Washington from the flame is Joan Miró's *Chicago,* a feminine figure with pitchfork, one of the many sculptures adorning downtown plazas and building interiors. If you happen to be in the city on a cold or rainy business day, you can get to the Plaza entirely underground; just go down to the subway station at State and Randolph and walk west, first to the courthouse; if you turn south you'll emerge in the lobby of the Brunswick Building on the south side of Washington at Dearborn. It's a pleasant walk where you'll encounter a variety of city workers and lawyers, as well as city exhibits. At the Brunswick Building, you'll find underground shops and a restaurant.

If you go west to the huge neoclassical City Hall–Cook County Building from the Plaza, enter off Clark Street and walk through to the City Council Chambers on the La Salle Street side.

In the spring of 1983, the city elected its first black mayor, Harold G. Washington, a former congressman. The election, one of the bitterest political battles in the city's history, resulted in a major split between the old-time Democratic machine, as personified in its white chairman, Eddie Vrdolyak, and the mayor. The same battle was re-enacted in 1987 and Vrdolyak is now a Republican. Despite the tumult, the city continues to work. Meetings of the city council on the second floor, often fiery these days, are open to the public. There is no regular schedule, but if you're in the town on a business day, the visitors' gallery could present an interesting insight into the workings of big city government.

## La Salle Street—The Financial District

Several blocks south of the City Hall–Cook County Building you'll find yourself amidst the frantic pace of Chicago's financial center, where all of the exchanges operate. The Chicago Board of Trade towers over the foot of La Salle Street at 141 West Jackson Boulevard like a benevolent mother. The statue of Ceres, goddess of grain, looks down from atop the 45th floor. The Chicago Board of Trade opened for business in 1848, but was housed elsewhere until the current Art Deco building was opened in June, 1930. In 1982 a large addition designed in the Art Deco style was completed in order to accommodate a second trading floor. Together, the old and new buildings occupy an entire city block. Now visitors to the fifth-floor gallery can look south to see traders in grain, and north to see the old but refurbished trading floor, where big-dollar futures contracts in financial instruments are traded. Witnessing the close of trading (shortly after 1 P.M. on any business day) makes the Board of Trade alone worth a visit to Chicago. Traders in more than ten different trading pits wind up the day in a hand-waving shouting match as they try to take best advantage of closing prices to buy or sell their remaining futures contracts. One of the south Loop's most popular restaurants, the Sign of the Trader, is open here for lunch, and the basement cafeteria, just below the Jackson Boulevard entrance, isn't bad either. Visitors are also welcome in the new quarters of the Chicago/Mercantile Exchange (established in 1874) at South Wacker Drive and Monroe. Trading there lasts till 3:00 P.M.

West of the Board of Trade, along Jackson, you come to Union Station, one of the city's two remaining major railroad stations and the center of all Amtrak travel into and out of Chicago. Union Station's magnificent interior has recently been renovated. Pedestrian commuter traffic here and in the nearby Northwestern Station (north along Canal Street) from 7:30 A.M. to 8:30 A.M. and 4:30 P.M. to 5:30 P.M. is a no-nonsense affair, as suburbanites by the thousand move quickly and efficiently to and from their jobs in the Loop or Near North.

## South Loop Area

Backtracking east again on Jackson to La Salle, you'll come to the Continental Illinois National Bank (1924) and adjoining Rookery (1886) across from the Board of Trade. Go inside the bank and be sure to take the escalator to the second banking floor to view the block-long panorama of tall columns supporting a magnificent ceiling. Dating from 1886, The Rookery (209 South La Salle) is rugged on the outside but delightfully warm and welcoming on the inside, the result of a design by Frank Lloyd Wright when it was remodeled in 1905.

Walk north across Adams to the stunning La Salle National Bank Building, an Art Deco structure dating from the 1930s. On business days, you can enjoy a good, reasonable lunch in the basement cafeteria and grill at the building's east side. Then cross Clark Street to the Commonwealth Edison Building and continue east to the 1894 Marquette Building (140 South Dearborn), where you'll see bronze reliefs at the entrance of an otherwise forbidding-looking building. Inside, the lobby mosaics depicting expeditions by explorers Marquette and Jolliet are well worth viewing.

As you leave the Marquette Building, look south to the Mies van der Rohe-designed Federal Center and Plaza. At this pristine federal office-building complex you'll delight in the great and colorful Calder sculpture entitled *Flamingo,* a striking orange-painted structure that seems like it would soar to the heavens were it unstuck from its concrete foundation. For modern history buffs, the Dirksen Federal Courthouse across the street was the site of the notorious "Chicago Seven" trial of radical "Yippies" in the late 1960s, presided over by the late Julius Hoffman. The single-story building at Clark and Adams, incidentally, is a convenient post office.

As you turn north on Dearborn from Adams, you soon encounter the 1980 Xerox Center at Dearborn and Monroe, one of the bold works by Chicago architect Helmut Joah Jahn. Its curving facade is a striking contrast to the older, more traditional Inland Steel Building of stainless steel with glass columns, diagonally across Dearborn on Monroe. Directly across Monroe from the Xerox Center is First Illinois Plaza, a lower-level center of lively music and box lunches in summer (wintertime events are held in a small, comfortable auditorium). Look up at the First National Bank building with its unique, sweeping design. And, as you walk north along Dearborn, look for the mosaic sculpture on the east side of the plaza, *The Four Seasons,* by Marc Chagall. A nice touch of color, especially in summer when the plaza is lively and people-watching is at its best.

Head west on Monroe to Wacker Drive.

## Sears Tower and North Wacker Drive

Only the Pentagon claims to have more office space than the Sears Tower, but it's the building's height that is most impressive. Rising 1,454 feet above Wacker Drive at the southwest corner of the Loop, Sears Tower long ranked as the world's tallest building. A Canadian edifice has now won that distinction. But the Sears building still outranks every other superstructure in Chicago, including the Standard Oil Building (1,136 feet) and the John Hancock Center (1,127 feet).

There is of course an entire floor, the 103rd, devoted to an observation deck, and it's here that visitors by the hundred flock daily, except when the dramatic views are blocked by clouds.

The best way to visit the tower is from the entrance on Wacker Drive, between Adams and Jackson. Climb the steps to the mammoth second-floor lobby, where you'll see the Alexander Calder mobile mural *Universe,* set in motion in October, 1974, and still moving.

To get to the observation floor, descend on an escalator to the lower level, pay a moderate entrance fee, and enter the express elevator, which whisks you up to the observation floor at a rate of 1800 feet per minute—you travel those 100-plus floors in less than one complete minute. Here on a clear day, you can look east to the eastern most shores of Lake Michigan, north to Milwaukee and Wisconsin, south to the factories of northwestern Indiana, and west to the vast expanse of residential area that is Chicago and her western suburbs. The best views, though, are of the immediate downtown areas. You can easily pick out many of the buildings such as the distinctive First National Bank Building, Marina City, the Art Institute, the Board of Trade, the Field Museum of Natural History, Adler Planetarium, McCormick Place, Meigs Field, the Standard Oil of Indiana Building, and the

Hancock Center. One of the best times to see the sights from the tower is about an hour before sunset (there's still enough light to see a great distance, and you can also watch the sun go down).

As you leave Sears Tower, walk north along Wacker Drive past the lineup of stunning new office buildings (including the unique U.S. Gypsum building at Monroe and Wacker) to the Civic Opera House, home of Chicago's well-endowed Lyric Opera, which attracts such stars as Luciano Pavarotti and Renata Scotto. (The opera season begins in late September and runs through mid-December.)

The Opera House is only a small portion of the block-long structure: the Civic Theater is located in the northern section, and in addition there are scores of offices and a cozy, ground-level bar and grill. Just north of the Opera House on the west side of Wacker you'll pass the old Morton Salt Building ("When It Rains, It Pours").

On any business day, walk east along Randolph to the Illinois Bell Telephone headquarters building at 225 West Randolph to see old-time telephones on display in a telephone museum. There are also new telephones on display, as well as exhibits and films explaining modern communications technology, from microwave transmission through the earth satellite systems.

Bigger, of course, isn't always better, but in the case of Chicago's Merchandise Mart, bigger has meant better for the city's home furnishings and apparel industries. At one time, not too long ago, Chicago was the hub of the nation's wholesale furniture trade; the city even had a separate Furniture Mart (still an imposing building along the lakefront, but converted to exclusive condominiums). Back in the 1920s, a Marshall Field executive dreamed up the idea of building a huge structure to house the store's wholesale operations along with those of other major retailers. The biggest building of its kind in the world emerged on a two-block area bounded on the south by the Chicago River, on the west by Orleans, the north by Kinzie, and the east by Wells Street. The Great Depression of the 1930s and a certain amount of mismanagement led to near disaster until the building was purchased in 1945 by the late Joseph Kennedy, father of John F. Kennedy. Since then, the Merchandise Mart has been converted into a lavish showcase for interior decorators, furniture wholesalers, and related businesses; two floors are devoted to the radio and TV Studios of the National Broadcasting Company.

More recently, the adjoining Apparel Center has risen to become a major enterprise for the Midwestern wholesale clothing industry, with over 4,000 lines of women's children's, and mens-and-boys wear in permanent showrooms. Another sign of the times: a 527-room Holiday Inn occupies the Apparel Center's top floors and features a good bar, attractive atrium, and exposition center.

## Greek Town and Chicago Circle

About a mile or so west of the Loop, along Halsted between Monroe and Van Buren, you can see most of what's left of Chicago's original Greek Town, once a concentration of immigrants from Greece, who have since moved north to the Lawrence and Western area. There remain any number of small shops—butchers and bakers mostly—and some really interesting restaurants where dining is something of an adventure. The cuisine is invariably interesting and moderately priced, and the interiors of such spots as the Parthenon, between Van Buren and Jackson, are well-appointed but decidedly informal, with shirt-sleeved executives and students lingering over long lunches of a Chicago favorite, gyros and Roditos.

Farther south on Halsted beyond the Eisenhower Expressway, you come to the University of Illinois Chicago Circle campus which dates from 1965. It's a pleasant place to visit, even when school is out, as you amble through a labyrinth of buildings enjoying an interesting combination of low- and high-rise architecture. The administration tower is larger at the top than on the bottom, and most of the classroom buildings are interconnected by overhead walkways, which literally keep the students off the streets.

Actually the University of Illinois in Chicago comprises more than 25,000 students on two campuses. The liberal arts and engineering campus, formerly known as Chicago Circle, is the new one. The older Medical Center to the west, is part of a major medical, teaching, and hospital complex of some sixty health-care institutions. They include Cook County Hospital, St. Luke's Rush-Presbyterian Hospital, and the $60 million University of Illinois Hospital, which opened in 1981.

A historically significant building in the area is Jane Addams' Hull House (800 South Halsted), a landmark memorializing the social-service pioneer Jane Addams, who established the first settlement house in Chicago. Her efforts, combined with those of other reformers, led to such pioneer welfare laws as tenement-house regulations, an eight-hour work law for women, workmen's compensation, and insurance for all workers. She was a staunch advocate of women's rights and co-winner of the Nobel peace prize in 1931. The old Hull House is an exhibit now, and the building diagonally across the street is a modern parking garage for students—but vestiges of the old "settlement" style neighborhoods remain to the west along Taylor Street.

You can still find some great Italian neighborhood eateries on Taylor. One favorite is Florence restaurant at 1030 West Taylor, an informal place frequented by medical students; the linguini is mouthwatering, as is made-to-order chocolate rum torte.

If you're in a shopping mood, walk south on Halsted from Taylor to Roosevelt Road and turn east across the Dan Ryan Expressway to the little-known Jeffro Plaza shopping center at 555 West Roosevelt. Look especially for the Conte di Savoia international food market and be prepared to spend a half hour taking in the sights and smells of this unusual shop with its open kegs of parmesan and oregano plus sausages and huge rounds of cheese. There are gourmet condiments and cookware, too—a great place, even though it's a bit off the beaten path.

On the other side of Roosevelt, at Jefferson, look for Manny's, a modern version of a cafeteria-style Jewish deli, where the food quality is high, portions are large, and the price for a lunch, say of Kreplac soup and a corned beef sandwich for example, is under $5.00.

Maxwell Street at 2000 South on Halsted in the not so distant past was a galaxy of surprises, with a memorable cigar store Indian, which stood in the middle of swarms of shoppers who haggled endlessly, European-style, over the price of a pair of shoes, a girl's dress, or a set of that prickly, long-handled wool underwear that little boys of the time hated with a passion. Now, though, Maxwell Street shows signs of age and visitors should exercise considerable caution in this very changing neighborhood. Head back northeast to Jackson and return to Grant Park.

## Grant Park West to Chinatown

In Grant Park immediately east of the Art Institute, between Monroe and Jackson, you'll come to the James C. Petrillo Bandshell, site of free summer concerts by the Grant Park Symphony Orchestra. The concerts, presented each Wednesday, Friday, Saturday, and Sunday evening between late June and the end of August, feature popular as well as classical music. Around Labor Day, the area becomes even livelier when a free festival draws some of the jazz world's greatest musicians. A limited number of seats are available for early arrivals (concerts usually begin around 7:30 or 8:00 in the evening) so check local newspapers for dates.

If you were lucky enough to hear the concert, walk south to the Clarence Buckingham Fountain for the hour-long, computer-programmed light-and-color water display. Children especially are fascinated as the lights turn the huge sprays of water from deep red to blue, yellow and green, and all shades in between. The huge, rococo-style fountain dates to 1927.

The Field Museum of Natural History is the first of three major museums located at the south side of Grant Park, the others being the Shedd Aquarium and the Adler Planetarium. Of the three the Field is the largest—in fact, it's one of the largest marble buildings in the world—and is likely to impress you the most. Recently the museum has mounted major exhibits of national stature, making it even more popular with both Chicagoans and visitors. The gift shop is small but unique, with many items imported from the exotic lands depicted in the anthropological exhibits of the museum. From here it's only a short walk under Lake Shore Drive to a museum of living beings, the Shedd Aquarium.

John G. Shedd, president and chairman of Marshall Field and Company in the 1920s, bequeathed $3 million to establish the aquarium, but died before construction began in 1927. The octagonal building was completed in 1929, and all the galleries were fully stocked with fish by 1931. Located between the Field Museum and Adler Planetarium, the Shedd Aquarium houses 7,000 aquatic animals of 777 species ranging from exotic tropical saltwater fish to freshwater ones taken from adjoining Lake Michigan. Favorites (only to look at) include the sharks, moray eels, penguins, and huge sea turtles that seemingly could break through their glass enclosures. New star is the freshwater otter display with otters frolicking beside a waterfall whose banks are landscaped with native Illinois prairie plants.

A leisurely stroll east of the aquarium brings you to the Adler Planetarium, the structure built because Max Adler, a wealthy Sears, Roebuck Company executive, wanted to bring the first artificial "sky" to the United States from Germany and have it installed in a planetarium in his hometown. Sky shows now are given on a Mark VI Zeiss planetarium projector, successor to the original Zeiss unit that intrigued Adler. Each show depicts the stars, nearby planets, and distant galaxies as seen from Chicago, and after an evening show, visitors are invited to view the actual sky through the Doane Observatory telescope. Moderate admission is charged for the sky show, but the other exhibits are free. These cover astronomy, space exploration, telescopes, (including one used to discover the planet Uranus), navigation, and antique scientific instruments. There's even a moon rock returned to Earth by the *Apollo 15* mission crew.

Soldier Field, just south of the Field Museum, is a huge lakefront stadium that is home to the Chicago Bears and the city's professional soccer team, the Chicago Sting. It's a mammoth place, singularly suited to mammoth extravaganzas such as the American Legion's annual Fourth of July pyrotechnic displays.

McCormick Place, the commanding lakeside structure, at Cermak (22nd Street) and Lake Shore Drive, is Chicago's leading exhibition center, attracting up to 100,000 conventioners for a single show. It is surprisingly ill situated in relation to Chicago's restaurant and hotel center. Most trade shows are closed to the public, but one important exception is the annual Chicago Auto Show, held in late February. The

Arie Crown Theatre in McCormick Place presents road tours of Broadway plays, concerts, dance programs, and other special events.

West of Lake Shore Drive along Cermak is McCormick Center Hotel, a tall, isolated hotel catering mostly to convention clientele. Immediately west of the hotel, you'll come to Donnelley Hall, a city exhibition center that once housed the huge four-color presses that printed *Life* magazine. The R. R. Donnelley Plant, due north of here, still prints scores of national magazines and catalogs in two gigantic buildings.

As you leave Donnelley Hall and head west toward Chinatown, continue north a few blocks to 18th Street and Prairie, site of the Prairie Avenue Historic District and lifework of the Chicago Architecture Foundation. Prairie Avenue was known as Chicago's "Gold Coast" when tycoons started building mansions along it after the great fire of 1871. By the turn of the century, however, it had become unfashionable, and the area started to go to seed and then became a warehouse district. Today, only a handful of houses remain, most carefully restored. Here you can tour fortress-like Glessner House, built in 1886–87 for John Jacob Glessner, a vice-president of International Harvester. See, too, the interior of the brightly restored Greek Revival Widow Clarke house, built in 1836 (at another site and moved to this one in 1977), the oldest surviving residence in Chicago. Other distinctive buildings are the 1891 Kimball mansion (Kimball pianos) and the 1870s Joseph Kohn house.

From there, it's a convenient bus ride west along Cermak to Clark and Chinatown. Chinatown was first centered around Clark and Van Buren Streets but settled into the area around Cermak Road and Wentworth Avenue around the 1920s. Like New York City's Chinatown, Chicago's abuts a Little Italy, making this an area rich in mix of ethnic culture. There are some very interesting shops to browse around in Chinatown—and don't be surprised to hear mostly Chinese spoken. Some of the residents do not speak English at all. Plan to have lunch or dinner here—the food in selected restaurants can be extraordinary and quite reasonable. A personal favorite is the Three Happiness, on the north side of Cermak.

Backtrack east to Michigan Avenue and head north.

## The Cultural Center—North Michigan Avenue

Chicago is not always kind to its historic buildings. The old Stock Exchange Building, long a landmark (but not an official one) on La Salle Street, fell to the wrecker's ball years ago, with only its Trading Room salvaged for posterity as a special exhibit in a new wing of the Art Institute. But in the case of the Main Library at Michigan and

Randolph, the city has held its own, converting the old Italian Renaissance building into the charming Chicago Public Library Cultural Center, which should be included on any walking tour of the Loop.

The building dates from 1897, when it became the first permanent quarters of the city's library system. (The library system itself dates from the Chicago Lyceum of 1834, but all of that 30,000-volume collection was destroyed in the Fire of 1871; much of the new collection derived from a British donation of several thousand volumes.) Renovated over three years (1974 to 1977), the Cultural Center has become a focal point of special fine arts events—concerts, films, and art exhibits —as well as a general interest reading room for thousands of Chicagoans.

Most visitors are attracted mainly by the building's fascinating interior. Here you see majestic, stained-glass domes, one at each end of the block-long (and half-block wide) building. One of the domes (nearest the Randolph Street entrance) tops the Grand Army of the Republic Museum, a permanent collection of Civil War memorabilia, with special emphasis on the Union Forces from Illinois. Abraham Lincoln of Illinois was president during that bloody war, while Ulysses S. Grant, who had lived at Galena in western Illinois, served as a leading general.

Even more impressive, though, is the southern end of the building, where in Preston Bradley Hall you see a stunning, Tiffany-designed stained-glass dome. The room's supporting arches are adorned with mosaic scrolls and rosettes bearing the symbols of sixteenth-century master printers. The first floor circulation desk at the Washington Street entrance provides visitors with current information on special events at the Cultural Center and other places around town.

## Michigan Avenue and the Near North

As you work your way north along Michigan Avenue from the Cultural Center at Randolph past the international bank and tourism offices and an occasional McDonald's, you have to be impressed with the diversity of architecture, mostly new. The city's architectural renaissance dates from the 1950s. Its first lakefront high-rise observation tower was in the Prudential Building on Randolph just east of Michigan. Now it is dwarfed by the huge Standard Oil (of Indiana) Building, immediately to the east, and an even newer architecturally striking skyscraper at Randolph and Michigan, directly across Randolph from the Cultural Center.

The Chicago renaissance is partly due to the amazing growth of new and restored hotels. Some, like the Bismarck (Randolph at La Salle in the Loop), remain characteristically old and wood paneled, while oth-

## The Near North Side

### Points of Interest

1) Chicago Academy of Sciences
2) City Hall
3) Daley Center
4) John Hancock Center
5) Magnificent Mile
6) Marina City
7) Merchandise Mart
8) Museum of Contemporary Art
9) North Rush St. Night-Life Area
10) Old Town Night Life Area
11) Olympia Center
12) Prudential Bldg.
13) Tribune Tower
14) Water Tower (Information Center)
15) Water Tower Place
16) Wrigley Bldg.
17) Chicago Historical Society

ers, like the Hyatt Regency, on Wacker east of Michigan, are open and airy. The Hyatt, made up of two huge buildings, adjoins the modern office-shopping complex called One Illinois Center. You can almost get lost in the labyrinth of shops, bars, and restaurants in the combination hotel and office complex, but what a way to lose yourself! Both structures—and others to the south—are built on air rights looming over the old Illinois Central Railroad right-of-way. (As an historical footnote, Abraham Lincoln once served as a legal counsel for the Illinois Central Railroad.) By the year 2000, it is said, Illinois Center, the complex north of Michigan between East Lake Street and Wacker, will extend its labyrinth of shops and offices all the way to Lake Shore Drive.

Other hotels worthy of a visit, either for afternoon tea or cocktails, or just a look: The Palmer House, State and Monroe; the very prestigious Drake on Michigan; the Mayfair-Regent around the corner and half a block east on E. Lake Shore Drive; and the Whitehall and Tremont, two among several small, intimate hotels in the city, both located a half-block west of Michigan north of Chicago Avenue. Still others are the Ambassadors West, Omni Ambassador East West, at Goethe and State Street Parkway, north of Division, and the exclusive Park Hyatt, which is visited mostly for dinner. It's just west of the Old Water Tower at Chicago and Michigan with the main entrance off Chicago. And, of course, there's the Ritz Carlton on Pearson just off Michigan.

North along Michigan and Wacker look for the plaque commemorating the Fort Dearborn Massacre (Michigan Avenue Bridge), one of those ugly historic events that school children are taught along with details of the great Chicago fire in 1871, which destroyed the face of the old city in and around the Loop. Like any number of Midwestern cities, Chicago traces its roots to the late seventeenth-century French explorations by Louis Jolliet and Father Jacques Marquette, but the first permanent establishment was the U.S.-controlled Fort Dearborn, set up on the banks of the Chicago River and Lake Michigan in 1804. The Fort Dearborn massacre occurred in 1812 about two miles south of the Fort while the settlers were in full retreat. The fort was reestablished and remained functional until 1837. Cook County was organized in 1831 with the village of Chicago as the county seat of justice. The city was incorporated on September 12, 1833.

Pioneer Court, just north of the river, honors many leaders of early Chicago, especially Cyrus McCormick, inventor of the reaper, which was to transform the Midwestern frontier into a veritable breadbasket for the world. In fact, the Equitable Building, is corporate headquarters of International Harvester Company (now Navistar International), a successor to the old McCormick Reaper Works, which was situated on the north side of the river, east of Michigan Avenue.

The McCormick family in the 1920s affiliated themselves with the Pattersons to form one of the nation's major communications empires, controlling the *Chicago Tribune* and the *New York Daily News*. Today the Tribune Company also owns Chicago-based WGN radio and super-television station and the National League Chicago Cubs baseball team.

Robert R. McCormick was instrumental in the construction of the Gothic Tribune Tower, immediately north of Pioneer Court. The news-paper provides conducted tours. (Most of the papers, however, are printed at a newer plant some distance northwest of here.) But check to see if they are still curtailed by labor problems, as a long-term strike was still in effect at press time.

Another Chicago family, the Wrigleys, of chewing gum fame, gave their name to the distinctive Wrigley Building (built 1921–24 and actually two buildings in one) on the west side of Michigan. Although now partially hidden from Lake Shore Drive by newer structures, the Wrigley Building remains especially attractive at night, when its near-white terra-cotta walls are beautifully lighted by floodlights beaming from the south bank of the Chicago River. In the rear of the north wing is the Wrigley Building Restaurant, one of those lesser-known spots where you can dine quietly and comfortably without spending a for-tune.

As you walk north along Michigan Avenue to Grand, you'll notice an occasional stairway in the sidewalk leading to lower Michigan Ave-nue. This phenomenon grew out of plans to create a series of streets under the Loop that would keep upper levels free of traffic.

Those plans never materialized, but examples of what might have been are to be seen below Michigan between Grand on the north and Randolph on the south (and also below Wacker Drive from Michigan all the way around the Loop to the Eisenhower Expressway). If you're interested, walk on either side of the Chicago River (in the daytime) and cross the lower Michigan Avenue Bridge, actually a two-tiered structure serving both levels of the avenue. You can board one of the sightseeing boats at the river or walk north to East Hubbard Street, where you'll spot Billy Goat Tavern, a favorite hangout for printers and other newspaper folk. It's a short-order cafe and bar where a grilled club-steak sandwich is considered to be an elaborate dish. But fun.

Around the corner, on Rush Street, you'll find Riccardo's, a regular restaurant where the bar has some dramatic Art Deco murals as a backdrop. Although the ambience is Italian, Greeks run the place. The sidewalk café at Riccardo's is especially congenial late in the afternoon of a warm summer's day. The relaxed atmosphere of the Corona Café at Rush and Illinois also is popular with Chicagoans. Wabash, just north of the Chicago River, is home to two major institutions, the *Chicago Sun-Times* on the east side of the street and the Chicago headquarters of IBM on the west. The *Sun-Times* is open year-round, and you can see a nice array of photography in the first-floor gallery. Just walk on through, or time permitting, tour the plant, which at one time also housed the now-defunct *Chicago Daily News.*

Moving north along Wabash, a bilevel street at this point, look down on Hubbard and take the westside steps to Andy's (11 East), especially around 5:00 on a week night. Chances are you'll encounter some of Chicago's popular jazz being played informally behind a huge and usually crowded bar. There's a modest cover charge but it's worth it. The music ends around 7:30 P.M., giving the musicians time for gigs at places where the cover charge isn't quite so modest.

Back on Michigan Avenue, turn east toward the Lake on Ontario for a block and a half to the Museum of Contemporary Art. Founded in 1967 in a building that once housed a bakery, the museum has established itself as a popular attraction in a city that traditionally has nurtured commerce and industry more than culture. Since 1979, when the museum added an adjoining remodeled townhouse, the Museum of Contemporary Art has occupied over 16,000 square feet in seven large, bright galleries. Here you are likely to find the unknown as well as the established artist of the avant garde, including such well-known twentieth-century names as Bacon, Braque, Calder, de Kooning, Magritte, and Picasso. The museum also delights in bringing forth the new names in film and video artistry. From here continue east past the local outlet of CBS at McClurg Court to Lake Shore Drive.

Chicago's past as a bustling lake port is best represented by the 3,000-foot long Navy Pier at the foot of Grand Avenue east of Lake Shore Drive. It was built in 1916 to receive ships plying the waters of Lake Michigan. Over the years commercial shipping has moved south to the huge Lake Calumet facilities of the Port of Chicago, leaving the city-owned Pier available to host all sorts of ethnic and cultural events.

As you wander the Pier Area near Lake Shore Drive, don't overlook Lake Point Tower, between Illinois and Grand, one of the city's most stunning skyscraper apartments. Its especially attractive late in the day when the western sides of the building literally glow in the fading light of the setting sun.

### The Magnificent Mile

Returning east to Michigan Avenue and heading north toward Ontario until you come to Erie Street, you will pass a number of classy but not necessarily well-known shops and an occasional art gallery. Here Saks Fifth Avenue maintains its main Chicago-area outlet, a multilevel store that has just about everything you'd find at the original in New York City. In a sense, this is the beginning of what is known as Chicago's "Magnificent Mile," a Chamber of Commerce phrase for a series of exclusive stores that cater to the well-to-do and those who aspire to become so. Along this stretch of Michigan there's an Elizabeth Arden, of course, along with Tiffany's, Gucci's, and any number of small, exclusive shops including Stuart Brent's popular bookstore. These are intermingled with I. Magnin, Bonwit Teller, Marshall Field, Lord & Taylor, and the new Neiman-Marcus in what is called Olympia Center, an office and apartment conglomeration that wraps itself behind the southeast corner of Chicago and Michigan avenues with entrances on both.

Long before you reach that intersection though, you'll easily pick out its distinctive landmark—the Water Tower—on the northwest corner, and across the street, the Water Pumping Station, home of the "Here's Chicago" multimedia promotional view of the city. Most of the area you've walked—from the Art Institute north to Chicago Avenue—was totally devastated by the fire of 1871, so any of the older buildings left in the area, other than the Water Tower and its pumping station, postdate the fire. (The fire actually started west of the Loop and swept east and north, killing 250 people and wiping out the homes of 100,000 others. One result: Chicago has long had one of the strongest building fire codes in the nation.) Today the Water Tower on the west side of Michigan houses a small air-conditioned information center where you can find out schedules and places of current happenings, from plays to festivals to concerts. There are also a visitor events line, fine arts hotline, and direct phonelines to selected restaurants.

Latecomers notwithstanding, the big event on North Michigan Avenue remains Water Tower Place, occupying the entire block bounded by Michigan, Pearson, Seneca, and Chestnut. A score of stores, eateries, and shops on the Michigan Avenue side attract literally thousands of shoppers every day—Sundays included. The complex also contains any number of offices, condominium apartments, movie theaters, and the hidden-from-view Ritz-Carlton Hotel, unique in that the hotel's main lobby is 12 floors up. When entering Water Tower Place for the first time, pass up the doors to Marshall Field or Lord & Taylor. Enter instead through the center doors on North Michigan Avenue leading to the stunning atrium lobby with its bevy of trees, a waterfall, and general feeling of solace and calm. Multilingual brochures at the information desk give the names and locations of all the stores and shops.

As you get off the second-floor escalator, you encounter an inner atrium with three glass-enclosed elevators that whisk you to the seventh floor for great views of the entire air-conditioned vertical shopping center. Watch your time: browsing here can consume a half day or more. You may want to stop on the mezzanine level at Vie de France for a croissant and cup of coffee; the light-lunch fare there is also

# EXPLORING 63

excellent, but for heartier cuisine you may want to try the adjoining highly regarded Chestnut Street Grill.

Tea at the Ritz-Carlton is one of Chicago's genuine pleasures. Enter the hotel at ground level, immediately behind Marshall Field, and take the elevator to the 12th floor. Here you enter a two-acre fountain-centered lobby and an atrium-like greenhouse. Views to the north from the plant-bedecked greenhouse are still open enough for you to see some of Lake Michigan as you sip tea, coffee, or cocktails and munch hors d'oeuvres, usually with relaxing live piano music in the background.

Immediately north of Water Tower Place, between Chestnut and Delaware, stands towering Hancock Center, the city's third-tallest building (at one time, it held the rank of world's tallest). Some say its architecture is so-so—some even call it box-like—but the fact remains that "Big John" is tall, and the ride to the 94th-floor observation level is worth the price of admission. Or for the price of a drink you can take in cocktails on the 96th floor, or a dinner on the 95th, with unsurpassed views of the lakefront as far south as Indiana or as far north as the northernmost suburbs. The lower floors of Hancock Center are devoted to shops and offices, while the upper ones (below the observation-dining-cocktail floors) contain condominium apartments and an upper-level garage.

Directly across Michigan from Hancock Center is Fourth Presbyterian Church, home for years to some of the city's leading families (including the McCormicks). This well-endowed facility is open to visitors and worth a short stop to see the richly paneled Blair Chapel, a reincarnation of something you'd find in a classic church in England.

A contrast of sorts is presented by the building at the southeast corner of Michigan and Walton, now known as the Playboy Building but originally the Palmolive Building. It houses the editorial offices of *Playboy* magazine, now presided over mostly by Christie Hefner, daughter of founder-publisher Hugh Hefner. The beacon atop this building originally served as a navigational aid to vessels sailing on Lake Michigan, but now it's cut off from view by taller buildings in the area (including "Big John"). The Knickerbocker Hotel, across from the Drake Hotel on East Walton, has been nicely restored (it formerly was a property of Playboy Enterprises, Inc.). Its lobby provides a nice respite for late afternoon or early evening cocktails with piano music. (Due east of here, at the lakefront, are two 1920s Mies van der Rohe buildings, which are noted on Culture Bus Tours of the North Side. They are at 860–80 North Lake Shore Drive.)

The Drake, also built in the twenties, is one of Chicago's revered hotels, catering to an upscale clientele that prefers the old to the glitz of the modern. The Cape Cod Room in the Drake has a reputation for fresh seafood that predates most living Chicagoans, but if it's completely booked the hotel's other eating establishments deliver good values for the price.

A few doors east of the Drake, but with its entrance on Lake Shore Drive East, is the Mayfair Regent, one of several smaller exclusive hotels that have gained tremendously in popularity. Afternoon tea and cocktails there are recommended, as is dinner in the Ciel Blue dining room.

Among the latest in fashionable shopping and dining sites along North Michigan Avenue (at Oak) is One Magnificent Mile, a 58-story combination of shops, offices, and condominiums. Here you find a three-level designer apparel department store, Stanley Korshak (A Chicago tradition that moved a block north from older, smaller quarters), the two-story Spiaggia Restaurant featuring northern Italian cuisine, and an informal Spiaggia Cafe.

Oak Street, west of Michigan, continues to feature exclusive shops, boutiques, and cafes—a great area for browsing on a warm summer's day.

## Rush Street Area

Rush Street intersecting Oak is synonymous with nightlife in Chicago. The street itself is less than a mile long, starting at the Chicago River just under (or behind) the Wrigley Building and stopping just north of Oak at State and Elm. From Chicago Avenue north to Elm, you'll find the glitter of discotheques and popular jazz spots: Billy's, Faces, and the Back Room. Singles, meanwhile, flock to The Ultimate Sports Bar and Grill, and the Division Street area just north of Elm and west of State: the Snuggery, and Butch McGuire's. Sweetwater, owned by former Bear linebacker Doug Buffone, attracts sports figures.

In its heyday, Rush Street was the center of the city's night life. Venture there carefully; it is pricey, crowded, and can be rough and tough. A public housing project just to the west has been the scene of many violent crimes.

To capture a sense of days gone by, continue north one block on State Street Parkway to Goethe and the twin hotels, Ambassadors East and West. Although they are owned and managed separately, the hotels attract much the same clientele; in the Ambassador East is the famous Pump Room, a place where visiting celebrities still like to dine. Just north of the Ambassador West you pass the former Playboy Mansion. It was here in the heyday of his time in Chicago that publisher Hugh Hefner held court until he up and moved to the West Coast.

While you're in the area, tour Astor Street, a block east of State, to see old-style homes tucked between modern apartments. Astor is historic enough to have gained landmark status for the entire street, from North Avenue to Division. Charnley House at 1365 North Astor, a national historic landmark, dates from 1891–92; its design is attributed to Louis Sullivan and David Adler, with a touch of Frank Lloyd Wright, a protege of Sullivan, thrown in.

At the North Avenue end of Astor, occupying a block-wide lot, is the residence of the Roman Catholic Archbishop of Chicago.

## Old Town

Backtrack south to Division Street again. As you move west along Division to La Salle, notice the unusual apartment building just north of Division. It's a photographer's delight, since the southerly facade is an unusual mural, and many of the windows on the building's east side are merely painted on to look like windows. At Wells and Division you encounter a Chicago tradition, the House of Glunz—the headquarters of a company that's been catering to wine lovers since the 1880s. Stop in for a taste of wine and a look at memorabilia that includes photos of the old days when this was one of meatpacker Oscar Mayer's favorite taverns.

Mayer, of course, founded the huge meat-processing plant known for the American hot dog. The original plant was located a block or so west of Wells as was Dr. Scholl's factory that produced helpful aids to aching feet. The latter, incidentally, like many former factories, is being converted to exclusive apartment units.

Walking north along Wells, you encounter any number of old standbys in an area that is undergoing a comeback in popularity for shopping and dining. Piper's Alley, at North and Wells, is worth a walk through as you move into what is known as the Old Town Triangle. You will also come to the Sullivan-designed Garrick Theater, home of the always popular Second City comedy review (Mike Nichols and Elaine May are among scores of top comedy acts who got a start here). Guests can buy a ticket for the main show, then stay to watch the improvisational performance afterward.

Northern Old Town is a good place to take a leisurely walk along the side streets west of Wells and Lincoln Avenue, where the chic and modern blends nicely with the chic and the old. Examples of architecturally worthy buildings are the Sullivan-designed town houses at 1800 Lincoln Park West that date from 1888, and many of which are beautifully restored. Other places to look for in this area of nineteenth-century nostalgia are the Crilly Court buildings at St. Paul and North Park Avenue; Concord Place; and old St. Michael's Church at Eugenie and Cleveland.

## Near North

The Chicago Historical Society at North Avenue and Clark Street is one of those easily overlooked museums that is well worth a one- or two-hour visit. Over the years the Society has developed a lively center of exhibitions. Among them are a stunning array of dresses worn by Chicago's leading ladies of the late nineteenth and early twentieth centuries and a series of pioneer craft demonstrations of spinning, weaving, dyeing, quilting, and candlemaking, all by docents in authentic period costumes. The Society is best known as a center of Lincolniana, with an entire gallery devoted to a biographic diorama of the Civil War president's life, plus rare memorabilia from his Springfield, Illinois, home and his Civil War years in the White House. (Although some distance from Chicago, Lincoln-related sites in Springfield and Salem are well worth a visit.) Saturdays and Sundays are good times to visit the Historical Society because there are often films and other events of special interest. The gift shop here is quite good.

One favorite stop, north of Old Town adjoining the west side of Lincoln Park at the foot of Lincoln Avenue, is Hemingways Movable Feast, a short-order restaurant with a "mile-long" menu of king-size sandwiches. You can feast inside or on the patio, or take your meal out for a picnic in the park.

## The Lincoln Park Zoo

Like Washington, D.C., Chicago still has its many free attractions that are true delights, and the Lincoln Park Zoo has to rank high on the list. Even in its moribund days, when the animals were seen in barred cages, the zoo held a fascination that drew literally thousands of visitors on a typical summer's day (the zoo is open year-round, but it's far less crowded in the fall-winter and spring). Today it is a natural-habitat-style zoo allowing the animals greater freedom and us a better look at them.

The most endearing exhibit, at the westerly entrance off Stockton Drive, is the Children's Zoo and Nursery. Although it's primarily for toddlers, you'll find that the child in you takes over, and you'll want to stop there to see the newborn of the Zoo's kaleidoscopic population. You may see tiny lion cubs frolicking in a glass-enclosed waist-high cage and tiny gorillas or chimpanzees exercising on miniature tires and other paraphernalia. There's even a petting area, where tots (young and old) reach out and touch a rabbit or a gerbil.

Nearby, seals cavort on rocks and in the water (there's an aquarium-like visitors passageway where you can see the seals swimming underwater), and in the huge lions' den, the big cats lounge in regal splendor. Most beguiling of all the mammal enclosures is the new gorilla house, where entire families of these fascinating beasts cavort on ropes and ledges to the delight of neck-stretching audiences. Polar bears also have their own swimming hole, while birds abound in the ultranatural setting of the Zoo Rookery, just off Fullerton and a block or so west of the Lake.

And there's even more. A bit south of the main entrance, off Stockton, look for the Farm-in-the-Zoo, a working farm with a fascinating array of animals indigenous to Midwestern farms: dairy cows, hogs, sheep, and horses, all working to keep the farm as in days long past. Don't expect flowing fields of grain, though; instead there's an enticing duck pond, where rental boats provide a welcome respite to all that walking you've been doing.

Just north of the zoo's western entrance you arrive at the Lincoln Park Conservatory, a Chicago landmark of sorts since the 1890s. A stunning array of live orchids greets the visitor at the entrance to the Palm House, one of four glassed buildings. Immediately beyond the orchids you'll encounter huge palm trees from India and Malaysia and a 50-foot Fiddle-leaf rubber tree from Africa. A curving walkway leads you through the Fernery and Tropical House to the Show-House, the greenhouse where major flower shows are staged, attracting thousands of Chicagoans every year. (The flower shows are usually staged over three or four weeks. They feature chrysanthemums in November, poinsettias in December, and a bewildering display of lillies at Easter. Admission, even to the major shows, is free.)

Note: If you're driving or have access to auto transportation, take the time to visit the Lincoln Park Conservatory's sister greenhouse in Garfield Park, on the West Side; it's even larger, and equally beautiful.

## Lincoln Park West

Lakeview Avenue from Fullerton north to Diversey and the area of Fullerton near the Park, boast examples of old Chicago living at its finest. The streets are bordered by Lincoln Park on the east and large, high-ceilinged, tailored apartment buildings on the west, with a smattering of hotels and dining establishments in between. It's an area where nannies used to stroll babies in the park, but nowadays you're as likely to see the one-half of an up-and-coming young couple walking their Weimaraner or some other pedigree. To capture the full flavor of a bygone era, watch for the Theurer-Wrigley House at 2466 North Lakeview and Dawes House at 503 West Lincoln. Along southerly parts of Halsted near Armitage (west of where Lincoln and Armitage intersect), you'll find a grand assortment of antique shops, hardware stores, and good clothing stores as well as a large variety of bars, restaurants, and the Chicago's equivalent of New York's Off-Broadway playhouses. Nightlife in this general area is more alive with Chicagoans than tourists, but that can be a plus if you want to mingle with the locals.

Enjoy much of the same type of strolling north of Lincoln Avenue along Cleveland and Hudson Avenues (they parallel each other) all the way to Dickens, where you can turn east and head directly for the Lincoln Park Zoo. Other pleasant walking areas to tour in this mid-north area are Fullerton Avenue, from Clark to Halsted and Lincoln; the De Paul University area west of Halsted and south of Fullerton (the campus and surrounding neighborhoods have undergone extensive restoration); and Lincoln Avenue immediately north of Fullerton (look for some great bookstores as well as the restored Biograph Theater, a fine arts cinema known historically as the site where the notorious John Dillinger was gunned down by Federal agents). Lincoln Avenue, incidentally, from its beginnings just south of Lincoln Park at Clark as far north as Belmont, is dotted with antique stores, bars, and trendy dining spots. For drinks and sandwiches, try the John Barleycorn Memorial Pub at Belden and Lincoln, where recorded and live classical music is played. For an added touch, slides of works of art are projected onto screens at both ends of the bar. The Barleycorn Pub goes mildly berserk every December staging Chicago's celebration of Beethoven's birthday.

### The South Side (Jackson Park and Hyde Park)

If you head south on Lake Shore Drive, you'll come to Jackson Park. Chicago, a city that loves a festival, big or small, has inherited many of its cultural institutions from the World's Columbian Exposition of 1893. The Palace of Fine Arts, built in Jackson Park for the Exposition, housed the Field Columbian Museum, now the Field Museum of Natural History, from 1894 to 1920. When that museum was moved to Grant Park in 1920, the Palace of Fine Arts fell into ruin. With $1-million from philanthropist Julius Rosenwald and a $5-million bond issue to restore the exterior and reconstruct the interior, the renovation led, in 1933, to the opening of part of the Museum of Science and Industry. It is now the nation's most popular museum of its kind with an annual attendance around four million—somewhat more than the population of the entire city.

Even Chicagoans who have been visiting the Museum of Science and Industry since childhood have yet to be anything but fascinated by its array of exhibits, ranging from the health sciences to physics to chemistry. One remarkable feature is the realistic indoor coal mine exhibit, where you ride an elevator down from a high point in the building to

THE SOUTH SIDE

the confines of the make-believe mine. Much of the free museum reflects Midwestern business interests in agriculture (you see live chicks on display), nuclear energy (the nearby University of Chicago was the site of the first splitting of the atom), and railroading (one of the world's largest miniature railroad setups is here). The newest exhibit is the Henry Crown Space Center, with its dramatic Omnimax Theater.

A general favorite is the annual Christmas Around the World display of evergreen trees decorated in the holiday traditions of many nations. This highly photogenic display is staged from late November to early January. Still fascinating, too, is the permanent exhibit of the German U–505 submarine captured in 1944. Allow at least a half day for rambling among the museum's 2,000 exhibits in seventy-five different halls—it's a long walk, but an exciting one, covering some fourteen acres of floor area.

The Columbian Exposition of 1893 was also associated with the park-like Midway Plaisance of the University of Chicago, immediately west of the Museum of Science and Industry between 59th and 60th Streets. Here you enter the domain of the University of Chicago, the main reason that the community of Hyde Park, founded in the 1850s and annexed to the city in 1889, still flourishes as a lively locale of arts, crafts, and advanced intellectual pursuits. Novelist Saul Bellow long lived in the area, and economist Milton Friedman to a large extent built his international reputation while at the University of Chicago.

Walk along the Midway, as it's known, to Rockefeller Memorial Chapel, at 58th and Woodlawn, which stands out as the tallest and perhaps most interesting of the many University Buildings that face onto the parkway. The chapel is named for the university founder, John D. Rockefeller, who started things rolling in 1892 at Cobb Hall, at 58th and South Ellis, a year before the opening of the Columbian Exposition.

In the early '40s, some of the nation's leading scientists were assembled here on Ellis, including Enrico Fermi and Glenn T. Seaborg. It was Seaborg who led a group of scientists in the isolation of plutonium, the basic fuel of nuclear reactors, and Fermi who on December 2, 1942, directed the first successful nuclear chain reaction, which led to the development of the atom bomb. The laboratory where the plutonium was isolated is a national historic landmark: Room 405, of George Herbert Jones Laboratory on Ellis between East 57th and 58th Streets. Old Alonzo Stagg Field stadium, where the university's Big Ten football teams played, was the site of the nuclear chain reaction. The stadium is long gone; the site on Ellis between 56th and 57th Streets is marked by the Henry Moore sculpture appropriately titled *Nuclear Energy.*

More benign, certainly, are the memories evoked in the famous Oriental Institute, at 58th and Ellis, around the corner from Rockefeller Chapel. Here you'll find an amazing array of artifacts, the result of years of archaeological research in Egypt, what was once Persia, and other areas of the Middle East going back to the times of the pharaohs, Babylon, and other sites named in the Old Testament. The display of Egyptian mummies is extraordinary as are a towering likeness of the young Egyptian ruler King Tutankhamen and a winged bull (from Iraq circa 705 B.C.).

From here walk east to the corner of Woodlawn and 58th to an outstanding example of Frank Lloyd Wright's Prairie School design, Robie House, built in 1909 and now occupied by offices of the university. Continue north along Woodlawn to East 55th Street and then east to the commercial center of Hyde Park. The entire area is a great place for browsing, especially Harper Court at Harper Avenue between 52nd and 53rd Streets. There are Illinois Central commuter stations at 53d, 55th, and 59th Streets, where you can catch a train that will take you back to the Loop in 15 minutes.

Incidentally, the Midway connects Jackson Park with Washington Park. Both parks were originally designed by the firm of Olmsted and Vaux. When Washington Park opened in 1874 it was a most fashionable place for Chicago's wealthy to roam. The 1893 Columbian Exposition brought great attention to Jackson Park, and since that time, Washington Park suffered a decline in favor. The park's main attractions are the DuSable Museum of African American History and the Lorado Taft Sculpture, *Fountain of Time*. It is used, however, on weekends by neighborhood families for ball games and barbecues.

## Sheridan Road and the Northern Suburbs

From the Loop you can tour Sheridan Road, named for a Civil War general, Philip Henry Sheridan, by car or sightseeing bus. It's a drive that keeps you close to Lake Michigan and still introduces you to many outstanding neighborhoods and institutions. Sheridan Road actually begins a few blocks west of Lake Shore Drive at Diversey Boulevard, and trail-like, ambles west for a half mile or so where it right-angles into a straight north route to Devon. Reflecting the changing positions of the shoreline (Lake Michigan widens as you move north), Sheridan continues to present sharp, right-angle turns to the west and then north as you make your way into Evanston and beyond.

Your best bet is to pick up Sheridan Road at Foster Avenue, just west of Lake Shore Drive. The Saddle and Cycle, one of the city's rare surviving old-fashioned tennis clubs, is located off Foster just west of the Drive. Turning north on Sheridan, you drive past stunning high-rise apartments and what's left of the old Edgewater Beach development (for years the Edgewater Beach Hotel, now extinct, was a Chicago institution), dating from the days when the lake water literally bordered the city a short distance east of Sheridan Road, as it continues to do north of Hollywood. Most of Lincoln Park was built on landfill, which also permitted construction of northern Lake Shore Drive.

Immediately north of Hollywood, where Lake Shore Drive terminates, you will pass a score or more of high-rise apartment buildings that front on the lake. A few blocks beyond, you come to a complex that is Mundelein College and the undergraduate campus of Loyola University, the state's largest privately endowed college. (The Loyola downtown campus is in Lewis Towers, immediately west of the Chicago Water Tower.) Pull off Sheridan Road at the south entrance to the Loyola Campus and ask directions to the Madonna Strada Chapel, a little-known jewel of a church right on the lakeshore. The modern library, a few steps from the chapel, houses a small, interesting art gallery.

Continue north to the 7400 block of Sheridan, where you can spot a landmark home designed in 1915 by Frank Lloyd Wright, the Emil Bach house. As you enter Evanston drive around Calvary Cemetery, which also fronts on the lake.

After you pass Calvary Cemetery and turn north on Sheridan once more, you'll immediately get a sense of old Chicago suburbia: large homes, large lawns, large shrubs, and frequently, large automobiles. You can turn off at practically any side street north of Main Street (which cuts into Sheridan) to view any number of extraordinary dwellings. Forest Avenue north of Main can be especially rewarding with examples of Prairie School architecture at 1000 and the old Oscar Mayer mansion at 1030. There's a Michigan Avenue in Evanston, too. It's immediately west of Sheridan Road and replete with turn-of-the-century mansions. Farther west, at 1730 Chicago Avenue, the 1865 Willard House has been restored and is open for tours. The original owner, Frances Willard, was a temperance leader, and the home now houses the national headquarters of the Women's Christian Temperance Union.

Sheridan Road actually bypasses downtown Evanston, but if you're interested in seeing a relatively thriving shopping area, turn west on Davis Street.

Not long ago, Evanston was dry as a bone—remember, it's the home of the Women's Christian Temperance Union—but now the restaurants serve beer, wine, and liquor. Being the home of Northwestern University, Evanston is something of an oversized college town. In fact the university's first president, John Evans, circa 1855, prompted the name of the town. At that time, Evans presided over ten scholars in a three-story frame structure. Today the university has two large campuses (the professional/medical one is at Chicago Avenue just west of

Lake Shore Drive) with overall enrollment of some 10,000 students. The Evanston campus is primarily devoted to liberal arts and engineering, with outstanding music and drama departments. You can tour the campus on your own: pick up a self-guided pamphlet at the Norris University Center, 1999 Sheridan Road. Farther north, at 2100 Sheridan, you can visit the Shakespeare Garden, a quiet, formal garden of roses, rosemary, and other flora mentioned in the works of the Bard.

Not many remember the vice-president who served under Calvin Coolidge—in fact, many have trouble remembering Coolidge. But his vice-president, Charles Gates Dawes, lived in a turreted, 28-room chateau at 225 Greenwood Street in Evanston. The building is nicely restored and open for tours.

Just north of the Northwestern Campus, you'll spot on your right a rare Lake Michigan lighthouse, called the Gross Point Lighthouse, which dates from 1860. There are weekend tours of the tower from May into October.

Sheridan Road continues to jog to the north, as you wend your way through Evanston and into Wilmette. Wilmette is noted architecturally for the famous Baha'i House of Worship, a distinctive temple-like structure that seems to combine the dome of St. Peter's with the flying buttresses of the Cathedral of Notre Dame, but all with a definite Middle Eastern flair. This is a must stop for any photography enthusiast.

The Temple serves as the national center of the Persian-born Baha'i faith, which happened to be represented at the Columbian Exposition of 1893. Construction of the Temple began in 1903 and was completed in 1953.

Continuing north, you'll see even more opulent examples of suburban living stretching all the way to Lake Bluff. Soon you arrive at Wilmette's pleasant little shopping center, Plaza del Lago, with a Spanish motif. Stop for lunch or a little shopping. Burhops, one of Chicago's leading seafood vendors, has a store there, as do any number of small, classy boutiques.

The North Shore's biggest and most popular community event is the Ravinia Festival in the town of Highland Park. It plays every summer in Ravinia Park from late June through early September at a 36-acre wooded park a couple of miles west of the lake. It's a community event because countless volunteers help finance and put together the annual series of symphonic concerts, recitals, chamber music, and popular musical events from rock to country to Dixieland jazz.

Ravinia Park is to Chicago, therefore, what Tanglewood is to Boston or the Hollywood Bowl is to Los Angeles. Featured for the first eight weeks of the season is the Chicago Symphony Orchestra with its summer director, James Levine, and any number of renowned guest conductors. It's all very informal, with normally straitlaced musicians appearing tieless in short-sleeved sport shirts (white, of course).

A large percentage of the audience arrives as early as 6:00, allowing time to dine in one of two restaurants (one features buffet) or to picnic (with wine) on pleasant little tables in a delightful gazebo.

For best listening and viewing, a reserved seat in the Pavilion is definitely in order, but if you are satisfied with just hearing the music piped over loudspeakers, you can join hundreds of other concertgoers who recline on their blankets on the lawn outside the Pavilion and listen under the stars.

Commuter trains from the Chicago and North Western station at Madison and Canal provide direct service between the Loop and the Ravinia Park concerts, or you can reserve space on a chartered bus (through any major hotel).

North of Highland Park, Sheridan Road leads you past historic Fort Sheridan, which served as a major processing center for Army recruits during World War II. Established in 1887 on 695 acres stretching along 1 1/3 miles of shoreline, the fort contains an impressive collection of 93 brick and stone buildings dating from the 1890's. The buildings are still in use, and about 40 percent of the post has been designated a national historic landmark. The post is open to daytime visitors, and it is definitely worth a detour. The fort's museum and military cemetery are also of interest.

Barat College on Sheridan Road, at the southern entrance to Lake Forest, is a small, private, liberal arts college serving resident and commuter students. Lake Forest itself is among Chicago's most exclusive suburbs, with tree-lined streets that are breathtaking any time of year, but especially so in October, when full fall color comes to areas along Lake Michigan.

Other places of interest nearby include the Marriott Lincolnshire Resort at Lincolnshire and Six Flags Great America at Gurnee, a few miles north and west of Lake Forest. The resort is a combination hotel/motel featuring swimming, dining areas, cocktail lounges, a well-regarded theater-in-the-round that draws professional performers, and an 18-hole golf course.

Six Flags Great America provides attractions for the entire family, from thrill rides like The Edge, a nearly vertical roller coaster, to musical shows in the Theatre Royale. The park is open from early May to October with a full seven-day schedule from June through early September. Admission is fairly high, so plan to spend the day.

Tempel Farms, west of the Tri-State (I-94) at Rte. 132, is the only place in America where rare Lippizan stallions perform their paces in the same style as Vienna's Spanish Riding School. Check "Special

Interest Sightseeing" in the *Practical Information for Chicago* section for details about these exciting performances.

### Western Suburbs (Oak Park, Brookfield)

You can reach Oak Park from downtown Chicago by driving west along the Eisenhower Expressway (I-290). Oak Park is known for two major Chicago figures: Ernest Hemingway, who lived there as a youngster, and Frank Lloyd Wright, who accomplished much of his Prairie Style architecture in and near this western suburb. Vestiges of the Hemingway boyhood are hard to find, but Wright's works are easy to see. The Hemingway birthplace is at 339 North Oak Park Avenue, and his boyhood home is at 600 North Kenilworth.

Two of the more prominent structures on public tours of the area are the Frank Lloyd Wright Home and Studio, 951 Chicago Avenue (a National Historic Landmark built in 1889, when Wright was 22; the restored studio dates from 1898), and the Wright-designed Unity Temple (built between 1905 and 1909 at Lake and Kenilworth; it presents an interlocking complex of abstract geometric forms).

Begin your tour of the Oak Park Historic District at the Visitor Center, 150 North Forest Avenue. The center provides a slide show to introduce you to the area, an annotated walking-tour map so that you can guide yourself, a recorded tour for self-guidance, and a host of pamphlets. A guided tour that covers the temple and Wright's home and studio is offered as well. The historic district is bounded roughly by Lake, Clyde and Division Streets and Harlem Avenue.

While at the Center, also inquire about the River Forest Historic District north of Oak Park, where you can see six Wright-designed homes. River Forest is adjacent to Oak Park and its historic district is just a couple blocks from Oak Park's. It contains a number of houses by other architects of the Prairie School as well as some in the classical and medieval styles dating from the 1920s. Edgewood Place, just east of Auvergne, is especially rewarding.

Chicago, incidentally, is ringed by a series of massive forest preserves, and while you're in the Oak Park–River Forest area, you're close to one of the finest. Just drive west on Lake, Division, Chicago, or North Avenue to Thatcher. A Trailside Museum at 738 Thatcher, a building dating from 1874, houses a modest small-mammal zoo.

The Brookfield Zoo, 14 miles west of the Loop in suburban Brookfield (southwest of Oak Park), has been attracting animal lovers to 200 acres since 1934. It was the first zoological park in the country allowing animals to roam freely while visitors gaze at them over waist-high fences and deep protective moats. Over recent years, the zoo has added a popular dolphin show, "Seven Seas Panorama," and a delightful children's zoo. The zoo's largest addition is Tropic World, said to be the largest *indoor* exhibit of animals—mostly primates—in the world. Actually Tropic World is three "worlds" in one: Africa, Asia, and South America—each depicting the rain-forest ecology of the subcontinents.

### West of Chicago

Even farther to the west, Oak Brook, one of the newest of the Chicago suburbs, is the epitome of a planned, high-income community. The Oak Brook Shopping Center is replete with upscale shops and a major branch of Marshall Field & Co. Hotels, reflecting a trend of business to migrate closer to O'Hare Field, abound in the area.

Beyond Oakbrook, the popular Morton Arboretum, just north of the East-West Tollway at Illinois 53, is at its peak in May, when the flowers are in bloom and early October, when leaves changing turn the area into a rainbow of color. Ducks paddle in a pond near the main entrance of this 1,500-acre preserve of woody plants from around the world. The formal gardens here are especially attractive.

# PRACTICAL INFORMATION FOR CHICAGO

**TELEPHONES.** The area code for Chicago and the surrounding area is 312. You do not need to dial the area code if it is the same as the one from which you are dialing. Information (known as directory assistance) for Chicago and communities within the 312 area is 411. For numbers outside the 312 area code, dial 1 plus the area code plus 555–1212. An operator will assist you on person-to-person, credit-card, and collect calls if you first dial "0." All long-distance calls must first be prefaced by dialing 1, followed by the area code and number. Pay telephones start at 30¢.

**HOTELS.** Like all major cities, Chicago has had its share of glamour hotels ever since multimillionaire Potter Palmer built his grand old Palmer House. Most of the prestigious, big-name chains are here, and competition being what it is, these tend to refurbish, redecorate, and generally gussy-up their properties with some regularity. They span the super deluxe to expensive categories and feature all the high standards associated with their names.

The usual percentage of slick, ultramodern new hotels exists, catering to high-volume business and pleasure travelers. They are comfortable, full of the latest in modern conveniences, and exude a flashy veneer of sophistication.

Then there are the old grand dames, the prestige mainline names where your grandmother stayed when she came to Chicago and which feature a more formal elegance, richly paneled lobbies, acres of polished marble, genuine antiques, and service in the old manner. They offer the kind of wide aisled, grand staircase grandeur impossible to duplicate in today's world.

Over the past few years an interesting new trend has been developing toward creating small personalized English-type hotels. These tend to be very posh, low-key, and upper-class and exude the quiet rustle of old money. Their mood is understated, comparable to London's finest.

Some of the moderate finds are often so priced because of location, which may be a bit out of the center for some travelers or perfect for others. There are fashions in hotels, just like clothes. Being older, down the street, around the block, and perhaps not as "in" today simply because newer, flashier spots may have captured the limelight, some of the moderately priced hotels are excellent and have very devoted followings.

Inexpensive is a relative term. This year's inexpensive price range was probably considered deluxe not too many years ago. Those chosen here are selected from the many for specific reasons. Some are close to downtown and feature on-site parking, others cater to families interested in adequate, comfortable, and clean surroundings but who have no need of a concierge, imported bath oil, and a posh decor.

Price categories for double occupancy are as follows: *Super Deluxe* $175–$230 and up; *Deluxe* $135–$200; *Expensive* $95–$140; *Moderate* $70–$95; and *Inexpensive* $65 and under.

Interestingly, a wide spectrum of all categories offers escape weekend packages at bargain prices. So investigate before you invest. Chicago Hotel Association, 100 W. Monroe, 60603, offers a brochure outlining weekend specials.

### Super Deluxe

**Mayfair Regent.** 181 E. Lake Shore Dr.; 787–8500. Gracious, traditional, new 209-room beauty totally refurbished. (Formerly Lake Shore Drive Hotel dating from late 1920s.) 19th-floor rooftop dining with sweeping lake view. Accent on old-world service. Arriving guests register with bilingual concierge at antique Louis XVI desk. Quiet residential Gold Coast mood close to North Michigan Ave., across from Oak St. Beach. Lobby lounge is decorated with hand-painted Chinese murals and, with its fireplace, has the living room look of a town-house mansion. 24-hour room service. Umbrella and plush robes in room. Private telephone-equipped limousines for airport transportation or local sightseeing. *Palm* restaurant. Even their garbage is refrigerated!

**Park Hyatt.** 800 N. Michigan Ave., on Water Tower Sq.; 280–2222. This is the former Water Tower Hyatt, and anyone who knew it then would never recognize the place. It has been turned into a remarkable Cinderella, an intimate jewel of a hotel where the arrival of each guest is treated like a special event. The doorman who welcomes you is wearing a coachman's coat and cape made of mink with black leather Gucci boots. Check-in is personalized, a concierge is there to smooth the way, and housekeepers are stationed on every floor to unpack your luggage and take care of any necessary sewing or pressing. The 255 rooms have marble-topped dressers, rosewood and Chinese lacquer pieces, designer bed linens, and hand-painted watercolors. The lobby's marble floors are covered with Oriental rugs, and Oriental art, velvet sofas, and lush palms provide a relaxing, low-key decor. The style is definitely upper echelon. This is the first of the "small wonderfuls" planned by the Hyatt chain.

**Ritz Carlton Hotel.** 160 E. Pearson, just off Michigan Blvd.; 266–1000. Shoppers can practically fall out of bed and into the temptations of Water Tower Place across the driveway. An unusual hotel that does not begin until the 12th floor, although there is luggage check-in at the lower level. The spectacular lobby is a marvelous place to promenade—large, splashy fountain, acres of lounge space, fountain-side dining room. The hotel offers the kind of grandeluxe service and facilities that the name implies. For the absolute ultimate in baths, the Anniversary Suite has a 5½-by-7-ft. white marble tub set on a pedestal with a chandelier overhead and silver trees etched on walls and mirrors.

**Tremont.** 100 E. Chestnut; 751–1900. A prestige property where there are only suites. Antique English prints and large Flemish-style vases decorate the unpretentious lobby—rather like the entrance to an English country house. Fireplaces, overstuffed chairs, everything quiet, unobtrusive, and very classy.

Elizabeth Taylor likes to stay here when she's in town. Good location 1 block from Upper Michigan Ave. Its *Crickets Restaurant* is locally popular.

**Whitehall.** 105 E. Delaware Pl., just off Michigan Blvd.; 944–6300. Very prestigious, has the understated low-key, high-quality mood of a private upper-class London club. Everything about the place is so restrained that even the dining room is private, open only to members and guests. For the ultimate, the elaborate Terrace Suite has its own formal dining room, kitchen, terrace complete with garden furniture and plants, sitting room, and bedroom. Even guests like Gregory Peck, Katherine Hepburn, Richard Burton, and Donald Sutherland have found their privacy protected here. Do not expect a lot of flash and glitter. The entrance and lobby look like a high-rent town house just off Knightsbridge. 222 rooms function with quiet efficiency, fresh Rogers and Gallet soap magically reappears in bathrooms, and the food is always good.

*Deluxe*

**Ambassador West.** 1300 N. State Pkwy.; 787–7900. Prestigous Near North Side address. One of City's long-time society queens. Excellent service, beginning of quiet residential Gold Coast neighborhood.

**The Barclay-Chicago.** 166 E. Superior; 787–6000. Under the same management as The Knickerbocker-Chicago, is another very special personalized hotel. Soft French Provincial decor; 75 percent of the rooms are suites. 120 suites have fully equipped kitchens and stocked liquor cabinets.

**Chicago Hilton and Towers.** 720 S. Michigan Ave.; 922–4400. Its 1620 rooms make it one of the world's largest hotels, almost a self-contained city in itself. Big and busy. South of downtown with beautiful views overlooking Grant Park and the lakeshore. Ideal location for museum-goers. Art Institute, Goodman Theatre, Field Museum, Shedd Aquarium, and Adler Planetarium all close by.

**Chicago Marriott.** 540 N. Michigan; 836–0100. Opened May 1978. Good location along south fringe of "Magnificent Mile" of carriage-trade shops and prestigious restaurants. Ultramodern, eclectic decor. Lots of convention business. Rooms functional but quite standard.

**The Drake.** 140 E. Walton Place at Michigan Ave.; 787–2200. Across the street from the Oak Street Beach. Truly deluxe suites, the kind of baronial grandeur no one can duplicate today. Some people with familiar society names maintain apartments here. Noted for variety of exceptional restaurants. Outstanding luxury in the grand manner with a sense of tradition.

**Hyatt Regency.** 151 E. Wacker Dr.; 565–1234. East of the Michigan Ave. Bridge. So popular it is constantly expanding, now has 2,033 rooms and large convention center. Familiar Hyatt-style waterfall lobby with tropical plants. Lots of bustle, activity, innovative entertainment, and all those "touch of Hyatt" extras. Some suites have fireplaces. Underground garage.

**The Knickerbocker-Chicago.** 163 E. Walton; 751–8100. For a while this was the Playboy Towers. Now it has reassumed its maiden name, and the famous glass dance floor and everything else in the 265-room hotel just off Michigan Ave. has been restored. 94 of the rooms have 2 baths. You'll find Godiva chocolates on your turned-down bed and Vitabath in the tub; bathrooms are equipped with toothbrush, toothpaste, and dental floss. The blond oak-paneled walls of the *Prince of Wales Room* are a mellow background for the harp music played at dinner.

**The Lenox House.** 616 N. Rush St.; 337–1000. (Formerly the Croydon). Mostly suites, kitchens in all units. Completely refurbished.

**Omni Ambassador East.** 1301 N. State Parkway; 787–7200. No.-1 booth in the Pump Room here still marks the importance of celebrities. Long a favorite with movie stars who began settling in here between trains on coast-to-coast film promotions.

**Palmer House and Towers.** 17 E. Monroe; 726–7500. Millionaire founder Potter Palmer would be happy to check in here any time. One of the truly grand old hotels. Now a Hilton property. Built in an elaborate gilt-edge style no longer possible to duplicate, the Empire Room is one of the most beautiful dining rooms in the city. Second-floor lobby that leads to it is also worth a visit. Fine restaurants, lounges, excellent downtown location only steps away from all major State St. department stores. New luxury section in the Tower.

**Westin Hotel.** 909 N. Michigan; 943–7200. Formerly the Continental Plaza. Settle down into spacious quarters with period furniture and remote control TV. Newest "in" spot for the new generation Hollywood set. Another excellent location for shoppers along the avenue.

*Expensive*

**Americana-Congress.** 520 S. Michigan Ave.; 427–3800 in Illinois, 800–826–0900 outside the state. (Formerly Pick-Congress.) Another of those sturdy structures built to last. Modernized, face-lifted, and facing toward the Art Institute. 5 restaurants.

**Holiday Inn.** This chain maintains 2 quite sophisticated hotels near the downtown area: The **Mart Plaza** sits high atop the chic new Apparel Center at 350 N. Orleans St. across from the Merchandise Mart; 836–5000; and **Chicago City Centre** is on Ohio just off Michigan; 787–6100. All are high rise and offer in total over 1,000 rooms.

**McCormick Center Hotel.** 23rd St. and S. Lake Shore Dr.; 791–1900. A convention hotel-motel with 650 rooms. Always operating at full steam as conventioneers rush in and out for nearby McCormick Place. Fine for its purpose, but nonconventioneering families would find it noisy and fast paced. There is a health club with sauna, steam bath, and whirlpool.

**Midland.** 172 W. Adams; 332–1200. A recently refurbished hotel that has turned into a real European-style beauty while still preserving its rich architectural integrity. One of the new celebrities on the local hotel scene. In the heart of the financial district. Good food, definitely a rising star. 100 guest rooms have personal computers (Dialcom) with access to electronic mail as well as stock market, sports, airline, and entertainment information.

**Ramada Executive House.** 71 E. Wacker Dr.; 346–7100. Overlooks Chicago R. just ½ block off Michigan Ave. Located just north of the Loop. Caters to expense account travelers, very modern mood. Rooftop restaurant.

**Raphael.** 201 E. Delaware; 943–5000 or 800–327–9157. An elegant find with European atmosphere. 172 guest rooms on the Gold Coast one block east of

Michigan.Quality far surpasses its prices: such touches as a box of chocolates on arrival and Perrier water in your room refrigerator.

**Richmont.** 162 E. Ontario; 787–3580. (Formerly the Eastgate.) Another of the intimate-sized new finds located among the boutiques, galleries, and restaurants of North Michigan Ave. Rates include Continental breakfast. Completely renovated and decorated with European flavor.

**Sheraton-Plaza.** 160 E. Huron; 787–2900. A special bonus here is a rooftop pool offering a dramatic view of the city. Concierge.

*Moderate*

**Allerton.** 701 N. Michigan; 440–1500 or 800–621–8311. Recently renovated. 450 rooms at about the lowest rates to be found in the pricey North Michigan Ave. area. Older, but clean and a real bargain for budget travelers.

**Ascot Motel.** 1100 S. Michigan; 922–2900 or 800–621–4196. Large motel south of shopping and business district but close to McCormick Place and South Side attractions. Outdoor heated pool, 14 cabana rooms. Free parking. 200 rooms.

**Avenue Motel.** 1154 S. Michigan; 427–8200 or 800–621–4196. 80 rooms south of the city. Room service, waffle shop, cocktail lounge, and free parking. Decor is Far Eastern.

**Bismarck.** 171 W. Randolph; 236–0123. Well-known older hotel with loyal following. Located across from County Building-City Hall. *Chalet* restaurant is noted for Swiss-German specialties, and the hotel has something of a Germanic flavor. Good dollar value. Some recent remodeling in bedrooms. Garage facilities.

**Blackstone Hotel.** 636 S. Michigan; 427–4300. Has been around a long time and still going strong. Became known as a favorite with visiting Presidents a long time ago, but it has been a long time since one stayed there. Across from Grant Park and the Art Institute, close to the Auditorium Theater and Roosevelt College.

**Claridge.** 1244 N. Dearborn; 787–4980. Moderate prices on the fringe of the Gold Coast. Renovated (formerly Tuscany Hotel) with such upscale amenities as concierge, valet, multilingual staff, and airport limo.

**Gold Coast Group.** Three all-suite hotels: The Elms, 18 E. Elm St.; The Talbott, 20 E. Delaware; and Delaware Towers, 25 E. Delaware Place—all located along the Gold Coast. All rooms have kitchenettes or kitchens and dining rooms, breakfast, and a complimentary newspaper. European tradition. Call 943–0161 or 800–621–8506.

**Days Inn.** 644 N. Lake Shore Dr.; 943–9200. Formerly Holiday Inn. Excellent lake-view location near Navy Pier. Revolving rooftop Pinnacle Dining Room, also economy-priced Barn restaurant. Weekend packages.

**Essex Inn.** 800 S. Michigan; 939–2800 or 800–621–6909. Recently redecorated and well located for those headed for McCormick Place Convention Center and south-of-the-city attractions. Free bus to the Loop makes getting around easy. Outdoor heated pool, some cabana rooms. Free parking.

**Hyde Park Hilton.** 4900 S. Lake Shore Dr.; 288–5800. Only 5 min. to the Museum of Science and Industry and McCormick Place. Also a neighbor to the

University of Chicago and the treasures of the Oriental Institute. 330 newly appointed rooms and suites, a lake-view restaurant, lounge, and large outdoor swimming pool and sun deck. Lots of free parking. Hourly free shuttle service to North Michigan Ave.

Many other chain motels have what they consider showcase properties here. **Rodeway Inn,** 506 W. Harrison St.; 427–6969; with 154 rooms, is considered a convenient location. So is the 150-room **Best Western River North** at La Salle and Ohio Sts.; 467–0800; with its year-round rooftop swimming pool and free parking. Near the Merchandise Mart. **Quality Inn** is at 1 S. Halsted St. and Madison St., just off Kennedy Expressway (I–94); 829–5000.

*Inexpensive*

**Chicago Midway Airport Inn.** 5400 S. Cicero; 581–0500 or 800–621–0127. At the north edge of Midway Airport. 15 minutes from McCormick Place, with free shuttle service there and to the airport. Heated outdoor pool, 200 rooms.

**Lake Shore Hotel.** 600 N. Lake Shore Drive: 787–4700. A good address close by Northwestern University's Downtown Campus and the furniture Mart. Just across from lakefront Olive Park.

**Comfort Inn of Chicago.** 601 W. Diversey; 348–2810. 100 completely remodeled and modernized rooms with complimentary breakfast and hotel service. Close to Lincoln Park, beach, and about 10 min. from downtown. Coffee shop, cocktail lounge.

**La Salle Motor Lodge.** 720 N. La Salle; 664–8100. Called "the affordable motor hotel in downtown Chicago." Location is an important factor here. Just 7 blocks north of city center, within walking distance of Merchandise Mart and Apparel Center. You can park next to your room. 70 rooms, restaurant. No meeting facilities available.

**Ohio House.** At La Salle and Ohio, near the Merchandise Mart; 943–6000. This is a surprising find—a 2-story, 50-room motel complete with coffee shop and at-door self-parking and near the heart of the city. There is a free courtesy car to the Loop and major attractions. Easy access to expressways.

## O'Hare Airport Area

*Deluxe*

**Embassy Suites.** 6501 North Mannheim Rd., Des Plaines; 699–6300 and 1939 N. Meacham, Schamburg; 397–1313. All two-room suites; breakfast included.

**Hyatt Regency O'Hare.** 9300 W. Bryn Mawr Ave.; 696–1234. Striking copper mirrorlike exterior makes this a landmark. 1,100 rooms overlook 12-story atrium lobby in dramatic Hyatt tradition. All those "touch of Hyatt" extras. Close to O'Hare, but also only 20 min. from the Loop. Health club for stress-bound travelers, 4 restaurants and 2 lounges.

**Marriott-O'Hare Motor Hotel.** 8535 W. Higgins Rd. at Cumberland interchange on Kennedy Expressway; 693–4444. Business executives tend to gather here for fly-in corporate meetings. Families often come along to enjoy its 2 pools, ice skating, health club, and tennis.

Hotel Sofitel Chicago. 5550 N. River Rd.; 678–4488. New branch of French chain prides itself on presenting a Gallic personality.

The Westin Hotel, O'Hare. 6100 River Rd., Rosemont; 698–6000. Opened January 1984. Its 535 rooms are 4 min. from O'Hare. Facilities include year-round swimming pool, health club, and 2 racquetball courts. There are 2 restaurants and a sleek lobby lounge in the Westin tradition, plus an entertainment lounge.

### Expensive

The Hamilton Stouffer Hotel. 400 Park Blvd.; west of airport, near Itasca; 773–4000. Eye-opening, 12-story atrium lobby; over 400 luxurious rooms; complete health facilities.

O'Hare Hilton. Directly across from main terminals in the world's busiest airport; 686–8000. All 886 rooms are soundproofed. Usual Hilton standards, lots of conference space and 7 restaurants to accommodate guests. Underground moving sidewalks offer direct access to airport terminals.

Sheraton O'Hare North. 6810 N. Mannheim, Rosemont; 297–1234. This 500-room facility is 3 miles north of the airport. Features indoor and outdoor pools, sauna, and recreation facilities. Recently renovated.

### Moderate

Holiday Inn. Three additional locations near airport: Touhy Ave. and Mannheim Rd., Des Plaines; 296–8866. 1000 Busse Hwy., Elk Grove Village; 437–6010. 5440 N. River Rd., 1 mile east of airport; 671–6350.

Ramada Hotel O'Hare. 6600 N. Mannheim Rd.; 2 miles north; 827–5131. Hotel and motor inn with indoor and outdoor pools, health club; 727 rooms; home of well-known *Henrici's Restaurant.*

Rodeway Inn. 3801 Mannheim Rd., Schiller Park; 678–0670.

### Inexpensive

Howard Johnson's. Two properties at 10249 W. Irving Park Rd., Schiller Park; 671–6000 and 8201 W. Higgins Rd.; 693–2323.

Quality Inn. 3939 N. Mannheim, Schiller Park; 678–4800. $5 million spent to completely refurbish Manny Skar's onetime headliner.

TraveLodge. 3003 Mannheim Rd. at Higgins Rd. 1 mi. north of airport; 296–5541. This smaller, 2-story facility has 95 rooms and offers family rates as well as a free airport shuttle bus.

For rock bottom economy, there is **Royal 6**, 6450 Touhy Ave., I–94 (Niles), 647–7700, **Motel 6**, I–80 and Halsted St., East Hazelcrest, 957–9233, and **Regal 8 Inn**, 2448 N. Mannheim (Franklin Park), 455–6500.

 **BED AND BREAKFAST. Bed & Breakfast, Chicago.** P.O. Box 14088 Chicago, 60614. (312) 951–0085. $45–$120 double with breakfast (rates vary by season). Some hosts multilingual. Information on 100 different locations in homes, highrises in Evanston, Chicago, and North Side. Some accommodations are self-catering.

 **RESTAURANTS.** Ever since its days of brawling adolescence, Chicago has been identified as "strictly a meat and potatoes town." However, residents who do even a modicum of dining out these days are well aware that this characterization has long since become obsolete. For the rest of the world, though, the image dies hard.

Excellent meat, with or without potatoes, will doubtless continue to be a prime factor in the repertoire of the city's restaurants. The significant point is that it is no longer the only feature of dining out in Chicago worth noting. A diner who fancies continental cuisine, Mexican-style trout prepared with cucumbers and cilantro, or tandoori murg from India currently can indulge his dining whims almost as easily as can one who wants a 2-in. porterhouse with a baked potato and sour cream on the side.

In recent years Chicagoans have shown a greatly increased interest in fine food of all kinds. This may be due to the influence of the diverse ethnic groups that have been drawn to the city or the great popularity of international travel, which has exposed Chicagoans to the delights of fine food from Paris to Tokyo and points in between.

To cater to the public's expanding tastes, more and more restaurateurs have sought out chefs with backgrounds in the classic European schools of cuisine or in various ethnic styles of cookery.

The result is a lively and infinitely varied reservoir of restaurants. Some statistically minded observer employed by the city's Convention and Tourism Bureau calculated that Chicago's eating establishments are so numerous that a person could dine out in the city every day of his or her life without duplicating a single restaurant. Such an intinerant diner would, of course, encounter some exceptionally bad food along the way. But he would also be served many meals that range from satisfactory to memorable.

As an aid to finding meals in this last category we offer a carefully selected list of recommended establishments. We have listed first restaurants which fall under the headings **Local Specialites, American-International, Seafood, Steaks and Beef.** Next, those restaurants serving **ethnic cuisine** are listed by nationality.

The price categories we use are approximate; figure for an average 3-course meal (appetizer, main course with vegetable, dessert) at a given establishment, per person. This does not include wine or drinks, taxes, or gratuities. For outstanding service you may wish to tip 20 percent, with another percent for an especially helpful maître d'.

**Super Deluxe** restaurants will cost $40 and up. Meals at **Deluxe** restaurants run between $30 and $40. **Expensive** dinners will usually cost between $20 and $30. **Moderate** meals should run between $10 and $20. A tab at an **Inexpensive** restaurant will cost $10 or less.

Today, credit cards, "plastic money," are a very acceptable commodity. Most–although not all–restaurants accept credit cards. These are indicated by the following abbreviations, which appear at the end of each listing; AE - American Express; CB - Carte Blanche; DC - Diners Club; D -Discover; MC - MasterCard; V - Visa.

## LOCAL SPECIALTIES

Some foods have been popular in Chicago for generations, yet are rarely found outside the metropolitan area. Here are some of the best examples you can find.

### Pizza

Chicago-style "pizza in the pan" has developed dozens of variations in hundreds of pizzerias throughout the metropolitan area, and Chicago residents are intensely loyal to their favorite kinds and places. Some of the best ones are located in the cosmopolitan area north of the Loop.

*Inexpensive*

**Giordano's.** 747 North Rush St.; 951–0747. The newest popular variation on deep-dish pizza was invented by Giordano's in the '70s. Double-crust pizza has its fillings inside and tomato sauce on an upper-crust that comes from the oven puffed like a soufflé. Best variety: cheese with fresh spinach and sliced mushrooms. Also conventional thin-crust and single-crust "pizza in the pan." AE, CB, DC, D.

**Pizzeria Uno.** 29 East Ohio St.; 321–1000. This is where "pizza in the pan" was born. With a thick, pastry-like crust, whole tomatoes, and great gobs of zesty sausage without casing, two slices will keep you functioning for hours even in a Chicago winter. Very busy, it's a good late-night choice. The same pizza is served a block north at the sister restaurant, **Pizzeria Due** (619 N. Wabash; 943–2400). AE, DC, MC, V.

### Chicago Red Hots

Take a steamed poppy-seed bun, add a garlicky smoked frankfurter, and top it with sunny yellow mustard, bright green sweet-pickle relish, red tomatoes, and a kosher dill pickle and you have a Chicago classic. If you're adventurous ask for hot peppers—tiny pickled varmints called "sport peppers," grown almost exclusively to be eaten on Chicago hot dogs. Celery salt, sauerkraut, and pickled tomatoes are also sometimes added, but never ketchup for anyone over 12. Some of the best hot-dog stands and shops are in the north suburbs and in North Side Jewish neighborhoods, but good ones are all over Chicago.

*Inexpensive*

**Gold Coast Dogs.** 418 N. State St.; 527–1222. Bustling from early morning to late at night, this family-run shop does a brisk trade with office workers as well as those in the neighborhood, who carry out or find a spot on one of the tidy place's tall stools. Upscale aspirations lead them to offer Perrier with the soft drinks and grilled swordfish sandwiches, but the real draw is good Chicago red hots with the works and crisp French fries. No credit cards.

## Italian Beef Sandwiches

Sold in shacks and snack shops all over Chicago, these hearty sandwiches are made from thinly sliced beef steeped in a hearty broth of natural juices, black pepper, and garlic with herbs. Stuffed into dense, resilient French bread dripping with the gravy, the sandwiches are often ordered with roasted sweet peppers and-or giardiniera, and oil-packed mixture of olives, celery, and hot peppers.

*Inexpensive*

**Mr. Beef.** 777 North Orleans St.; 337–8500. Located cater-corner from the packing house that supplies most of the city's stands (and will sell bulk quantities to take back home), there's stand-up dining indoors and picnic tables in the parking lot. This is nothing fancy, but it's clean and their sandwiches, sold from early morning, are the best in town. No credit cards.

## AMERICAN-INTERNATIONAL

### Traditional

*Expensive*

**The Pump Room.** 1301 N. State Parkway, Ambassador East Hotel; 266–0360. The look is sleek and contemporary with clean lines and a feeling of spaciousness. Culinary offerings are imaginative and palate-pleasing, with nice extra touches. There is a varied and reasonably priced menu and an extensive dessert selection. Dancing. AE, CB, DC, D, MC, V.

**Sessions Pullman Club.** 605 E. 111th St.; 785–7578. One of Pullman's famous mansions has emerged as a pleasant place to dine while touring that community's many historic sites. Menu at the entrance changes nightly, but fresh fish, veal, steak, and lamb chops are available year round. MC, V.

**Wrigley Building Restaurant.** 410 N. Michigan Ave.; 944–7600. Although it is now dwarfed by taller neighbors, the wedding-cake Wrigley Building is still one of the outstanding landmarks of the city's skyline. This twin-tower edifice houses a restaurant whose fare seems to be unfailingly pleasing to a legion of regulars who somehow just never seem to go anywhere else for lunch. There are so many of them the general air is almost that of a club. The varied menu includes steaks, whitefish, chops, special salads, and unusual appetizers and desserts. Steak tartare, with raw egg and anchovies, is a long-time menu favorite. If you sample one of the martinis, you'll know why the bar always does a stampede business. Dinners, too. AE, CB, DC, MC, V.

*Moderate*

**Carson's—The Place For Ribs.** 612 N. Wells St.; 280–9200. This popular, large restaurant often has long waits for tables, but an adjacent carry-out store will sell you most items to take back to your hotel. What everybody waits for are lean and meaty barbecued baby back ribs served with a caramelized, rather mild, sweetish sauce. The value's terrific: Main course prices include rolls, an immense iceberg-lettuce salad with good scratch-made dressings (or cole slaw), and a choice of oven-bubbly cheddary potatoes au gratin, crisp potato skins, baked potato, or fries. The barbecued rib-and-chicken combo is especially enjoyable, and you can specify all light or dark meat. Costly, but among the best anywhere, is a giant New York sirloin steak with an optional (and worthwhile) charcoal crust. AE, CB, DC, D, MC, V.

**R.J. Grunts.** 2056 Lincoln Park W.; 929–5363. Humorous graphics and copy make the menu here a delight to read, and set the stage for fun, casual dining. Among the wide range of offerings, burgers, sandwiches (particularly the roast beef), nachos, and soups are good choices. Plus there's an imaginative, all-you-can-eat salad bar. Portions are immense, and prices moderate; service friendly and efficient. AE DC, MC, V.

**Hamburger Hamlet.** 44 E. Walton Pl.; 649–6600. As the name implies, you find hamburgers here—giant, juicy things seasoned to perfection and served with a choice of toppings. The chili is excellent. AE, DC, MC, V.

**Hillary's.** Water Tower Place, 845 N. Michigan Ave.; 280–2710. There's lots of brass, glass, and greenery at this chic watering hole and eatery. If you like your hamburgers in a sophisticated setting, try the half-pounder here. It comes plain or juicy or flavored with minced vegetables. Quiches are popular, and the salads are well made. If you're hungry (or want to share), try the huge fried-onion loaf as an appetizer. Nachos also are good starters. Rounding out the menu are steak and seafood selections and rich cheesecake for dessert. AE, DC, D, MC, V.

*Inexpensive*

**Chicago Claim Company.** 2314 N. Clark St.; 871–1770. With exposed brick and mining artifacts, an old rooming house has been happily transformed into a comfortable and rustic setting. Juicy, charbroiled hamburgers, made with top-quality meat, are the attraction here. Try the "Motherlode," a huge hamburger with any of 4 cheeses and other accessories, or the steak sandwich with tomato, bacon, cheese, and onion. You can also choose from fresh fish and chicken specials, and a fresh salad bar with a choice of 30 items, including dressings. Serves late. AE, MC, V.

**Ed Debevic's.** 640 N. Wells; 664–1707. Step into Ed's and you step back into the 1950's revived by Coca Cola, Orange Crush, and homemade signs ("Our coffee is so good we drink it ourselves."), juke boxes at each booth loaded with '50s tunes, and waitresses who crack their gum and call you honey. The food—good, simple, homemade, and inexpensive—suits the decor. Hamburgers and fries are the big things here, but you'll find scores of other down-to-earth items on the menu: meat loaf, pot roast, turkey, fried chicken, spaghetti, chicken pot pie, and tuna salad. The fountain serves up great chocolate, strawberry, and vanilla malts, sodas, and black cows, and a full bar even has Ed Debevic's beer. The place is popular but doesn't take reservations; shortest wait is for counter seats. No cards.

**D.B. Kaplan's.** 845 N. Michigan Ave.; 280–2700. Essentially a deli, but what a deli. Thoroughly delightful, semisophisicated atmosphere on the 7th level of the Water Tower Place shopping complex. A 3-ft.-long menu offers hundreds of items and provides great reading with its collection of outrageous puns. Single item sandwiches are available, but the larger ones are more intriguing. Also omelettes, soups, knishes and other side dishes, fish platters, hot plate specials, and desserts. Naughty double-entendre ice cream and drink menus. Often rushed service. Serves late. No cards.

**Santa Fe Cafe.** 800 N. Dearborn Parkway; 944–5722. One of the most recent regional food trends to reach Chicago is the smoky cookery of the Southwest. This corner, fast-food restaurant is an example of the genre at its best and cheapest. Slabs of tangy, barbecued ribs may be savored sitting down, at standup tables, or from carryout containers. Other smoked selections, available in sandwiches, include pork loin, brisket, and turkey breast. Grilled chicken is crispy outside, moist inside. Side orders of smoky beans and slaw accompany barbecued orders. A meaty chili is satisfying hot and spicy. AE, MC, V.

## New American

### Deluxe

**Gordon.** 500 N. Clark St.; 467–9780. Here you can sample inventive nouvelle American cuisine in a slick, sophisticated setting softened with orignial pieces of art and fresh flower displays. Signature appetizers include eggplant duxelle with glazed blue cheese, and fresh smoked meat and fish; while entrées vary from crispy sweetbreads, and free range veal and chicken imaginatively prepared to grilled salmon with a Chinese mustard glaze and grilled swordfish with ginger, soy, and miso. Gordon has long been known for its luscious flourless chocolate cake with chocolate mousse, but you might also consider the homemade sorbets and ice creams, lemon souffle with hot caramel sauce, or best of all, a tasting platter with tantalizing samples of six desserts. Half orders of main courses at $1 over half price. Pre-and post-theater menus. Weekend dancing. AE, CB, DC, MC, V.

**The 95th.** John Hancock Center, 875 N. Michigan Ave.; 787–9596. It's a lofty view from the 95th floor of "Big John," but the cuisine also rises to commendable heights. Although à la carte prices also tend to be on the lofty side, a *prix fixe* dinner of American cuisine, which includes appetizer, seafood course, salad, entree, dessert and coffee, provides excellent value in luxury dining. Conch fritters, pate of hare en croute, and quennelle of sole are recommended appetizers, while good entrée choices are stuffed pork loin with fig sauce, and various game specialties. The attractively priced wine list has more than 300 entries, and the cocktail lounge, one floor up on the 96th, offers a spectacular view of the city and Lake Michigan. AE, CB, DC, D, MC, V.

### Expensive

**Buckingham's.** Chicago Hilton, 720 S. Michigan Ave.; 922–4400. In restful, club-like surroundings decorated with artists' renderings of nearby Buckingham Fountain, Chef David Friedman's offerings intrigue the imagination, the eye, and—best of all—the palate. Innovative dishes such as grilled quail in a filo-pastry nest with crisp vegetables; hickory-smoked chicken breast with mango and raspberries; and grilled fresh tuna with avocado make for exciting, memorable dining. Desserts are beautiful and the small wine list is moderately priced. Open for lunch; low-priced, early-evening menu. One of the city's best brunches is served Sundays upstairs in the Normandie Lounge, decorated with furnishings from the French luxury liner of the '30s. AE, CD, DC, D, MC, V.

**Foley's** 211 E. Ohio St.; 645–1261. Brilliant presentations of original cooking in modern, elegant surroundings. Even strange dishes have well balanced flavors; they include "tuna tempura sashimi," bullseyes of crisp tempura batter surrounding seaweed-wrapped nearly raw fresh tuna ringing crisp blanched asparagus; and a delicious soup is made of curried eggplant, banana, and apple. Many of the more traditional dishes have innovative, pleasant surprises: grilled veal medallions are served with puff pastry filled with sweet onions and leeks; mushroom-stuffed chicken breasts are sauced with pinot-noir butter. Don't miss soufflé-like saffron-rice pudding. AE, DC, D, MC, V.

**Printer's Row.** 550 S. Dearborn St.; 461–0780. Comfortable, clubby surroundings belie the avant-garde cooking by chef Michael Foley. Most items are beautifully presented on oversize china with colorful vegetable assortments. Don't miss the New York State foie gras prepared any way; venison dishes are invariably tender and moist; and fresh fish dishes are uniformly good. The best desserts tend to be chocolate or fresh fruit; home made ice creams and sorbets are also worthwhile. There's also a daily, understated apple-dessert special. Lots of nice wines by the glass and a big American list of by-the-bottle choices. AE, DC, D, MC, V.

## Creole-Cajun

### Expensive

**Dixie Bar & Grill.** 225 W. Chicago Ave.; 642–3336. Once an old factory, Dixie lures diners who enjoy a theatrical ambiance and Cajun cuisine. In a setting of floor-to-ceiling palms, slow-turning fans, ceramic tile, a neon clock, and artifacts like stuffed sharks suspended from the ceiling, you can sample everything from gumbo and mud bugs (crayfish) to voodoo chicken, Cajun mixed grill, and an array of so-so blackened dishes—rib eye, New York steak, scallops, and lamb chops. Desserts include Key lime pie and Creole bread pudding. Special drinks include Cajun martinis, mint juleps, mimosas, and Dixie beer. Dixie serves five daily specials. AE, DC, D, MC.

**Maple Tree Inn.** 10730 S. Western Ave.; 239–3688. The feel is that of a neighborhood restaurant in New Orleans, but the cooking is often better. Start with savory andouille sausage, then move on to a garlic-bread boat packed with crisply fried soft-shell crabs, oysters, catfish, crawfish, or shrimp. Entrées include oyster-stuffed carpetbagger steak, terrific hickory-buttered shrimp, catfish pecandine, and savory jambalaya. Etoufée and blackened dishes change daily. There are pecan pie and sweet potato-praline cheesecake for dessert—with chicory coffee, of course. Jazz lounge upstairs, oyster bar below, and a garden out back for summer dining. MC, V.

## Varied

### *Deluxe*

**Cricket's.** 100 E. Chestnut; 280–2100. A collection of business-corporation artifacts decorates the walls and hangs overhead in this bright, carefree spot that very successfully achieves a chic, clubby ambience reminiscent of New York's "21" Club. The kitchen is first class, the Continental menu innovative and extensive (18 appetizer selections, for example). A good way to start your meal is with crême Senegalaise, a chilled, velvety smooth chicken soup with just the perfect hint of curry seasoning. Entrées include vension, quail, veal sweetbreads, and fettuccine with prosciutto and shrimp First-rate Creole brunch Saturday and Sunday. AE, CB, DC, MC, V.

### *Expensive*

**The Bakery.** 2218 N. Lincoln Ave.; 472–6942. The restaurant is as dinstinctive as its chef-owner Louis Szathmary. The atmosphere is bright and lively, with unpretentious furnishings, snowy white linens, and a tuxedo-clad serving crew. There's no printed menu. Instead, your waiter or waitress describes the 8 to 10 entrées available each evening as part of a 5-course dinner that includes a duo of appetizers, soup, and dessert. Entrées usually include Chef Louis' justifiably famous beef Wellington, duck with cherry sauce, and roast pork loin stuffed with Hungarian sausage. AE, CB, DC, D, MC, V.

**Biggs.** 1150 N. Dearborn St.; 787–0900. Stylish cooking by Chef John Terczak in an opulent Victorian mansion. Soups are very nice; so are creamy seafood ragouts and fresh fish dishes. On Thursday evenings the diners become part of a murder mystery enacted in and around the dining rooms. For mystery-night information call 337–2126. AE, CB, DC, MC, V.

**Geja's.** 340 W. Armitage St.; 281–9101. The mood is romantic, menu is fondue—cheese, chicken, beef, seafood, chocolate—and other tasty treats. For a finale, try one of the hot coffee and liqueur combinations topped with whipped cream. Live flamenco guitarists. A great wine list and cheeses to go with them. Serves late. AE, CB, DC, D, MC, V.

## SEAFOOD

### *Deluxe*

**Cape Cod Room.** 140 E. Walton St.; 787–2200. If it swims, crawls, or slithers in ocean, lake, river, stream, or brook, you're apt to find it at this seafood restaurant in the Drake Hotel. There are more than a dozen preparations of lobster alone. Fresh clams and oysters are shucked to order. Soft-shelled crabs are cooked to perfection; the famous Bookbinder red snapper soup is superb. Décor is nautical and the staff attentive. AE, CB, DC, MC, V.

**Chestnut Street Grill.** Water Tower Place, 845 N. Michigan Ave.; 280–2720. Fish cooked over hickory and oak hardwood coals at this charming restaurant.

Décor features turn-of-the-century-style architecture and an open display kitchen where you can watch fish being grilled. Swordfish is a perennially popular choice, as is fried calamari with tartar sauce as an appetizer. Other grilled selections include brook trout, seafood brochette, lobster tail, prawns, and scallops. Pork chops, veal chops, lamb chops, New York strip steak, and sirloin are other grilled options. Crusty sourdough bread accompanies entrées. On the lighter side are low-cal spa dishes, a seafood quiche, seafood omelette, and shrimp and crabmeat salad. Cappuccino ice cream is a delicious dessert. AE, CB, DC, D, MC, V.

**Nick's Fish Market.** First National Bank, 1 First National Plaza; 621–0200. The finest seafood available flown in fresh from seemingly everywhere is the big drawing card at Nick's here in Chicago and at Nicholas Nickolas in Honolulu. These restaurants have attracted a sophisticated clientele who don't mind paying a lot for excellently prepared sea delicacies from far and local waters. You'll find abalone and whole baby salmon on the menu, as well as Hawaiian mahi mahi and opakapaka. Serves late. AE, CB, DC, D, MC, V.

### Expensive

**Shaw's Crab House and Blue Crab Lounge.** 21 E. Hubbard; 527–2722. Seafood reigns at this popular spot, a recreated 1930s New England seafood house. Start with an appetizer from the raw bar, then choose from an à la carte menu featuring crabs, oysters, clams, shrimp, lobster, scallops, and an array of fresh fish specials that change daily. Garlicky frog legs are delicious and so are the seafood stews. Desserts include a wonderful pecan pie, as well as tarts, Key lime pie, vanilla pudding, and fresh fruits. AE, CB, DC, MC, V.

### Moderate

**Shucker's.** 150 E. Ontario St.; 266–6057. Named for the folk who shuck (open) fresh oysters and clams for a living, this restaurant properly puts the emphasis on fresh fin and shellfish preparations. Housed in a former private club, the operation serves guests either on a lower bar/lounge level or in a balcony area. Shucker's New England clam chowder has won critical acclaim as one of the best in the city and, accompanied by a hot loaf of bread and a well-made spinach salad, makes a nice light lunch. AE, CB, DC, D, MC, V.

## STEAKS AND BEEF

### Deluxe

**Gene & Georgetti's.** 500 N. Franklin; 527–3718. Beef's the thing to order here, although pasta offerings are also commendable. The steaks come in huge portions that often overlap the edges of the generous-sized platters on which they are served. A house salad and crispy cottage fries accompany all entrées. Side orders of pasta are also available. Friendly relaxed service by old-time waiters sporting long white aprons and favoring "regulars." A popular, crowded bar at which you're liable to spot more than one well-known personality. No reservations, but the bar wait can be fun. AE, CB, DC.

**Morton's.** 1050 N. State St.; 266–4820. This basement restaurant in Newberry Plaza deals superbly with those bottom-line favorites of American taste: steak and lobster. The open grill is central to the wood-and-stucco décor. Make your selections from a cart presented by your waiter: 24-oz. T-bones, double-cut prime rib with the bone in, sirloin, 3-lb. lobsters, and cheese-breaded veal chops. Everything comes with a 1-lb. baked potato or perfect, golden hash browns. There's not much to the rest of the menu: salad, fresh asparagus with hollandaise sauce, good oysters on the half shell. There are dessert soufflés. Order one when you sit down, and it will emerge at just the right time, high and golden crowned. AE, CB. DC, D, MC, V.

**The Palm.** 181 E. Lake Shore; 944–0135. Located off the lobby of the Mayfair Regent Hotel, this steak house is a branch of a duo of successful New York restaurants. There's sawdust on the floor, old-fashioned fans whirling beneath the tin ceiling, and cartoons depicting famous patrons. The restaurant specializes in two entrees—steak and Maine lobster—and renders them both extremely well. The steaks are thick and juicy—top quality for top dollar; broiled lobsters are exceedingly tender and seldom under three pounds; call ahead for boiled ones. Tomato and onion slices make a simple, compatible appetizer. If you've room for dessert, the New York-style cheesecake is worthwhile. AE, CB, DC, MC, V.

*Expensive*

**Eli's the Place for Steak.** 215 E. Chicago Ave.; 642–1393. This restaurant nestled in the Carriage House is a favorite of show business, sports, and political names, as well as hosts of other folk. The menu concentrates on good quality beef, along with a limited number of poultry and seafood dishes, ribs, and the best beef liver in town. Eli's also has become equally well known for its cheesecake, varieties of which include chocolate chip, cinnamon raisin, blueberry, and strawberry. AE, CB, DC, D.

**Lawry's Prime Rib.** 100 E. Ontario St.; 787–5000. As its name implies, this is a specialty restaurant—housed in the elegant old McCormick mansion—and it delivers its raison d'etre very well indeed. Prime rib is tender, juicy, and sliced to the desired degree of thickness and doneness from a slab rolled to your table on a silver cart. Accompaniments are traditional crisp Yorkshire pudding, mashed potatoes, and a vegetable. Simple but delicious. Desserts are simple, too, and include chocolate ice cream and a rich trifle. Luncheon offers a more varied menu, including salads and fish-of-the-day. More than 100 wines are available. Serves late. AE, CB, DC, D, MC, V.

**That Steak Joynt.** 1610 N. Wells St.; 943–5091. The former home of Pipers Bakery has been artfully transformed into a setting that's reminiscent of a Victorian bordello. A collection of antiques, quality oil paintings, and Tiffany-style lamps is set off against red velvet. Aged beef and ribs dominate the menu; less successful are some of the side dishes and seafood offerings. There is a popular piano bar. Tourists abound. Good Second City theater/dinner package is sometimes the only way to get tickets to that show.

## CUISINE BY NATIONALITY

### Afghan

*Inexpensive*

**The Helmand.** 3201 N. Ashland Ave.; 935–2447. A romantic neighborhood place with Oriental rugs and lots of hanging plants, it serves a seldom seen, complexly seasoned, mostly mild cuisine that seems a hybrid of Indian and Middle Eastern cooking. Aromatic soups, shishkebabs, zesty stews; try brown rice with lamb, glazed carrots, and raisins. AE, CB, DC, MC, V.

### British

*Expensive*

**Cafe Royal.** 1633 N. Halsted; 266–3394. Part of the lively Halsted Street restaurant scene, this elaborate complex was a candle factory in the late 1800s. Now it's a restaurant specializing in British and Scottish dishes and drinks. You can choose a variety of settings in which to enjoy your meal: a formal dining room with English antiques, fresh flowers, and soft hues of blue and pink, or five private dining rooms with closing doors, ideal for business or romance. Drinks are served at á spacious bar. Among the interesting listings on the menu are shepherd's pie, veal jockey club (loin of veal roasted and garnished with boiled eggs and served with sautéed potatoes), jugged hare, and fresh seafood. For appetizers you might consider crab cakes, potted meat in aspic with egg, and Cullen Skink soup (smoked haddock in a cream broth with onions and potatoes). Desserts fluctuate, but you can usually order a rich trifle. Drinks include a large variety of British and Irish beers and a selection of 150 to 200 wines. A special cruvenet machine pressurizes, thus preserving, 16 bottles of wine so that guests can sample fine wines by the glass. The 440-seat Royal-George Theater adjoins the restaurant. AE, CB, DC, MC, V.

*Moderate*

**Atlantic Fish & Chip Restaurant.** 7115 W. Grand; 622–3259. A no-nonsense place with the area's largest selection of English, Welsh, Irish, and Scottish foods and potables (many of draught). Roast beef with Yorkshire pudding, meat-and-potato pie, Cornish meat and onion pasties, black pudding, mixed grill with lamp chop, pork sausage and thick Irish bacon, soda bread, and other simple, good dishes in a family-run establishment. Rousing entertainment on weekends. Darts in an English-style pub. Buffet Sundays. MC, V.

### Chinese

*Moderate*

**Chiam.** 2323 S. Wentworth Ave.; 225–6336. 50-some meat, poultry, and seafood courses, not counting more than a dozen different chow meins, chop sueys, and egg foo yung variations. As if that weren't enough, the management is prepared to produce an array of other Chinese or American dishes. One of the better known of the Chinatown restaurants, Chiam features family-style dinners that are suitable for groups of from 2 to 8. The food is American-Cantonese in style. Try the diced lobster prepared with mushrooms, snow peapods, bok choy, bamboo shoots, water chestnuts, and whole almonds. A less well-known but worthy option: Dim Sum lunch of dumplings and pastries. AE, CB, DC, D, MC, V.

**House of Hunan.** 535 N. Michigan Ave.; 329–9494. An impressive range of Mandarin and Hunan-Szechuan dishes, including several not usually found at other local restaurants, indicates the creativity of the establishment's chefs. High praise for such entrées as beef with tender sliced scallops in hot sauce, Szechuan noodles in spicy vegetable-shrimp sauce, and chicken stir-fried with bamboo shoots and garlic sauce. Other good choices include moo-shu dishes and diced chicken with honeyed walnuts. It's fun to come with a group and share. AE, CB, DC, D, MC, V.

**Szechwan House.** 600 N. Michigan Ave.; 642–3900. Large restaurant has good selection of the spicy cooking of Szechwan and Hunan provinces, with some rarely seen treats, such as snails in a beefy-tasting hot sauce and crunchy jellyfish. More commonplace appetizers can be uncommonly good: dainty pot sticker dumplings, juicy shrimp toast, and plump stuffed crab claws. The best main courses include moo-shu pork; ginger duck with black mushrooms; and ma-po bean curd, made with hot peppers and ground pork. The big lunch buffet is a good buy. AE, CB, DC, MC, V.

*Inexpensive*

**Cantonese Chef.** 2342 S. Wentworth Ave.; 225–3232. In the heart of Chicago's Chinatown, this restaurant is done in attractive modern style with pleasant Oriental touches. It's a perfect place to stop for a meal before or after browsing through the many interesting shops in the area. The menu offers all the usual Cantonese favorites, with interesting preparations of beef, pork, chicken, duck, and seafood. Unusual dishes are also available. Try going with a group so you can share many different selections. AE, CB, DC, MC, V.

**Lee's Canton Café.** 2302 S. Wentworth Ave.; 225–4838. Some of the best food in Chinatown is to be found in this lunchroom modern setting. You'll do well enough stepping in off the street and ordering at random. The ideal approach is to have a knowledge of Chinese cookery or a Chinese friend to guide you in selecting some of the more unusual dishes. AE, CB, DC, MC, V.

## Ethiopian

*Inexpensive*

**Mama Desta's Red Sea Restaurant.** 3216 N. Clark St.; 935–7561. It's fun to eat the home-style cooking in this friendly, decorated-on-a-shoestring place. The food, mostly stews of chicken, lamb, or beef, is spooned onto huge, thin, pancakes called injera, pieces of which are torn off, folded, and eaten by hand. By meal's end what's left of the injera is stained many bright colors from the highly seasoned gravies; use it to sop up the last of the goodies. Fermented-honey wine is served with the dishes. Best bet: a combination plate. AE, CB, DC, MC, V.

## French

### *Super Deluxe*

**Ambria.** 2300 N. Lincoln Park West; 472–5959. This restaurant in the Belden-Stratford Hotel offers light, inventive nouvelle cuisine, with an emphasis on seafood. Every dish is beautifully garnished and presented. Sautéed fresh goose liver makes an excellent starter. Grilled fresh fish is consistently good. White chocolate mousse makes a delectable dessert. Or let the chef do his best by phoning ahead for a multicourse "degustation" dinner. Recorded classical music plays in the background. The service crew is young, but what it lacks in polish it makes up for in enthusiasm and friendliness. AE, DC, MC, V.

**Café Provençal.** 1625 Hinman, Evanston; 475–2233. Antiques, pink linens, classical music, and an inviting fireplace evoke a country-French ambiance in this cozy room. The seasonal menu, changed four times a year, continues that theme with inventive preparations of fresh veal, beef, duck, lamb, game, and fish of the day. Representative offerings include cream of lentil soup, saddle of American spring lamb roasted and served with fresh herb, cassoulet, and home-baked breads and pastries. Desserts include homemade sorbets and ice creams, fresh fruit, simple custards, and luscious tarts. More than 75 wines are available, including some 30 to 40 rare cellar wines. AE, CB, DC, MC, V.

**Carlos'.** 429 Temple, Highland Park; 432–0770. Thought by many to be the best restaurant in the region, this small suburban spot features efficient service, a great wine list, and careful, beautiful, original cooking by Roland Liccione, a Vietnamese-Corsican chef. From gratis hors d'oeuvre to complimentary sweets (by master pâtissiere Mary Beth Liccione, his wife) the meal is a spectacle to be long remembered. First courses can include an airy puff pastry case of delicate scallops with asparagus, or tiny soft-shell crabs with crayfish in sweet-garlic butter, or meltaway foie gras with truffles and citrus sauce. Squab, veal, and fish dishes are great, and include brill, grilled or steamed, with three-mustard sauce and two-color pasta; or grilled swordfish and pompano with a pair of fresh-herb sauces. Desserts range from spectacular, multi-chocolate creations to dainty cookie-and-fruit options. AE, CB, DC, D, MC, V.

**Ciel Bleu.** 181 E. Lake Shore Dr.; 951–2864. This showcase restaurant on the 19th floor of the Mayfair Regent Hotel offers a stunning view of Lake Michigan. As you sit and watch the billowing sails by day or shimmering lights at night, you'll bask in elegant surroundings and enjoy cosseted service by attentive waiters and a watchful maitre d'. The seasonal menu includes such items as marinated Norwegian salmon or hot goose-liver appetizers and medallions of veal, escallop of halibut, and salmon in a creamy mustard sauce. There is a fine version of vichyssoise and an admirable creamy tomato soup. The dessert cart is laden with sinfully rich temptations. AE, DC, MC, V.

**The Everest Room.** The LaSalle Club, 440 S. LaSalle St.; 663–8920. This little-known newcomer is already one of the city's top restaurants. The view of Chicago is spectacular, the service Midwestern friendly but polished, and the cooking, by Jean Joho from L'Auberge d'Il, is deft, light, and highly original.

Appetizers include a crisp filo-pastry bag filled with fresh shrimps and leeks, a first-class black risotto of squid in their ink, and velvety foie gras. Main courses include roasted John Dory fish encased in wisps of crisp potato, poached beef tenderloin with foi gras, and sautéed breast of squab with truffles and napa. Best desserts are simple berry-and-sauce creations. AE, DC, MC, V.

**Le Français.** 269 South Milwaukee Ave., Wheeling; 541–7470. You may have to wait weeks for a reservation, but a visit should take priority on any discriminating diner's calendar. The kitchen is larger than the dining room, but guests are not crowded, the ambience is genial and comfortable, but not ostentatious—the whole show is the food. Specials are displayed on silver platters. Portions served are large and accented with sauces and elegant garnishes. Chef Jean Banchet, a perfectionist, checks every dish that leaves his kitchen. This is serious dining on culinary creations that you are unlikely to find anywhere else—from delightful seafood mousses, through roast veal loin wrapped in pastry, to elegant and unforgettable souffles. AE, CB, DC, D, MC, V.

**Jimmy's Place.** 3420 N. Elston Ave.; 539–2999. Strictly for opera lovers, this friendly, cozy restaurant has opera playing from the time it opens until after it closes; the décor includes colorful opera posters and stained-glass windows of opera scenes. But the best reason to come is for the wonderful classic cooking on a menu that changes monthly. Gingery tuna tartare and pâté assortments are memorable beginnings; soups are wonderful; and main courses come with a vast array of dainty baby vegetables. Seafood is always a good choice. For dessert: great pecan tart, light poached pear with chocolate sauce, or, of course, an opera torte. AE, CB, DC, D, MC, V.

**Le Perroquet.** 70 E. Walton; 944–7990. A tiny private elevator takes you to the 3rd floor, where you alight in a spacious, cheerful, and elegantly appointed dining room, the most civilized in town. The walls are adorned with vivid foliage murals by Chicago artist Meg Abbot. The tables lining the room are decorated with fresh flowers in lovely, delicate vases. Mussels are a great beginning to a nouvelle cuisine dining experience that is excellent throughout. Choose from several light mousses, fresh fish lightly grilled, pigeon en dodine, and a selection of meat dishes. Save room and a few superlatives for the pastries and souffles. AE, CB, DC, D.

**Ritz Carlton Dining Room.** 160 E. Pearson; 266–1000. The Ritz Carlton Hotel may be a sleek, modern building, but this formal room belies its location, recalling an earlier age of elegance, with beautiful chandeliers, elegant table settings, and formally attired waiters. The à la carte menu features light appetizers such as foie gras of duck, and truffle and carrot tarts, as well as fish, lamb, veal, beef, and duck entrées. As an alternative, a *prix fixe* menu includes soup, appetizer, entrée, imported cheeses, dessert selection, and coffee or tea, and a menu degustation enables two diners to try two appetizers, entrées, and desserts from the same menu. Those who watch their calories will appreciate the alternative cuisine with less than 650 calories. This option may sound Spartan, but the choices include a gourmet appetizer, meat or fish entrée, and salad. Lunch and Sunday brunch are also served. AE, CB, DC, MC, V.

**La Tour.** 800 N. Michigan Ave.; 280–2230. Just off the lobby of the intimate Park Hyatt Hotel, La Tour is romantic and elegant, with rich carpeting and a soft palette of peach and gray. The superb cuisine draws from continental, nouvelle, and classic themes. You can begin with a choice of select hors d'oeuvres, such as Petrossian smoked salmon or casserole of grilled scallops with zucchini and thyme. Salads include a warm quail salad with radishes and watercress, ginger and lemon vinaigrette. Fish, meat, poultry, game, and fowl appear as entrées in interesting preparations, among them sautéed breast of duck with fresh thyme and artichoke, and lamb chops with honey and black pepper. Desserts are homemade; the wine list is comprehensive. A lighter lunch menu offers sandwiches, and the lavish Sunday buffet includes coffee or tea, juice, fresh bakery selection, and choices from the appetizer, entrée, and dessert buffets. A lovely place to dine, with the added bonus of a view overlooking Chicago's historic Water Tower. AE, CB, DC, MC, V.

*Deluxe*

**Jackie's.** 2478 N. Lincoln Ave.; 880–0003. Chef Jackie Shen's neighborhood restaurant lures distant customers with its unique combination of French and Chinese cooking. A veteran of Le Français, the Hong Kong-raised chef turns out beautifully arranged dishes with unique treats such as wontons with snails and goat cheese, or roasted baby chicken with cloud-ear mushrooms and green peppercorn sauce. Most of the cooking is classic French with a light touch; fish dishes excel. Signature dessert: a bittersweet chocolate sack filled with white-chocolate mousse and berries. Wine list, one of Chicago's best, includes more than a dozen half bottles and a great many by the glass. AE, CB, DC, MC, V.

**Les Plumes.** 2044 N. Halsted St.; 525–0121. A pair of husband-wife teams operate this chic but noisy place that serves some of the loveliest arrangements of classic French cooking in town. Rich cream of brie soup with sliced mushrooms is a memorable opener; so is delicate scallop sausage or a varied array of pâtés. Delicious seafood dishes include a trilogy of grilled fish, each filet in its own isolated pool of contrasting sauce. The roasted, carved chicken ringed by crisp disks of potato and served in natural juices is a visual spectacle with flavors to match. Desserts are among the city's best, and most are garnished with a homemade ice cream in a crisp pastry cup adrift in a satiny sauce. AE, MC, V.

**Yoshi's Café.** 3257 N. Halsted St.; 248–6160. Comfortable, restful ambiance is combined with a unique cooking style. Japanese-born, French-trained Chef Yoshi Katsumura adroitly blends the classic techniques of European cookery with exotic Oriental flavorings: sesame oil, sweet sake, radish sprouts, ginger. Presentations—often in oversize, austere Japanese vessels—can be spectacularly beautiful. Typical: tempura-fried soft-shell crab escabeche drizzled with sweet sake and garnished with sweet diced red pepper; veal medallions with candied ginger and lemon zest; green-tea ice cream. A tiny place with fine service; reasonable wine prices. AE, MC, V.

**L'Escargot.** 701 N. Michigan Ave.; 337–1717, and 2925 N. Halsted St.; 525–5522. Ensconced in bright, attractive quarters within the Allerton Hotel, this country French restaurant features high ceilings, attractive posters, lots of greenery, and French pop music. White-washed walls serve as backdrops for large antique cabinets and breakfronts. L'Escargot introduced cassoulet to Chicago and still features this tasty and very French peasant dish. But there are many other temptations as well. The changing array of dishes usually includes more than a dozen entrées plus innovative appetizers, soups, and desserts. Recommended are cream of watercress soup, rich with potato and leek flavor, roast duck, and for dessert, a buttery bread pudding. AE, CB, DC, D, MC, V.

**Un Grande Café.** 2300 N. Lincoln Park West; 348–8886. The tables may be covered with paper and the floors with tile, and the atmosphere may be rather noisy, but this informal bistro-like room serves some very sophisticated cuisine at reasonable prices. Appetizers include snails in a pastry shell, cold ratatouille, and spinach, tomato, and cheese terrine; entrées range from a superb steak and fries to grilled calves liver in mustard sauce. Daily specials, including a fresh fish of the day, vary the offerings. Light entrées are available too, among them an omelette with seasonal vegetables and smoked trout with celery root remoulade. AE, DC, MC, V.

**Yvette.** 1206 N. State Pkwy.; 280–1700. This fashionable Art Deco spot in essence is 3 establishments in 1. There's a small sidewalk café in front, in warm weather the place to be "seen." This leads into a bistro and, in back of that, an informal dining room. 10 or more appetizer selections include oysters Provençale and brie soup. Duck with cherry sauce and beef with a peppercorn sauce highlight the entrées. Desserts feature a variety of tortes, tarts, and other pastries. There's piano entertainment during the evening. AE, DC, MC, V.

### Moderate

**Rue St. Clair.** Richmont Hotel, 640 N. St. Clair St.; 787–6974. A cozy little bistro with terrific bread, cute posters, friendly servers, and good cooking. Great steak and fries, nice salads, good wines by the glass. Daily low-cal specials don't taste like diet dishes. A plus: sidewalk dining when the weather's nice. AE, CB, DC, D, MC, V.

**Zincs.** Presidential Towers, 555 W. Madison St.; 902–2900. A French brasserie in two sections. One, in the atrium lobby of this luxury apartment complex, is best for casual sandwiches and snack plates; it often features live music. Terrific pizza-like tarts are an attraction; so are good sausages and Alsatian dishes with sauerkraut. At one side is a cozy bar with a great selection of beers and European soft drinks. The other part is the adjacent, glassed-in dining room decorated with French posters and serving an enormous selection of authentic bistro dishes, including good roasted chicken, couscous specials, and great bistro steak with skinny fries. Look for dishes with "angel-hair" fried onions, a real treat. Low-priced early-evening special. AE, CB, DC, MC, V.

## German

### Expensive

**Golden Ox.** 1578 N. Clybourn Ave.; 664-0780. The décor alone makes a visit worthwhile. There's an amazing collection of German paintings, woodcarvings, steins, and what-have-you. Beamed ceilings, leaded windows, and handset tile floors add to the mood. The menu offers traditional German classics and American cuisine in enormous variety. AE, CB, DC, D, MC, V.

*Moderate*

**The Berghoff.** 17 W. Adams; 427–3170. This Chicago institution tends to defy classification. Certainly, it is German, with excellent roulade of beef, Wiener schnitzel and kassler rippchen. But you'll also find such selections as mahi mahi, grilled or broiled fresh swordfish steak, Boston scrod, and broiled tournedos au povire. Appetizers, too, are an international melange with escargot, and Bismarck herring. The dessert menu is largely Teutonic with strudel, tortes, and Black Forest cake. Draft beers are custom-brewed for Berghoff's. This 2-level, spacious old dining establishment has oak paneling and bustling, black-attired waiters. AE, MC, V.

**Heidelberger Fass.** 4300 N. Lincoln Ave.; 478–2486. Sauerbraten is a specialty here. Schnitzels also rank high, along with beef rouladen, smoky kasseler ribs, wienerrostbraten, hearty sausage platters, pot roast, roast duck—even several fish selections. Enjoy German draft beers, non-pareil liver dumpling soup, hot apple strudel, and Black Forest cake. Located in the heart of the old Germantown area, the restaurant has a décor reminiscent of an old European village, complete with homes and shops and costumed waitresses. AE, CB, DC, MC, V.

**Schulien's.** 2100 W. Irving Park Rd.; 478–2100. This gemutlichkeit German restaurant has been in business for 100 years and was a speakeasy during Prohibition. Things are quieter now, but the Wiener schnitzel remains the same. The menu features four or five other German favorites and also a selection of steaks, chops, fish, and sandwiches. Bartenders perform magic tricks and there are also guest magicians. AE, DC, MC, V.

## Greek

*Moderate*

**The Courtyards of Plaka.** 340 S. Halsted St.; 263–0767. Style and hospitality are the charm of this upscale restaurant in the heart of Greek Town. All the usual Greek favorites are on the menu, along with some less familiar dishes like tzatziki, crisp slices of cucumber marinated in a thick garlic yogurt sauce, or cold octopus uniquely prepared in a special wine sauce. Moussaka is memorable, so is moschari stamnas, a flavorful Greek beef stew, tsipoura (sea bass) and sweet desserts like baklava and sokolatina. AE, CB, D, MC, V.

**Greek Islands.** 200 S. Halsted St.; 782–9855. Located in large attractive quarters, this popular Greek Town spot continues to offer fine value. The grilled red snapper and sea bass are outstanding and the gyros excellent. Lamb is prepared in a host of styles. Octopus stewed in hearty tomato-wine sauce and deep-fried squid are specialties. As an appetizer, try taramosalata, a fish-roe spread delicious when slathered on crusty bread. If you're undecided, ask for a family-style combination dinner. Serves late. AE, DC, MC, V.

**Parthenon.** 314 S. Halsted St.; 726–2407. Greek music blares from the juke box as flames leap high from saganaki (cheese spiked with brandy and lemon juice) appetizers. The front window provides clues to pleasures to be found within Passersby can watch a whole lamb slowly spit-broiled to browned perfection. Tasty, crisp, outside cuts of lamb and beer barbecued in this manner are served along with onions and parsley as gyros. Seafood selections range from cod and sea bass to squid and octopus. Broiled snapper and sea bass are consistently good. Special family dinners (not on the menu) offer a good sampling of this traditional Greek kitchen. And, befitting a Greek restaurant, there are more than a dozen different lamb dishes. Serves late. AE, CB, DC, MC, V.

## Indian

### *Moderate*

**Bombay Palace.** 50 E. Walton; 664–9323. A very chic atmosphere offering a menu so varied it is hard to choose. Some consider it the city's finest Indian restaurant. Murgh keema masala and lamb vindaloo are among favorites. Combination platters offer a chance to sample varied entrees. Modestly curried, but a helping of minted yogurt with cucumbers will cool the palate. Smoky tandoori dishes include chicken, fish, and breads. Save room for mango ice cream and kulfi, a luscious combination containing rosewater and ground almonds. AE, CB, DC, MC, V.

## Italian

### *Super Deluxe*

**Spiaggia.** 980 N. Michigan; 280–2750. One of the city's showplaces, this beautiful room overlooks Michigan Avenue, Lake Shore Drive, Oak Street Beach, and the blue vastness of Lake Michigan. But the view inside is equally impressive, with marble-rich Art Deco styling in tones of green, plum, and mauve, tiered seating, and a grand piano high above in a specially constructed loft. The food served here is northern Italian, and the beautifuly presented specialties range from thin crust pizza baked in brick ovens and wonderful pastas to fresh fish, veal, chicken, and tagliata (roasted sirloin with fresh rosemary, olive oil, lemon, and peppercorns). For dessert, try the poached pear dipped in chocolate and presented in zabaglione sauce with pistachio nuts. Less expensive but no less beautiful is Spiaggia Café next door. It's a bit more casual offering pizza, cold antipasti, several entrées including grilled fish, and pasta dishes. Spiaggia has an extensive list of Italian wines; selections are served in the Café. AE, CB, DC, D, MC, V.

### *Deluxe*

**Avanzare.** 161 E. Huron; 337–8056. The atmosphere here is Milanese, with austere, high granite walls, Italian bronze sculptures, hardwood floors with oriental carpets, and tables and banquettes dressed in a rich bluish green. The set menu and 15 to 20 daily specials celebrate northern Italian cuisine with a nouvelle touch. Some good choices include grilled veal chops, sautéed duck breast in port wine sauce with sautéed cabbage, radicchio, pancetta and raisins, and roast leg of lamb stuffed with spinach and pesto. The menu also lists an array of antipasti, pasta, and fresh fish. Desserts include ricotta cheesecake and homemade ices, ice creams, tarts and tortes. The full bar offers more than 100 wines, many Italian, and a pleasant outdoor cafe is open from May through September, weather permitting. AE, CB, DC, MC, V.

**La Strada.** 155 N. Michigan Ave.; 565–2200. There's a big-city feeling about this large, North-Italian restaurant that has some of the finest quality veal dishes in town. Pasta, which is home made, is typically carefully cooked; it's worth waiting for the risotto alla Milanese, the saffron-scented Italian rice first course cooked in rich veal-stock. Large, expensive wine list; disappointing desserts, sometimes indifferent service. Best buy: the four-course pre-theatre dinner (order before 6:30). AE, CB, DC, D, MC, V.

## Expensive

**George's.** 230 W. Kinzie, 644–2290. A sophisticated, contemporary northern Italian restaurant. There are a dozen or so appetizers ranging from mussels with white wine and tomato to cold fettuccine with smoked meats and fresh oysters. Pastas are creative and unusual, such as penne made with either a 4-cheese combination or with a liver-and-tomato sauce. Entrées include scampi, shrimp, veal chops, lamb chops, and sole. Each day brings a supplementary menu with a handful of specials in all categories—sometimes including abalone. For dessert try the white chocolate mousse. There's entertainment some evenings, often featuring modern jazz groups. AE, MC, V.

**Salvatore's.** 525 W. Arlington Pl.; 528–1200. Northern Italian food develops an intimate kind of connoisseurdom of its own among its ardent advocates. In Salvatore's two rooms, a large high-ceilinged green dining room and a formal paneled room on a second level, you'll find a quorum of just such fans, drawn here for classic antipasti, and fresh soups. Good entrée choices from an extensive menu include a delicious pasta with spinach and ricotta cheese, and chicken Vesuvio, rich in garlic, olive oil, and herbs, served with well-seasoned roasted potatoes. There is complete bar service and a fine wine list. Serves late. AE, CB, DC, D, MC, V.

## Moderate

**Convito Italiano.** 11 E. Chestnut St.; 943–2984. The large food store downstairs (which has one of the country's biggest selections of Italian wines and olive oils) sets the tone for the dining rooms upstairs in this cosmopolitan, unstuffy place. Fresh, seldom seen dishes come from all of Italy's regions. The menu can include such items as lasagna filled with chicken, tomato, onion, green olives, and two cheeses; sautéed calf's liver in sweet-and-sour sauce with raisins and pine nuts; and grilled strip steak marinated in olive oil, balsamic vinegar, and garlic, served with white beans, Italian bacon, and onions. Enormous selection of good Italian wines by the glass. AE, MC, V.

**Da Nicola.** 3114 N. Lincoln Ave.; 935–8000. A homey restaurant with checked tablecloths, friendly service, and cooking that goes beyond the expected. Begin with bruschetta, crisp toast topped with soft, fresh mozzarella, flavorful tomato, and whole basil leaves. Light pizzas and a delicious leek omelette also make good starts. Broad range of homemade pastas (many of them stuffed); delicious veal and poultry dishes. Large wine list has a fine Italian collection, with many under $15. AE, MC, V.

**Febo.** 2501 S. Western Ave.; 523–0839. Famous for nothing! The slogan of this southwest side family restaurant is intriguing but inaccurate. For years Febo's has been known for its good quality pasta—cooked al dente—veal, and other specialty dishes, all reasonably priced. Hard-line trenchermen go there for its well-known Fiesta specials (for 4 or more persons), sumptuous feasts that include doubles of pasta and entrée and much, much more. A long-time favorite at this sprawling, multiroomed corner restaurant in one of Chicago's Italian enclaves is garlicky chicken Vesuvio. Saltimbocca also is good. AE, CB, DC, D, MC, V.

**The Italian Village.** 71 W. Monroe St.; 332–7005. 3 operations in 1, each on a separate floor and each with its own kitchen. On a subterranean level, you'll find La Contina, with a cozy setting for seafood and Italian-American specialties, plus selections like steak Diane, flamed tableside. Just off Monroe St. is the plushest of the facilities, the Florentine Room, where the emphasis is on northern Italian cookery and fine steaks. The décor is handsome, the staff efficient and courteous, and the tortellini first rate . . . and the prices much higher. Upstairs, the décor recreates an Italian village. There's a huge selection of reasonably priced dishes, including nearly 3 dozen pasta preparations. The balance of the menu ranges from pizza to saltimbocca. AE, CB, DC.

**Scoozi!** 410 W. Huron St.; 943–5900. The theatrical, carnival spirit is contagious in this enormous, noisy restaurant that's decorated to look as if it's been around for centuries. Exotic, thin-crust pizzas (such as one of caramelized onions, walnuts, gorgonzola, and escarole) are a draw; so are terrific pastas and other dishes available in small "grazing" portions: matchsticks of crisply battered fried zucchini with fresh sage; smoked pheasant with mushrooms and polenta; sautéed potatoes with artichokes; and literally dozens more. Plan on at least three or four dishes a person; this is a great place for sharing. AE, MC, V.

*Inexpensive*

**Mama Mia! Pasta.** 711 N. State St.; 787–5606. This counter-service restaurant 4 blocks west of Michigan Avenue's Magnificent Mile is to cafeterias what the Queen Elizabeth II is to river tugboats. A masterpiece of high-tech design, highlighting the Italian national colors of red and green, it has gleaming showcases loaded with ready-to-cook pastas and a reasonable selection of compatible Italian wines and imported beers. More than 20 different kinds of pasta are available, including whole wheat, tomato basil, beef, and spinach—all made fresh daily. There are 5 homemade sauces, plus daily specials such as lasagne sauce and eggplant Parmesan. Desserts are freshly baked. Eat in (using plastic utensils), carry out, or buy pasta and sauce by the pound for parties and at-home dining. AE.

## Japanese
*Moderate*

**Benihana of Tokyo.** 166 E. Superior St.; 664–9643. A floor show comes with your meal at the local branch of this successful Japanese steak house chain. It's provided by the colorfully neckerchiefed, white-garbed chef who displays his culinary talents as he cooks your food on a hot metal grill set right into the center of your table. He skillfully cuts steak, shrimp, and chicken into bite-size morsels to facilitate handling with chopsticks. As accompaniments there are mushrooms, onions, and bean sprouts grilled on the same surface as the meat. Seating is communal-style, with 8 to a table. If there are fewer in your party, you'll be seated with anyone else who happens along. AE, CB, DC, MC, V.

**Hatsuhana Restaurant.** 160 E. Ontario St.; 280–8287. Construction experts from Japan huddled with a creative young Chicago architect to fashion this open, airy, attractive setting for Japanese cuisine. Just the right Oriental touches create a welcoming, yet slightly exotic, feeling without sacrificing creature comforts. Customers dine either at handsome, unclothed butcher block tables or perch on stools at a long sushi bar. If you choose the latter, you'll be able to watch a fascinating show as nimble-fingered chefs create some of Chicago's finest sushi specialties (raw fish slices on vinegared rice balls) to customers' orders. The sushi is also available for those seated at tables. Charts help you figure your way around ordering these raw delicacies. In addition, the menu offers regular entrées, dinners, and specials, with an emphasis on fin and shellfish. Shrimp and vegetable tempura, for instance, is particularly noteworthy. AE, CB, DC, MC, V.

**Itto Sushi.** 2530 N. Clark; 871–1800. This simple, attractive place is conveniently located in the Lincoln Park West neighborhood. You can sample the amazing creations of the sushi makers or choose from a variety of other options that include beef teriyaki, shrimp and vegetable tempura, and yosenabe, a mixture of vegetables, noodles, and seafood in broth. AE, CB, DC, MC, V.

**Ron of Japan.** 230 E. Ontario St.; 644–6500. Skilled cooks do their work at your table, as at Benihana, while a telescoping exhaust hood over the cooking surface wafts away the smoke and heat. Excellent beef is grilled teppan-yaki style, along with shrimp, mushrooms, onions, and bean sprouts. The shrimp, in particular—with a unique creamy topping concocted from eggs and vegetable oil—are worth a double order. Diners wear oversized aprons instead of using napkins, and eat with chopsticks from metal plates resting right on the cooking surface. The room is handsomely done with some remarkable decorative embellishments, including Japanese antiques. AE, CB, DC, MC, V.

## Korean
*Moderate*

**Seoul House.** 5346 N. Clark St.; 728–6756. An interesting assortment of authentic Korean dishes is available at this storefront restaurant. All are cooked to order, and come with rice and kim chee, fiery-hot pickled vegetables that are almost a staple of Korean meals. Be sure to try fried mahndoo, which is somewhat like a won ton, with a seasoned filling of ground beef, bean sprouts, onion, cabbage, and green onions. Many dishes are spicy-hot. Among the milder selections are shrimp tempura and chap chae (beef with vegetables and noodles). Serves late, MC, V.

## Mexican

### Moderate

**Cafe La Margarita.** 868 N. Wabash Ave.; 751–3434. A little bit of Mexico just south of the bordering Rush St. nightclub belt, with lots of Mexican artwork and a cantina-like ambience. Cesar Dovalina, the owner, is interested in food and takes pleasure in discussing it with his guests. The bill of fare is extensive, offering traditional Mexican favorites, such as chicken in mole sauce and peppers stuffed with beef or cheese, plus unusual items, such as beef with onions and vegetables. Good seafood selections, such as stuffed crabs with a mild cream sauce and melted cheese. Very good margaritas, as you would expect. AE, CB, DC, MC, V.

**Frontera Grill.** 445 N. Clark St.; 661–1434. High-style Mexican dining with polished servers and refreshingly "different" dishes, including tacos al carbon, flour tortillas you fill with great guacamole, black beans, grilled vegetables and a choice of hardwood-grilled meats or seafood. Grilled game hen with garlic and "sweet spices" is good; so is the fresh fish baked in banana leaves. Chiles rellenos are the most delicate in town. A large selection of small dishes includes venison-and-pork "Texas chili." Good chocolate-pecan pie, chunky rich mango ice cream, too. AE, MC, V.

**Su Casa.** 49 E. Ontario St.; 943–4041. This converted coach house is now a charming 17th-century-style setting for one of the most elegant and handsome of the local Mexican restaurants. Chicken-filled enchiladas, cheese tacos, chiles rellenos, and other classic dishes highlight the menu. A number of more unusual Mexican dishes include shrimp Veracruz (served in the shell with a spicy sauce) and several steak preparations that use tender, good-quality meat. There's also a hearty Texas chili. A strolling guitarist entertains evenings. Serves late. AE, CB, DC, MC, V.

**Mi Casa-Su Casa.** 2524 N. Southport; 525–6323. It's well worth a trip off the beaten path to find this no-frills Mexican restaurant. Felix Gomez and his wife are warm, friendly hosts who make customers feel right at home. Prices are modest and the food top-notch. Skirt steak covered with onions, green peppers, and melted cheese is a specialty. Chiles rellenos, shrimp shish-kebab, arroz con pollo, and combination plates of tacos, enchiladas, tostadas, flautas, rice and beans for two are also good. AE, CB, DC, MC, V.

## Mideast

### Moderate

**The Casbah.** 514 W. Diversey; 935–7570. "Come with me to the Casbah" was Charles Boyer's line. Within recent years, more and more Chicagoans have been using it because of this fine establishment, which features Middle Eastern cuisine. You can start your meal with cheese borek, tissue-thin strudel leaves wrapped around a tasty filling, or kibbeh nayyee, a mixture of raw lamb and cracked wheat. Follow it with Shish kebob in various forms or a puff-pastry envelope filled with Cornish game hen, almonds, and cinnamon. Or your choice can be sarma, a combination of ground meat and rice wrapped in grape leaves, or a fine preparation couscous. Serves late. AE, CB, DC, MC, V.

## Polynesian

### Expensive

**The Kona Kai.** Marriott O'Hare Hotel, 8535 W. Higgins Rd.; 693–4830. This is the largest of the South Seas restaurants in the Chicago area and features such delectable exotica as Konakai egg flower soup, lobster or crab curry, and flaming ice cream. The Royal Hawaiian is a meat-and-shellfish feast with Polynesian pork, shrimp and fresh vegetables served with Yang Chow fried rice and fresh pineapple. The adjoining lounge has a repertoire of 50 exotic drinks—the kind of rum-and-tropical-fruit-juice creations that are as good-looking as they are spirit raising. There is Polynesian entertainment Friday and Saturday nights. AE, CB, DC, D, MC, V.

**Trader Vic's.** 17 E. Monroe St.; 726–7500. Plates of barbecued spareribs, fried shrimp, sliced barbecued pork, and crepe Rangoon are a popular accessory for cocktails in this atmospheric restaurant in the venerable Palmer House. If there are at least 15 in your party and you have given a week's notice, you can have a whole barbecued pig fresh from the Chinese ovens. Indonesian roast lamb, several kinds of steak, game hen, chicken, and chops are among the other meats prepared in the ovens. There is also a roster of curries, plus dozens of other selections, which are mostly Cantonese in origin. You also can order hard-to-find (in Chicago) abalone. Serves late. AE, CB, DC, D, MC, V.

## Scandinavian

### Inexpensive

**Ann Sather's.** 929 W. Belmont; 348–2378. No fuss. No frills. Just a very plain, clean, reliable establishment that seems to be a favorite of Scandinavian old-timers and family groups with lots of children. The menu is relatively limited, but the Swedish fare is top-notch. This is a popular breakfast spot (jammed on Sunday mornings) with thin pancakes served with tart lingonberry sauce and Swedish potato sausage—two popular items. Scandinavian handicrafts fill the attractively arranged window. Delicious fruit soup is usually available, as are Swedish meatballs, chicken, and a variety of desserts, complemented by offerings from a full bar. AE, MC, V.

### Serbian

*Expensive*

**Miomir's Serbian Club.** 2255 W. Lawrence Ave.; 784–2111. Attractive decor, recreating European street scenes, is a perfect setting for superb food. Start your meal with corba (traditional Serbian soup with beef and vegetables) or with 2 tasty and unusual spreads—kajmak (fermented milk) and ajvar (grilled eggplant, sweet green peppers, and celery in olive oil). Then proceed to other Serbian specialties—all deliciously seasoned. Try, perhaps, chicken cooked in wine sauce or skewered pork tenderloin. There's an extensive selection of wines to go with your food. Entertainment and dancing on weekends with Gypsy fiddlers, Cossack dancers, and assorted singers and vocalists. MC, V.

### South American

*Moderate*

**El Criollo.** 1706 W. Fullerton, 549–3373. With a variety of Argentine dishes on the menu, this unassuming place off the beaten path is a haven for meat lovers. Options include a mixed grill of short ribs, blood sausage, and sweetbreads, plus steaks and brochettes with meat and vegetables. A number of Mexican and Puerto Rican dishes are also served, along with a variety of South American wines. AE, CB, DC, MC, V.

**Machupicchu.** 5427 N. Clark St.; 769–0455. Moises Asturrizaga and his staff lovingly prepare unusual and tasty food that is authentically Peruvian. So are the handicrafts displayed on the restaurant's walls. The selection isn't extensive, but there's a good variety of well-seasoned dishes that generally are not hotly spiced. Many of the ingredients are familiar ones, but the end results achieved with chicken, beef, and fish dishes are a new taste experience for most. Moises himself tells you what's available each evening. There's no printed menu, but $9.95 and $20 complete dinners. Among the dishes that turn up frequently are escabeche, a chicken dish; potatoes stuffed with beef, onions, tomato, raisins, boiled egg, and herbs; anticuchos, sort of a Peruvian mixed grill; and hearty soups. Bring your own wine. AE, CB, DC, MC, V.

### Spanish

*Moderate*

**Cafe Ba-Ba-Reeba!** 2024 N. Halsted; 935–5000. This stylish re-creation of a rustic 1960s Spanish restaurant serves tapas, those delectable and varied small snacks you sample with glasses of dry sherry. Amid colorful murals and the hanging garlic hams and salt cods that festoon the tapas bar, you can choose from 35 hot and cold tapas, 8 daily specials, and 25 sherries. Delicious options include Spanish ratatouille, cold marinated seafood, baked fennel wedges with anchovy and capers, baked chicken wings, and a wonderful baked goat cheese. Traditional and seafood paella for two is available as an entrée, and you can wind up your leisurely meal with a choice of fresh tarts, caramel flan, baked bananas, and homemade ice creams. AE, CB, DC, MC, V.

**La Paella.** 2920 N. Clark St.; 528–0757. As you'd expect from the name, the featured dish at this small but attractive storefront restaurant is paella, a traditional Spanish stew-like dish. The delicious house version combines bits of meat, chicken, and seafood with saffron-seasoned-and-colored rice. Polite, attentive service makes customers feel welcome and relaxed as they enjoy the paella or other dishes, such as roast duck enhanced with mangoes and brandy sauce; chicken braised with wine, almonds, and garlic; marinated baked trout; and seafood casserole with lobster. Although this small, comfortable restaurant features Northern Spanish cuisine, daily specials highlight dishes from various regions of Spain. AE, CB, DC, MC, V.

## Thai

### *Moderate*

**Ananda.** 941 N. State St.; 944–7440. Especially high quality foodstuffs, nice tableware, and better-than-average service set apart this Gold Coast restaurant. A fairly large menu touches all the familiar bases. For a mild and unusual beginning, order crisp rings of deep-fried squid stuffed with seasoned ground pork; for something zestier, try fiery Chiengmai style beef tartare. There are wonderful salads zipped up with green chilis; a favorite combines red grapes with shrimps, cashews and young ginger. Coconut-milk curries and noodle dishes such as pud thai are also good choices. MC, V.

## Vietnamese

### *Inexpensive*

**Mekong House.** 400 N. State St.; 222–9191. The city's nicest looking Vietnamese restaurant also serves some of its best food, though with toned-down hotness. Try soft, rice-paper egg rolls, tart beef salad with lemon juice, and a hearty duck soup with a meal's worth of noodles. Sweet iced coffee is a traditional finish. AE, DC, MC, V.

**Pasteur.** 4759 N. Sheridan Rd.; 271–6673. The helpful servers will guide you through the huge menu of delicious dishes such as whole Dungeness crab salad, beef grilled over charcoal at the table, and lots of soup and noodle dishes. Try the salad with lemon-flavored rare beef, sugar cane coated with shrimp paste, and sweet iced coffee with dessert. AE, MC, V.

**TEATIME.** Several of Chicago's most posh hotels have a very definite upper-class, understated English mood—the kind of places where one hears the rustle of quiet old money in low key but elegant surroundings. In many of these places, tea carts, laden with rich, tempting pastries, bite-size sandwiches, and the sort of taste temptations more often encountered in Britain, roll out at 3:00. Relaxing music usually drifts across the lobby while these hotels pour:

**The Drake,** 140 E. Walton Place at Michigan Ave.;787–2200. Eight different varieties of teas served in the Palm Court from 3–5:30 P.M. $9.25 fee includes hot scones with clotted cream and jam, currant buns, assorted finger sandwiches and a selection from the pastry cart. Harpist provides the mood music. **Mayfair Regent,** 181 E. Lake Shore Drive; 787–8500. Served in Lobby Lounge decorated with hand-painted Chinese murals from 3–5:30P.M. $9 complete or selections may be made à la carte. 18 varieties of tea available. Violin, piano or harp music is always played, adding to the atmosphere. **Park Hyatt Hotel,** Water Tower Square, 800 N. Michigan Ave.; 280–2222. Served in the Park Hyatt Salon from 2:30–5 P.M. 6 different teas offered. Cost is $9.75 for tea including sandwiches and pastries. Live piano music except Monday. **Ritz Carlton Hotel,** 160 E. Pearson at Water Tower Place,; 266–1000. Served in the Greenhouse. Several varieties of tea featured daily from 3–5 P.M. Service includes a selection of finger sandwiches, scones and miniature pastry at $5–$9.75. Daily.

**HOW TO GET AROUND. By bus:** Chicago has an extensive bus system that will take you long distances for 90¢. For 25¢ extra you can get a transfer that allows you to spend an hour shopping or sightseeing before you ride back. Only change may be used—no dollar bills. If you need information on public transportation, call RTA 24-hour information at 836–7000 or 800–972–7000. Tell them where you are, and where you want to go, and they will tell you how to get there.

*CTA Culture Bus* operates every Sunday and holidays from the Art Institute, mid-April through September, on 3 routes that serve over 30 museums and cultural attractions. These operate between 11:00 A.M.–5:15 P.M., allowing passengers to get off at a particular destination, then later reboard another bus. Fare is $2.50 adults, $1.25 children.

**By subway:** Subway maps are available from *Chicago Tourism Bureau* and the same fare structure applies.

**From the airports:** O'Hare Airport, at Mannheim and Kennedy Expressway, is by far the most frequently used. Many hotels have their own airport shuttle service. For $9, *Continental Air Transport* will take you to downtown Chicago. The stops for the limousine are listed by hotels, so just get out at the hotel nearest your destination. A rapid-transit train offers direct service to Chicago in about 35 min. Pick up the subway which operates every 20 minutes at Terminal 4. Free courtesy buses are provided by about 30 O'Hare area hotels. (See *O'Hare Airport Area* hotel listings.) Midway Airport, only 11 mi. from downtown, is connected to Chicago by Continental Air Transport at $6.75 per person.

**By taxi:** Taxis currently charge $1.00 base fare and 90¢ for each additional mile. There is a 50¢ charge for each additional rider. **Note:** Fares are constantly being changed. There is a shared system from O'Hare and Midway airports via taxis identified by orange "Shared Ride" pennants. Minimum load is 2, maximum 3. Major cab companies are Yellow and Checker, 829–4220, and Flash Cab, 561–1444.

**By car:** Get a good road map and be wary of parking regulations; they are strictly enforced. Beware of parking in a posted area or you may fall victim to one of the infamous local towing companies and their extortionlike rates. Downtown State St. is now a pedestrian mall closed to cars, and there are many one-way streets complicating matters. U-turns are not permitted at intersections in Chicago, but are allowed in middle of block, unless prohibited by signs. In most suburbs, the opposite is true. Right turns are permitted on red lights after stopping if there is no oncoming traffic and signs do not say otherwise. Garages are increasingly expensive, with city-owned lots offering lower, but not cheap, rates.

**By limousine:** For those who want to arrive in style, there are a number of limousine services advertised in the Yellow Pages. *Carey Limousine Service* (tel. 663–1220 or 800–336–4646), *Chicago Limousine Service* (726–1035 or 800–621–7307), and *Metropolitan Limousine* (751–1111 or 800–922–0343), are a few of them. *Elegant Motor Cars* (867–8203) rents antique and classic chauffeur driven limos of '30s through '50s vintage.

**By rental car:** *Avis, Budget, Dollar, Hertz, National, Rent A Wreck, Thrifty, Ajax, Econo-Car, Airways, Alamo,* and *Sears* are among car rental agencies.

**By boat:** The summer shuttle service from the boat dock below Michigan Ave. Bridge to Northwestern Station is a popular ride. Commuters use it regularly, but visitors also enjoy it. Runs April through September, takes 10 min., and transports passengers along the Chicago R. in comfort for 75¢ each way (tel. 337–1446). 7:45–8:45 A.M. from station, 4:45–5:15 P.M. from bridge.

**On foot:** Several areas are ideal for walking. Michigan Avenue's Magnificent Mile, the Downtown Loop, Old Town, and Near North neighborhoods are examples. In all cases, no matter what conditions may appear to be, make local inquiries as to the safest way to go. As in all cities, there are certain trouble spots, and the world being what it is, it does not pay to take chances.

**By horse-drawn carriage:** *Chicago Carriage Company* has a stand at Pearson St. and Michigan Blvd. just south of Water Tower Place and offers carriage rides daily from 9:30 A.M. to 3:30 P.M. and again from 6 P.M. to 3 A.M.; Saturday and Sunday 10:00 A.M.–3 A.M. (tel. 280–8535) *Coach Horse Livery* is located 1 block west of Michigan Blvd. between Chicago Ave. and Pearson St. with rides available Monday – Friday from 10 A.M. to 3:30 P.M. and 6:30 P.M.–12:30 P.M., Friday to 2 A.M., and Saturday and Sunday from 10 P.M. to midnight Sunday, 2 A.M. Saturday. (tel. 842–8500). Rates vary but average $25 for one-half hour for 1–4 people.

**Getting out to the suburbs:** A number of major expressways, some paralleled for part of their route by elevated trains, make access to suburban areas easy. Dan Ryan (I–90 and I–94) goes south, Stevenson (I–55) southwest, Eisenhower (I–290) west, Kennedy (I–90) north-northwest, and Edens (I–94) north. Tri-State Tollway (I–294) skirts the metropolitan area on the south and west. For the most spectacular drive, follow the Outer Drive both north and south along the lake. The North-West Tollway feeds into Chicago from Beloit, Madison, and Janesville, Wisconsin, and the East-West Tollway (Ill. 5) comes in from Iowa.

*Northwestern Railroad* leaves Northwestern Station at Canal and Madison and heads north to Evanston, Wilmette, Kenilworth, Winnetka, Glencoe, Highland Park, Highwood, and Lake Forest, carrying executive commuters to their lakeshore suburbs. The railroad also has a northwest run to Des Plaines, Arlington Hts., Mt. Prospect, Palatine, Fox River Grove, Cary, and Crystal Lake. The *Milwaukee Road* angles slightly northwest en route to Glenview, Northbrook, and Deerfield. The *Illinois Central-Gulf* extends south to Park Forest. *Burlington Northern* goes west, and *South Shore* south.

## City Streets

Travel around Chicago is made easy by a simple grid pattern. It all begins at the intersection of State and Madison in the heart of downtown, which is the zero-zero point. From this center the numbers go up in all directions covering about 100 numbers to a block. If you are looking for an address at 2000 North State, expect to find it 20 blocks north of that corner. One at 400 E. Madison would be 4 blocks east and very close to the lake. The suburbs are another story, although many of the old traditional ones follow a similiar simple system. New subdivisions are more apt to be meandering. If all else fails, a call to a local police department will bring helpful directions.

 **TOURIST INFORMATION SERVICES.** Contact the *Chicago Tourism Council,* 806 N. Michigan, 60611 (tel. 312–280–5740). The new *Chicago Visitor Information Center* is in the historic Water Tower, open 7 days a week; multilingual. The state maintains a walk-in information center at 310 South Michigan Ave. (tel. 793–2094), and the *Conservation Department* is at 100 W. Randolph St. (tel. 917–2070). *International Visitors Center* is at 520 N. Michigan Ave. (tel. 645–1836). O'Hare Airport has a multilingual service in Terminal 3 (686–2304). *Travelers Aid* has facilities at the Greyhound Bus Station (tel. 435–4537); Union Train Station (tel. 435–4543); and O'Hare International Airport (tel. 686–7562). There are nearly 60 foreign consulates in the city, ranging from Argentina to Yugoslavia, who can help native residents with problems. *Mayor's Eventline* (tel. 744–3370). *Illinois Travel Line* offers a 24-hour recorded list of events at 800–252–8987.

For information on facilities for the handicapped call 744–4016.

Both newspapers, the *Chicago Tribune* and *Sun Times,* are good sources of information, listing current attractions, entertainment, and special events. The *Tribune* has a Friday section, titled "Weekend," full of suggestions and ideas for local and out-of-town visitors.

*Chicago* magazine, published monthly and available on newsstands, covers restaurants, shopping, and entertainment in depth. *North Shore Magazine* does the same for the suburbs stretching north along the lake. A variety of local newspapers geared to what's going on downtown on the restaurant and entertainment scene are available free at hotels and parking garages. Among the most popular is the *Reader,* free on Thursday afternoons after 1 P.M. at 11 E. Illinois

St. or from any of 100 merchants downtown and north. *State of Illinois Office of Tourism* publishes *Illinois,* covering 82 pages of statewide attractions, including Chicago. Their twice-yearly calendar of events is also helpful. Write 310 S. Michigan, Chicago 60601. Businessmen can keep up with what's happening by reading *Crain's Chicago Business.*

For weather forecasts dial 976–1212, time 976–1616. For Police, Fire, or Ambulance dial either 911 or 0. Medical Referral Service is 670–2550; Dental emergency 726–4076.

*CBS* has an all news station (80 on radio dials) that has frequent updates of local expressway traffic conditions.

 **SEASONAL EVENTS. January** and February bring a flurry of boat, travel and outdoor shows. With them comes the latest in everything from rowboats to ocean-worthy yachts. North country fishing-camp owners are on hand to fascinate anglers with tales of their wilderness adventures. Assorted attractions from artificial trout streams to casting contests attract visitors.

Meanwhile out in Chinatown, a dragon leads the way as a gala parade and celebration welcome the *Chinese New Year.*

**February** means flowers as the azalea and camelia flower shows bloom at Lincoln and Garfield Park conservatories. Celebrity sports figures appear at the *Chicago Sport Show,* which tends to change locations some winters. Stars of the *Ice Capades* make it all look so easy at the Chicago Stadium. The late February-early **March** auto show features everybody's dream buggy.

They put dye in the Chicago River to turn it green for *St. Patrick's Day* in March, and an always grand and glorious parade follows the green line painted down State St. come rain or shine.

*Old Town Art Fair* brings out artists and admirers in **June.** From June through September the *Ravinia Festival* takes place in Ravinia Park, Highland Park. This annual event is a series of symphonic concerts, recitals, chamber music, and popular music events that include rock, jazz, country.

The **July 4** holiday attracts food samplers with dozens of big-name restaurants dishing up *A Taste of Chicago* and serving their most popular specialties in Grant Park. Massive crowds, long lines, and some rowdyism and reports of underage drinking have been reported. A pickpocket's haven. Daily attendance has been as high as three-quarters of a million with well over one million on July 4, 1987, creating a traffic jam of mammoth proportion.

Big names in golf make sports headlines at July's *Western Open Golf Tournament* held at the Butler National course in suburban Oak Brook. Lake Michigan's version of the Tall Ships depart for the challenging Chicago to Mackinac race the third weekend in July. Free Wednesday, Friday, and Saturday evening concerts begin in Grant Park in the Petrillo Music Shell at the northeast corner of Jackson Blvd. and Columbus. Phone 294–2420 since hours may vary.

A series of weekend neighborhood ethnic festivals was formerly climaxed by *Chicago Fest,* a 12-day musical extravaganza in July or August, featuring music from rock to jazz, and blues to country. A couple years ago it was one of the city's headline events attracting huge crowds to Navy Pier. More recently there have been boycotts of performances. It did not do well in a new location at Soldier Field in 1983 and was cancelled in 1984. Still, many are struggling to keep the idea alive and the very popular event may resurface in the future. Meanwhile a very popular *July Air and Water Show* featuring the Armed Forces jet aerobatics precision flying teams attracts large crowds to the lakefront.

The *Gold Coast Art Fair,* usually in **August,** on Rush St. and Wabash, attracts the arts and crafts crowd. *Venetian Night* later in the month inspires colorful animated floats and brilliantly illuminated yachts, turning Monroe St. into a sort of St. Tropez for a night.

A special Olympics for the handicapped is held in Grant Park during late summer. Giants of jazz show up for another free, city-sponsored event, the 7-day *Chicago Jazz Festival* around Labor Day (first Monday in **September**). Its continuance in 1988, however, is dependent on the same factors influencing Chicagofest.

In **December,** Santa Claus arrives for the *State Street Parade* and the Museum of Science and Industry opens it month-long exhibit *Christmas around the World,* displaying Christmas trees from most major countries, along with their traditional foods.

Chicago is a parade town and any occasion calling for a celebration gets a much-applauded march downtown. Make local inquiries; if it's not Columbus Day, Veterans Day, the Shriners, American Legion, or whatever, it is just as liable to be a welcome home to world champion Chicago Bears.

**TOURS. By land:** Chicago and nearby areas of interest are covered in tours offered by *Gray Line of Chicago,* 33 E. Monroe (tel. 346–9506), *American Sightseeing Tours,* 530 S. Michigan Ave. (tel. 427–3100). Everything from Chinatown and some surprising city sites to plush suburbs and after-dark destinations. *Chicago Motor Coach Co.,* 5601 N. Sheridan, (tel. 989–8919) uses open-top double-deck buses in summer. All operate year around.

*On The Scene Tours,* 505 N. LaSalle (tel. 661–1440), covers just about any aspect of the city one can imagine. They offer special Amtrak all-inclusive packages into Chicago and are noted for guided tours of the massive, otherwise off-limits Merchandise Mart. There are "Hot Tix" discounted theater tours, leisurely excursions along the North Shore to the Baha'i Temple, or "Go Go Chicago" for a basic overview of the city's high points. Their guides also conduct specialized Art Institute tours. "Offbeat Chicago" visits the very different Graceland Cemetery, with its grandiose Victorian monuments and tours the University of Chicago and the antiquities of its Oriental Institute. There are History and Landmarks tours, adventures to Six Flag's Great America, lunch in the architectural splendor of 35-room Glessner House—you name it, they will arrange it. Anything from Abraham Lincoln's carriage to a multimedia recreation of the Chicago fire. These range from a couple hours to all day, and this very creative organization is constantly coming up with new tour ideas.

Amtrak has an ever-changing collection of all-inclusive package tours into the city, as do various airlines and bus companies. Chicagoland hotels offer special packages throughout the year with budget-priced fringe benefits. *Chicago Tourism Council* can tell you about them; so can your travel agent.

For something really different, consider the *Chicago Supernatural Tour,* "a unique bus guided tour to haunted and legendary places." These are held Saturday and Sunday afternoons at 1:00 P.M. and last 5 hrs. The $19.50 fee includes snacks. Departure is from De Paul University, Lincoln Park campus. Call 735–2530 for reservations. Tour usually includes what guides label "psychic hot spots, some interesting burial grounds, and a search for Resurrection Mary, Chicago's most famous ghost." Also some evening trips. Chicago's *Haunted City Tour* is another conversation-stopper that spends 5–6 hours delving into the City's lively ghost lore via bus. $25. (Tel. 895–5750). Reservations necessary for both.

**By water:** There are boating tours on Lake Michigan by the *Mercury Scenicruiser* (tel. 332–1353) and *Wendella Streamliner* (tel. 337–1446). Both offer views of the photogenic shoreline and skyline and leave from below the Michigan Ave. Bridge, passing through locks at the mouth of the Chicago R. into the lake. A dazzling, eye-opening view, even for residents. *Wendella* operates from mid-April to mid-September, weather permitting and offers 1, 1½, and 2 hr. trips at 10:00 A.M., 11:30 A.M., 1:15 P.M., 3:00 P.M., and 7:30 P.M. Prices are $5, $6, and $8, children under 12 half price. *Mercury* has 1½ and 2 hr. trips variously scheduled at 10:00 A.M., 11:30 P.M., 1:15 P.M., and 3:15 P.M., for $6 adults, $3 under 12. Their 2-hr. 7:30 P.M. cruise costs $8 adults, $4 children. They also have a program of 1-hr. lake rides. These are not operated on a fixed schedule, but generally leave at 2:30, 5:00, 9:00 P.M. and also at 6:00, 10:00 P.M. and weekends. Adults $5, children under 12, $2.50. It is wise to check both lines, since schedules change.

*Shoreline Marine Sightseeing* (tel. 673–3399) offers numerous 1-hour lake cruises from 3 locations: Shedd Aquarium, the Planetarium dock and evenings from Buckingham Fountain. These operate from Memorial Day to Labor Day, plus off-season weekends weather permitting. Fare is $4.00 adults, $1.50 children under 10. S.S. *Clipper,* now docked at Navy Pier, was built in 1905 and once cruised the Great Lakes. Last major renovation was in 1940, so it is wonderfully restored Art Deco. It has now been restored and is open to visitors who can roam from the steam engine to the captain's bridge and staterooms. Open roughly from May 1 to October. We strongly suggest that you call ahead as 1988 hours were not firm at press time. Boarding fee is $3.00 adults, $1.50 children. Cocktails and snacks are served on board (tel. 329–1800).

*Star of Chicago,* 600 E. Grand Ave. (tel. 644–5914) On the pricey side. $20.95 luncheon cruise, $39.95 buffet dinner cruise, weekdays, $44.95 Saturday and Sunday. Moonlight cruises, Sunday brunch, TGIF Friday afternoon cruises. New in 1983 and sails from Navy Pier.

**SPECIAL-INTEREST SIGHTSEEING.** For an overview, start at the country's tallest building, 110-story *Sears Tower,* at Wacker, Adams, Jackson, and

Franklin streets (tel. 875–9696). 2 nonstop elevators rush up to the skydeck 103 floors above the city, open daily 9:00 A.M. to midnight. Same hours apply to the only slightly shorter John Hancock Center Observatory, 875 N. Michigan (tel. 751–3681). On a clear day Michigan, Indiana, Wisconsin, and the Illinois prairie are visible, with superb shoreline views along Lake Michigan.

Chicago is a thriving financial center and institutions connected with its prosperity provide fascinating tours. The *Board of Trade,* housed in an imposing Art Deco structure with *Ceres,* the gilded Goddess of Grain, on the roof, is the largest commodities futures market in the country. Hostesses conduct tour-lectures every half hour 9 A.M.–12:30 P.M. Monday–Friday and help unravel the mysteries to budding brokers (tel. 435–3617).

*International Monetary Market* and *Chicago Merchantile Exchange,* 30 S. Wacker Dr., are the places to learn all about trading in gold, silver, and hogs. Hours and phone numbers are the same for both: 930–8200, Monday–Friday, 7:30 A.M.–3:15 P.M. Closed holidays. Noon tour.

The *Federal Reserve Bank,* 230 S. La Salle (tel. 322–5322) is certain to send visitors away with a better understanding of our monetary system, and so are the *1st National Bank of Chicago,* Dearborn and Madison streets—the world's tallest (tel. 732–4000)—and *American National Bank & Trust Co.,* La Salle and Washington (tel. 661–5897), which also offer tours.

To see what helps make this "the city that works," here are a few behind-the-scenes tours. You've been hearing about Chicago politics for years, why not tour *City Hall* at 121 N. La Salle St., (tel. 744–6671).

Some of Chicago's "finest" will guide visitors through the *Chicago Police Department,* 1121 S. State at 10 A.M. and 2:00 P.M., Tuesday through Friday. One week's notice required, children under 12 not admitted. (tel. 744–5571). Tour includes a look at the crime lab and some background on the city's livelier past.

Ever since Mrs. O'Leary's cow kicked over the lantern that legend insists started the Chicago fire, fire protection has been Chicago's prime concern. Here at 558 W. DeKoven St., where the fire supposedly started, the *Robert Quinn Fire Academy* trains future firefighters. To join an illuminating tour, call 744–6691. These are offered Monday through Friday at 11:00 A.M. and 1:00 P.M. by appointment only, when training sessions are not being held.

It seems appropriate that some of the country's best-tasting water comes from the world's largest water filtration plant. 50-min. tours at *James Jardine Water Purification Plant* at Navy Pier cover the entire purification process (tel. 744–3692). Advance notice required.

*O'Hare International Airport,* the world's busiest, also offers behind the scenes tours, Mannheim Rd. and Kennedy Expressway (tel. 686–2200).

If you're beginning to think Chicago specializes in the biggest, largest, tallest, etc., there is some truth in that. Even the post office is the largest postal building in the world (perhaps offering that many more nooks and crannies in which the mail can get "delayed"?). 2-hour tours daily except December (tel. 765–3009).

If "all the news that's fit to print" is your interest, both the *Tribune,* 435 N. Michigan (tel. 222–3993) and *Sun Times,* 401 N. Wabash (tel. 321–2032) offer tours—one-hour tours at the *Tribune* and 45-min. tours at the *Sun Times.* Those at the *Tribune* have been temporarily stopped because of a long-lasting labor strike still in process at press time. The Tribune Building, once labeled "exuberant Gothic Revival," is architecturally interesting and contains bits and pieces of such buildings as Westminster Abbey, the Arch of Triumph, and the Taj Mahal, near the entrance.

Here comes another "world's largest," this time the gigantic Kennedy family-owned *Merchandise Mart* at the Chicago R. and Wells St. This giant showcase of wholesale furniture, clothes, and gifts and furnishings measures displays by the mile and is usually closed to the public, but tours can be arranged when trade shows are not being held. Call 661–1440.

*Rockefeller Memorial Chapel* on University of Chicago campus is a vaulted Gothic wonder noted for its 72-bell carillon. Tours after Sunday services, 5850 S. Woodlawn.

*Tempel Farms* brings a touch of Vienna to Illinois with performances of its rare white Lippizan stallions. This one-hour program is well worth the trip to the farm west of the Tri-State (I-94) at Rte. 132. Indoor and outdoor performances, depending on weather. $7. Call 623–7272. Can be combined with a trip to the *Lambs Farm* (see "Children's Activities," below).

## Gangster Tour

"Scarface" Al Capone, "Machine Gun" Jack McGurn, "Baby Face" Nelson, Dutch Schultz, Bugs Moran, Paul "The Waiter" Ricca, Tony "Big Tuna" Accardo, Jake "The Barber" Factor, John Dillinger: not exactly a list of Chicago's Who's Who. But their names, for better or worse, became so indelibly associated with the city that nothing can ever erase them.

Certain city officials breathe a sigh of relief every time an old gangland monument like the infamous St. Valentine's Day massacre garage is torn down. But no one can ever forget that seven Bugs Moran henchmen were gunned down by other mobsters wearing policemen's uniforms at what used to be 2122 North Clark St. (The wall the seven were lined up against is now part of a restaurant in Vancouver, BC.) When asked who shot him, dying Frank Gusenberg said, "Nobody shot me."

Big Jim Colosimos Café (now an empty lot beside Lions Barb-B-Q at 2126 South Wabash) is where it all started. His own bodyguard reputedly arranged the underworld leader's "demise" in 1920, then assumed his empire. Honorary pallbearers included three judges, two congressmen, an assistant states attorney, assorted aldermen, and a future federal judge.

Dion O'Bannion, like Capone a graduate of the newspaper circulation wars, was shot down in his flower shop at 738 North State Street across from Holy Name Cathedral, and 26 flower cars followed his $10,000 casket to the cemetery. When Michael Merlo, head of Unione Siciliane, died, friends ordered a $25,000 floral tribute, including a wax effigy of him for the funeral cortege. Ironically, O'Bannion had been working on Merlo's funeral flowers when he was shot. The flower shop is gone, but the cathedral, which was riddled with 38 machine gun bullets two years later when O'Bannion's lieutenant Hymie Weiss and chauffeur were murdered, is still there.

By the time Capone assumed power, the Better Government Association wired the U.S. Senate, "Chicago politicians are in league with gangsters and the city is overrun with a combination of lawless politics and protected vice."

Then the massacre really began. In the first four months of 1926, there were 29 gang murders in Chicago, and at the end of four years over 200—with no convictions. Capone's income in 1927 was estimated at $105 million, and it was income tax evasion that ultimately sent him to prison. Today, he lies in an inconspicuous grave in Mt. Carmel cemetery in Hillside. The headstone was stolen in 1972.

Estimates put the number of assassinations on the corner of Oak and North Cleveland, in the heart of what was once the bootleg brewery district, at anywhere from 15 to over 40. And there was no safety in numbers for Antonio Lombardo, head of Unione Siciliane, gunned down near State and Madison, the world's busiest intersection, walking with two bodyguards.

Capone headquartered at the Metropole Hotel, 2300 South Michigan, where he occupied 50 rooms on two floors. He also had offices in another hotel connected to it by tunnel. His other known residences included 2222 South Wabash (the Four Deuces Brothel), 7244 South Prairie, and a summer home in Mercer, Wisconsin, where his brother Ralph died several years ago.

When Al went to the theater, he rode in a seven-ton bulletproof car with combination locks so no one could open it and plant a bomb inside. Eighteen bodyguards in tuxedos went with him. Today's visitor might feel more comfortable in the same kind of car when seeking out those South Michigan and South Wabash neighborhoods. (They're about three blocks west of McCormick Center Hotel and two or three blocks north off the expressway.) Neighborhood character changes within blocks in Chicago.

Jake Lingle, *Chicago Tribune* reporter who was also on Capone's payroll, was gunned down in the lower-level concourse of the Illinois Central Station, Randolph and Michigan, in 1930.

One by one these landmarks are disappearing—some making room for other construction, others through mysterious fires, to become vacant lots. But the alley just south of the still active Biograph Theatre, 2433 North Lincoln, where bank robber John Dillinger was shot, is still there. He had been hiding out in a flat behind the theater at 2420 North Halsted. The theater's Art Deco theme has been preserved, and it is still very much as it was the night Dillinger and "the lady in red" saw Dillinger's last film there.

The bullet-riddled car of "Baby Face" Nelson was found abandoned on the Winnetka Avenue bridge over the North Branch of the Chicago River in Northfield. His body was found dumped in a Skokie cemetery.

Grudges last a long time here. It was seven years and one day after the St. Valentine's Day massacre that 38-year-old "Machine Gun" Jack McGurn got his, gangland style, at what was then a bowling alley at 805 Milwaukee Avenue. He was always suspected as Capone's hit man for the St. Valentine's Day

SPECIAL-INTEREST SIGHTSEEING

headliner, and he was indicted, but the case never came to trial. Yes, he really did carry his machine gun in a violin case.

Roger "The Terrible" Touhy had been convicted on what he considered a "trumped up charge" involving kidnapping Jake "The Barber" Factor during Prohibition, and he spent more than 25 years in prison. There were always those who said he knew too much to survive. Twenty-three days after his release from Statesville Penitentiary in 1959 he was shotgunned down on the steps of his sister's house at 125 North Lotus.

Some local Chicago publications actually print the addresses and connections of surviving notorious residents, identifying them as "suspected gunman in the St. Valentine's Day massacre," "generally considered Capone's triggerman," and people ride around peering at them as though on some Hollywood movie star house tour.

In those early days, gangsters were an interesting ethnic mix; Sicilian, Irish, Jewish, Polish, etc. Things have changed. But they are a lot quieter now and Thompson .45-caliber machine guns are very passé. When reputed mob boss Sam "Momo" Giancanna was shot in his basement in suburban Oak Park a few years ago, his assassin used a .22-caliber revolver with a silencer, and his houseman very mysteriously disappeared.

The Chicago Crime Commission releases lists of syndicate-controlled businesses—these are regularly published in the paper, everybody knows about them, talks about them, and continues to patronize them. Chicago has always had a unique attitude about such things, a "live-and-let-live" philosophy, which also applies to business. Some city employees would rather bury the colorful past forever and pretend it never happened and is not, in some cases, still happening. However, recent restoration work on the Lexington Hotel, one of Capone's strongholds, is stirring up a lot of old memories. It is located on Michigan Avenue a few blocks from McCormick Place Convention Center.

Tourists, incidentally, need not worry. These fellows are only interested in killing each other off and go about it very professionally.

### Architectural Sites

This is where the skyscraper originated and names like Louis Sullivan, Burnham and Root, Mies van der Rohe, and Frank Lloyd Wright emerged as strong influences. So much has happened here architecturally that professionals refer to all the innovations as "the Chicago School" and a number of associations offer tours of major landmarks.

*Chicago Architecture Foundation.* Maintains the Archi-Center, 330 S. Dearborn, 60604 (tel. 782–1776), sponsoring a full schedule of walking tours, bus tours, and even bicycle expeditions to districts of architectural interest. They maintain 2 of Chicago's very historic houses. One is Glessner House, 1800 S. Prairie, near McCormick Place. Renovated 35-room Romanesque mansion designed by H.H. Richardson, in the historic district known as Millionaire's Row, now undergoing restoration. (tel. 326–1393). The other is the Widow Clark House, also located in the Prairie Avenue Historic District (tel. 326–1393).

*Sears Tower.* 233 S. Wacker Dr. The tallest building in the world, 110 stories and 1454 ft. high. Observation platform.

*The Rookery Building.* 209 S. La Salle. Vintage 1886, is one of the remaining early skyscrapers. Frank Lloyd Wright designed the lobby in 1905.

*Monadnock Building.* A few blocks away at 53 W. Jackson. Designed by Burnham and Root. Its 16 stories were completed in 1891. It is the tallest building with load-bearing walls in the world.

*Robie House.* 5757 S. Woodlawn (tel. 702–8370). This house, forerunner of the modern "prairie house," is one of the most important buildings of our century. Offers tours Monday–Saturday at noon.

*Oak Park.* There are 16 Frank Lloyd Wright buildings in Chicago, but suburban Oak Park, 25 min. from downtown, boasts 30, including the home and studio where he lived and worked for more than 20 years. The home is open to the public, guided tours. Call *Oak Park Visitors Center* (848–1978). The Center at Forest and Lake avenues is open daily 10:00 A.M.–5:00 P.M. year-round and provides maps, guidebooks and an audio-visual program, "Lightning on the Prairie." There are guided tours as well as tape-recorded walking tours in English, German, or Japanese. Guided tours of both Wright's home and the Unity Temple he designed are $4 each, $2 children and seniors. A $7 discount coupon includes the tour and the tape-recorded walking tour. Schedule is complicated so calling first is advisable. Annual house walk, covering a number of Wright-designed homes, is held 3rd Saturday in May and is a popular sellout. A property of the National Trust for Historic Preservation.

*Pullman Community.* 104th St. to 115th St. at Calumet Expressway. The first company town in America. Founded in 1880 by George Pullman, inventor of the Pullman sleeping car, it is an outdoor museum of architecture, city planning, and labor history. Victorian Hotel Florence serves lunch daily except Monday. Guided walking tours 1st Sunday of month, May–October. Open-house tours annually, 2nd weekend in October. Tours start at the Historic Pullman Center, 614 E. 113th St. Adults $3.50, students $2.00, seniors $3.00 (tel. 785–8181). A national historic landmark.

*Auditorium Theater.* 70 E. Congress. Designed by Louis Sullivan and beautifully restored. *Carson, Pirie, Scott & Company.* 1 S. State St. The cast iron in the store entrance, known as the rotunda, is often referred to as "iron lace." Also designed by Louis Sullivan. Both the exterior and vestibule interior were restored to their original style in 1979 to celebrate the company's 125-year anniversary, and the result is definitely a "designer original."

*Marquette Building.* 140 S. Dearborn. A 16-story steel-framed beauty finished in 1894. The life of Jesuit missionary Jacques Marquette, who wintered in Chicago in 1674–75, is shown on bronze reliefs above the main entrance. Inside, impressive mosaics trace Chicago history.

*Illinois Institute of Technology.* 10 W. 33rd St. Campus architecture designed by Ludwig Mies van der Rohe is the subject of a 1-hr. tour. Reservations (tel. 567–3025).

*State of Illinois Building,* covering square block bounded by Randolph, Lake, Clark, and La Salle streets. Completed in 1985, this steel and glass conversation stopper continues to generate controversy.

*University of Illinois,* Circle Campus. 750 S. Halsted. Tours (tel. 996–8686). *University of Chicago* 1116 E. 59th St. Special tours. Buildings designed by Eero Saarinen, Edward Durrell Stone, Mies van der Rohe, and Frank Lloyd Wright's Robie House (tel: 962–8374). 10:00 A.M. Monday–Saturday.

*Baha'i Temple.* Sheridan Rd. at Linden Ave., Wilmette. Looks like a modern Persian version of the Taj Mahal along the lakeshore. National Center for the Persian-born Baha'i faith, it took 50 yrs. to build and is unique in this hemisphere. Construction started on the white-faced ornamented dome in 1903 and by 1953 the lacy-looking marvel was finished. It is on the National Register of Historic Places. The faith came to the U.S. during the Columbian Exposition held in Chicago in 1893 and a site near the city was selected for the first Baha'i temple in the Western world. Open daily May 15–October 14, 10:00 A.M.–10:00 P.M. and October 15–May 14, 10:00 A.M.–5:00 P.M.

*Chicago's Famous Buildings: A Photographic Guide,* Third Edition, edited by Ira J. Bach; *A Guide to Chicago's Public Sculpture* by Ira J. Bach and Mary Lackritz Gray; *A Guide to Frank Lloyd Wright and Prairie School Architecture in Oak Park* by Paul Sprague; and *A Walk Through Graceland Cemetery* by Barbara Lanctot are sources for further information. These publications are generally available in the 2 shops of the Chicago Architecture Foundation.

*Landmarks Preservation Council of Illinois,* 407 S. Dearborn St. (tel. 922–1742), sometimes offers tours of Illinois historic architectural sites, both in the city and elsewhere in the state. Their members are active in working for historic preservation. *National Trust for Historic Preservation,* 407 South Dearborn St., (tel. 353–3419) is also becoming increasingly involved in local preservation.

## Plaza Art

It seems appropriate that the city that made such a name for itself architecturally should have equally unique art work decorating its buildings. There is practically a competition in which plazas try to outdo one another. In summer, office workers picnic, sunbathe, and in the case of Daley Center and First National Bank, enjoy free concerts in these plazas.

*Bertoia Sculpture.* Standard Oil Plaza, 200 E. Randolph. Truly unique "sound sculpture" in a reflecting pool. Meant to be heard as well as seen; natural wind currents determine the sound.

*Calder.* Federal Center Plaza at Adams and Dearborn. His 53-foot-high, 50-ton red stabile, entitled *Flamingo,* is here, while his mobile *Universe* decorates the lobby of Sears Tower.

*Chagall Mosaic.* First National Plaza, Monroe and Dearborn. Colorful 70-foot-long mural utilizes marble, stone, glass, and granite.

*Henry Moore's Nuclear Energy.* Recalls the historic spot on the University of Chicago campus where the first atom was split.

*Miro's Mystery.* Brunswick Plaza, 69 W. Washington. A 1981 addition, still the subject of much speculation.

*Claes Oldenburg's Batcolumn.* Social Security Administration Plaza, 600 W. Madison. Stands 100 ft. high with 1,608 pieces of welded steel.

*Picasso Mystery Sculpture.* Daley Plaza, Dearborn and Washington. Remains a 50-foot-tall object of considerable attention. It was a gift from that famed artist to the city. It has been variously described as a woman, a dog . . . or a vulture prepared to prey on the taxpayer. See what you think.

**PARKS.** Chicago had the good sense to do something few other cities considered—use its lakefront as a beautifully manicured frontyard rather than a series of docks and warehouses. Seemingly endless miles of parks stretch along the lake like jewels, interspersed with yacht harbors, a city golf course, some surprising statues, a conservatory, and grand views of the shore. *Lincoln Park.* Along the lake between North Ave. and Hollywood Ave. It houses the renowned Lincoln Park Zoo, Farm-in-the-Zoo, conservatory, outdoor gardens, lagoon, athletic fields, tennis courts, golf course, jogging paths, shooting range, and more. *Jackson Park.* 56th St., 67th St., Stony Island Ave., and the lake are its boundaries. This was site of the Columbian Exposition of 1893 and includes the exceptional Museum of Science and Industry. *Grant Park.* East of Michigan Ave. between Randolph St. on the north and Roosevelt Rd. on the south. 300 acres of attractively landscaped parkland adjacent to the Loop. The Field Museum, Adler Planetarium, Shedd Aquarium, and Art Institute are here (see *Museum* listing). Also noteworthy:

*Buckingham Fountain,* presented to Grant Park in 1927 by Miss Kate Sturges Buckingham in memory of her brother. A much larger version of one she admired at Versailles, it operates daily, Memorial Day to Labor Day, from 11:30 A.M. to 10 P.M., ending with a rainbow of color nightly. It is a dramatic spectacle, with waters rising 135 ft. above the marble base.

*Petrillo Music Shell,* also in Grant Park, is the setting of free concerts from popular music to classics during summer (tel. 294–2420).

**ZOOS.** *Lincoln Park Zoo* covers 35 acres just north near the lake and is especially noted for its gorillas. The Great Ape House has everything from chimpanzees to orangutans amusing viewers in their own private rain forest. The 550-lb. Bushman, most famous of them all, is now stuffed and in the Field Museum. Youngsters (and adults) who have never visited a farm are fascinated with the Farm-in-the-Zoo. Free. Contains about 2,500 mammals, birds, and reptiles. Its Rookery walkways wind past waterfalls, ponds, and bird sanctuaries. A world apart, yet minutes from downtown at 2200 N. Cannon Dr. in Lincoln Park. Open daily 9 A.M. to 5 P.M. (tel. 294–4660). Free.

*Brookfield Zoo* in suburban Brookfield, 11 mi. west, was the first zoo in the country to develop a moat system with completely natural outdoor landscaping, which makes it look like the animal is not caged. Monkey island can keep anyone amused for hours. A tropical African rain forest populated with gorillas, birds, monkeys, reptiles, and a pygmy hippo is one of its newest attractions. It was built complete with waterfalls and scheduled thunderstorms. Several dolphin shows are presented daily in the Seven Seas Panorama, and steam trains and motor safari trains make the zoo's 200 acres easier to visit. Open daily from Memorial Day to Labor Day, 9:30 A.M. to 6:00 P.M., other seasons to 5:00 P.M. Adults $2.25, seniors and children 75¢ (tel. 242–2630). Free Tuesdays. Parking $2.00. Both zoos have children's petting zoos, which are well maintained and tremendously popular.

 **GARDENS.** Partly because of the unique way Chicago's lakefront has been developed, the city seems to have a long, continuous garden strip for a frontyard. Within that strip, or often adjoining it, are several exceptional gardens, although some of the major botanical finds are a drive away.

*Garfield Park Conservatory.* 300 N. Central Park Blvd. Considered the largest in the world under one roof and covers 5.5 very exceptional acres. Special shows are seasonally scheduled, but the regular displays are always worth a trip. There is also a 175,000-sq.-ft. formal garden on the grounds and a Garden for the Blind. Open daily 9:00 A.M. to 5:00 P.M., 10 A.M.–6 P.M. during shows. Free (tel. 533–1281).

*Grant Park Rose Garden* near Buckingham Fountain. Over three dozen carefully manicured rose beds with 8,000 bushes.

*Lincoln Park.* Really a three-in-one delight. Grandmother's Garden, between Stockton and Lincoln Park West, dates back to 1893 and specializes in gorgeous old-fashioned flowers. 40,000 plants brighten this 130,000-sq.-ft. slice of tranquillity. The 3-acre Conservatory is the year-round pièce de résistance, with seasonal shows and rooms devoted to some of the most spectacular palms in captivity. Part of the Conservatory dates from 1891 and the great Victorian fondness for potted palms is part of its inheritance. There are also tropical plants and ferns in prime condition at all times. The flower garden to the south has over 25,000 plants surrounding Bates Fountain. The conservatory is open daily 9:00 A.M. to 5:00 P.M., 10 A.M.–6 P.M. during shows. Free (tel. 294–4770).

*Marquette Park Rose Garden.* 3540 W. 71st St. Features 4,000 of those beauties, plus a pool with live swans. Like parks in the world, these are all best enjoyed in the daylight. It is not wise to wander around in them after dark.

*Chicago Botanic Garden.* Lake-Cook Road just east of Edens Expressway in suburban Glencoe. 300 acres of gardens still undergoing development. Owned by Forest Preserve District of Cook County and managed by the Chicago Horticultural Society. Seasonal hours. Admission free, but $2 parking and tram ride $2 adults, $1 children and seniors. (tel. 835–5440).

*Shakespeare Gardens* on Northwestern University's nearby Evanston campus is planted with flowers Shakespeare wrote about in his plays.

**BEACHES.** Chicago has miles of beautiful sand beaches fully staffed with lifeguards in season. Open mid–June, closed Labor Day. Hours 9:00 A.M. to 9:30 P.M. Admission free. *Oak Street Beach,* which stretches along the Gold Coast, attracts a younger, avant garde city-dweller type, while *North Avenue Beach* attracts a mixed group. These 2 beaches are also most favored by vacationers. Up-to-the-minute information on all beaches is available by calling the Park District's Beach Information number, 294–2333. Swimming from rocks along Lake Michigan or in unpatrolled area is foolhardy and dangerous. Many suburban beaches along the North Shore accept paying guests. Heed red warning flags, which indicate undertow or other conditions that make swimming hazardous. Do not expect tropical temperatures—water in the 60s is normal; 72° here is considered absolutely spa-like!

**PARTICIPANT SPORTS. Bicycling:** Getting more popular every year. These several standout trails. *Chicago Lakefront Path* covers 20 mi., utilizing the city's lakefront parks, harbors, beaches, and ever changing skyline to great advantage. Park hours are 6:00 A.M. to 11:00 P.M., but for safety sake, it is wise to confine your cycling to daylight hours. *Illinois Prairie Path* extends 40 mi. into the western suburbs. A growing number of communities are utilizing abandoned railroad beds and parks to develop routes. *Schwinn Bicycle Co.* (tel. 454–7400), 1856 N. Kostner, Chicago 60639, is good source of information. *Spokes for Folks* rents bikes (and roller skates) daily during summer at Lincoln Park at Fullerton Parkway, and Cannon Drive. Open daily 10:00 A.M.–7:00 P.M., May 1–Labor Day and weekends in April, September, and October, depending on weather.

**Boating:** Big, broad, and deep, Lake Michigan is at the city's front door. Mooring slips are taken long in advance, but there are *launching ramps* at Diversey Harbor, Burnham Harbor, Calumet Park, Rainbow Beach, Wilson Avenue, and Jackson Park. There are 2 free launching ramps on Des Plaines and Calumet rivers. *Chicagoland Canoe Base,* 4019 N. Narragansett (tel. 777–1489), offers wide variety of canoe rentals, and many charter boats are available for fisherman attracted by Lake Michigan's coho runs. Hours, sunup to sundown. Summer Paddleboat rentals in Lincoln Park Lagoon; $4.00 for ½ hr., $7.00 per hour. $5 deposit.

**A word of warning.** Lake Michigan often displays the temperament of the inland sea it is. Never venture out in a boat before checking weather predictions. Sudden squalls are not uncommon. Call 298–1413 for extended forecast, including Lake Michigan wave and weather conditions. Also be wary of overloading small boats and heading too far out in small craft. Lake water levels have been extremely high, causing serious shore erosion.

**Golf:** Chicago Park District has 6 public courses and provides free winter golf school. *Waveland,* 3800 N. Lake Shore Dr. along the lake; *Columbus* at 5800 W. Jackson; *Marquette Park,* 67th St. and Kedzie; *South Shore Park,* 71st St. and South Shore; *Robert A. Black,* 2045 W. Pratt (the old Edgewater course) and *Jackson Park,* 1 block east of 63rd and Stony Island. All are 9 holes except 18-hole Jackson Park. Open daily dawn to dusk, April–September. Weekends and holidays $4.00, weekdays $3.50 for the 9-hole courses, and $5.50 weekends, $5.00 weekdays for the 18-hole course. Driving range is at *Lake Shore Drive and Diversey* along with a miniature-golf course, and another driving range in Jackson Park, open 8:00 A.M.–10:45 P.M. daily. Large bucket of balls costs $2.50. Park District phone is 294–2274. Many other fine courses are available for a greens fee in Chicago and suburbs. *Butler National* in Oak Brook is site of the Western Open.

**Jogging:** There are more than 20 miles of jogging paths along the lakeshore, from 5600 North to the Near South Side. There's plenty of company on the paths leading from the woods to the lakeshore. Between Fullerton and Belmont avenues there are wooden exercise spots, with advice to the runner and a seven-mile measured course. Be especially careful crossing streets at main intersections such as Fullerton Ave. There are plentiful water fountains during summer months. On May 8, 1988 the increasingly competitive America's Marathon should top in size the previous 12,000 runners. Write America's Marathon –Chicago, 223 W. Erie, Chicago, Il 60601 for information, or call 951–0660.

**Racquetball:** *Pottawattomie Park,* 7340 N. Rogers. Call 743–4313 for information and reservations.

**Tennis:** Park District has over 650 free tennis courts. Add to this the hundreds of courts in the suburbs and at the resort hotels. There are 2 major tennis facilities in the downtown district. Both are open daily April–October. *Daley Bicentennial Plaza,* Randolph and Lake Shore Dr. (tel. 294–4792), $5.00 per hour, 12 lighted courts, reservations required, and *Grant Park Tennis Courts,* 9th and Columbus Dr. (tel. 294–2307), $2.00 per day or $20 annual permit. 12 lighted courts, no reservations needed.

**SPECTATOR SPORTS. Baseball:** Baseball's National League *Chicago Cubs* play at Wrigley Field on the North Side. Season: April–October (tel. 281–5050). Daytime games only. The American League *Chicago White Sox,* at White Sox Park on the South Side, play ball April–October (tel. 924–1000). This is definitely a big baseball city, often with more news emphasis on major league scores than national events.

**Basketball:** *Chicago Bulls* play at Chicago Stadium, October–April (tel. 943–5800), which is also host to many college games and tournaments. Loyola, Northwestern, and DePaul usually field strong and exciting teams. The latter's *Blue Demons* have been in the headlines ever since they stepped into the limelight a few years ago as the nation's Number 1 team.

**Football:** *Chicago Bears* now play at Soldier Field, September–December (tel. 663–5408). *Northwestern* plays Big Ten and other teams at Dyche Stadium in Evanston.

**Hockey:** *Chicago Black Hawks* play at Chicago Stadium, making headlines October–April (tel. 733–5300). Newest team on the scene is the *Chicago Sting* soccer team, which plays at Soldier Field, outdoors May–September and at the Chicago Stadium indoors November–April (tel. 245–5425).

**Horse Racing:** Flat racing at *Hawthorne,* September–December (tel. 780–3700). Harness racing, mostly nights, at *Sportsmans Park,* February–September (tel. 242–1121), and *Maywood Park,* February–May and September–December (tel. 626–4816).

**Tournaments:** *Western Open Golf Tournament* is held in early summer at Oak Brook's Butler National. Sailors hope for a breeze the 3rd weekend in July for *Chicago to Mackinac boat race. Norge Ski Jump* at Fox River Grove has slide tournament in January. *Polo* matches at the Chicago Armory and at Oak Brook, May–October (tel. 654–3060), where some spectators cultivate such a way-out look that they compete with the ponies for attention.

For latest results on major sports nationwide, call *Sportsphone* 976–1313.

 **CHILDREN'S ACTIVITIES.** Both *Lincoln Park* and *Brookfield Zoo* have exceptional children's petting zoos, (see *Zoos* section in this chapter for details), and the *Lambs Farm* near Libertyville also has a children's farmyard, pet shop, and special programs ranging from pumpkin parties to hayrides and pony rides. The Sunday buffet breakfast, 11:00 A.M.–2:30 P.M. is popular with families (tel. 362–4636). Farmyard hours are 9:00 A.M. to 5:00 P.M. daily except holidays.

All the major museums offer very worthwhile programs for youngsters. The *Art Institute* has a Junior Museum, with unusual changing exhibits and attention-holding events. *Field Museums*'s trained volunteers guide children on carefully planned tours. At the *Museum of Science and Industry,* the thousands of gadgets, Colleen Moore's dollhouse, a newborn chick display, World War II submarine, and the working coal mine win youngster applause. *Adler Planetarium* has special Saturday morning Sky Shows for children. The kids would also enjoy seeing *Ripley's Believe It Or Not Museum* at 1500 N. Wells. See *Museums* section in this chapter for further details on hours and telephone numbers.

*Six Flags Great America.* North of the city off Rte. 94 at Gurnee. Theme park covers 200 acres, with roller coaster rides, cartoon characters, fantasy worlds, and enough general whoop-de-do to keep the whole family entertained. A 7-story-high movie screen almost puts viewer in the picture. New American Eagle roller coaster attracts the adventurous on a spine-chilling 66-mile-an-hour ride labeled the world's highest, longest, and possibly scariest. Open daily summer; weekends only in spring and fall (tel. 249–1776). Hours vary. Admission $15.95 plus tax, under 3 free and over 55 $10.95 plus tax. Parking $3.00.

*Doc Rivers' Roaring Waters.* Rte. 83 at Roosevelt Rd. in Oak Brook. Brings squeals of excitement from those who like to slide and splash on a warm summer day (tel. 941–1600). Open 11:00 A.M.–11:30 P.M. weather permitting.

*McFetridge Sports Center.* 3845 California Ave. Operated by the Chicago Park District and features ice skating and a hockey rink. Figure skating and hockey lessons. Rental skates available (tel. 478–0210).

*Goodman Theatre.* 200 S. Columbus Dr. (tel. 443–3800). Has a special children's theater.

*Second City.* 1616 N. Wells St. (tel. 337–3992). Youngsters are encouraged to participate at children's theater. This well-known talent center has been the launching pad for many big name stars.

The *Chicago Public Library Cultural Center.* 78 E. Washington. Features storytelling hours, puppet programs, films, and youth-oriented lectures. Call for recorded schedule. (tel. 346–3278)

The *Chicago Architecture Foundation.* Has special tours for youngsters to help them learn about buildings and what makes them special. Reservations necessary (tel. 326–1393, 782–1776 and 922–3432).

Hundreds of dolls make their home in an 1883 mansion at suburban Naperville's 11-acre *Naper complex,* 201 W. Porter Rd., (tel. 420–6010). Open May through October on Saturday, Sunday and Wednesday from 1:30 P.M. to 4:30 P.M. There is also a firehouse and old-time fort. Aurora has the *Blackberry Historical Farm and Village,* with a replica steam train ride to an 1840s farm, complete with a carriage museum housing 40 vintage buggies of all shapes and descriptions. Craftsmen demonstrate their skills in the village's 11 stores. Open May–Sept. 10:00 A.M.–4:30 P.M. (tel. 892–1550).

For those who like to plan ahead, there is the *Bozo Show.* There's a LONG waiting list to watch the clown with orange hair. To get your name on that list, write WGN TV, 2501 W. Bradley Pl. 60618.

 **HISTORIC SITES.** The picturesque *Water Tower* at Michigan and Chicago avenues is one of the most famous survivors of the disastrous Chicago fire, which swept across the city in 1871 and left much of it in ashes, including the central business district.

Just across the street, *Here's Chicago* is a new attraction utilizing the historic Water Tower Pumping Station at Michigan Ave. and the Water Tower. Also a survivor of the Chicago Fire, its museum section emphasizes that disaster. A tour of the Pumping Station is followed by multimedia shows in 2 different theaters. Some critics feel the presentations do not do justice to Chicago's attractions. It's more of a people show than a place show. Open Sunday through Thursday 9:30 A.M.–4 P.M., Friday and Saturday to 7:00 P.M. Adults $3.75, children and seniors $2.00. Cheerie O'Leary's is their on-site gift emporium emphasizing Chicago collectibles (tel. 467–7114).

*Fort Dearborn.* Just south of the Michigan Ave. Bridge. The site of Chicago's first settlement. The city's early history is depicted on bronze tablets on the bridge.

*Old Town.* Running from 1200 to 1700 north on Wells St. Includes some of Chicago's finest restored Victorian residences. It is a cosmopolitan area populated with distinctive shops, restaurants, and pubs. The entrance to 19th-century Pipers Alley at 1608 is marked by a large Tiffany lamp.

*Hull House,* 800 S. Halsted. Part of the famed social settlement established in 1889 by Jane Addams. Two buildings have been restored and are National

Historic Landmarks. Open 10:00 A.M.–4:00 P.M., Monday–Friday, also summer Sundays from noon to 5 P.M. (tel. 413–5353). Located on University of Illinois Chicago Circle campus. Ramp for handicapped.

*Chicago Historical Society.* In Lincoln Park at Clark St. and North Ave. Has everything to acquaint you with Chicago's history. Particular emphasis is placed on the state's popular native son, Abraham Lincoln, and the Civil War. There are exceptional exhibits pertaining to Illinois pioneer life and the Chicago Fire, plus an impressive costumes display. Pioneer craft demonstrations recall the frontier way of doing things. Hours are 9:30 A.M.–4:30 P.M., Monday–Saturday, and noon–5:00 P.M., Sunday. Adults $1.50, children and seniors 50¢. Admission free Monday (tel. 642–4600).

*Chicago Public Library Cultural Center.* 78 E. Washington St. and Michigan. The land was once part of old Fort Dearborn military reservation. When the city library outgrew this post-Chicago Fire landmark, it was preserved, with the soft-spoken help of Mayor Daley's wife, for its exquisite Tiffany glass domes, mosaics, grand staircases, and general architectural beauty. Built in 1897 in the style of an opulent Italian Renaissance palazzo. Noted for its changing exhibits and G.A.R. collection. Many cultural programs and exhibits are regularly cosponsored by the *Chicago Council on Fine Arts* and the *Public Library.* To find out what's on schedule call (tel. 346–3278). Open Monday–Thursday, 9:00 A.M.–7:00 P.M., Friday to 6:00 P.M. and Saturday to 5:00 P.M. To arrange for special guided tours call 269–2922. Admission is free.

Evanston just to the north has 3 sites worth a detour. *Gross Point Lighthouse* off Sheridan Road dating from the 1860s, has a Maritime Museum and Nature Center dedicated to native wildlife. Lighthouse tours are available Saturday and Sunday afternoons June through September (tel. 328–6961). The mansion-museum of former Vice-President *Charles Dawes* at 225 Greenwood St., a block from Lake Michigan, is now home of the Evanston Historical Society. Its 28 rooms are full of antique furniture, artifacts, and historical displays. Open 1:00 P.M.–5:00 P.M. Monday, Tuesday, Thursday, Friday, and Saturday. Adults $2.00, children $1.00. Friday is free (tel. 475–3410). The museum-home of *Frances Willard,* Women's Christian Temperance Union founder, is the 3rd site (tel. 864–1397).

**MUSEUMS AND GALLERIES.** Chicagoans tend to be modest when it comes to boasting about their cultural riches. But the treasures in their museums and art galleries are right up there in the big league with the best of them.

**Adler Planetarium.** 1300 S. Lake Shore Dr. A great observatory on the lakefront. Probably the best view of the city is across the water from this promontory (tel. 322–0300). Its exhibits range across history from man's earliest navigating techniques using antique instruments to the most modern astronomical developments—everything from navigating a historic sailing schooner to a space vehicle. Open daily 9:30 A.M.–5:00 P.M., Friday to 9:00 P.M., from mid-June through August. Other times Monday through Thursday to 4:30 P.M.; Friday to

9:00 P.M.; Saturday, Sunday, and holidays to 5:00 P.M. Exhibits free. Elaborate Sky Show presented in Sky and Universe Theaters focuses on nearby planets, galaxies, and distant stars. Sky Show costs $2.50 adults, $1.50 kids. Children under 6 are not admitted to Sky Show, but there is a special children's Sky Show on Saturday mornings. Senior citizens free.

**Art Institute.** Michigan at Adams St. Truly one of the world's great art museums. Noted for its Impressionist collection, Renaissance oils, Thorne miniature rooms, garden restaurant, and children's museum (tel. 443–3500). There are works by El Greco, Monet, Renoir, Rembrandt, Cézanne, Degas, and Picasso. Grant Wood's *American Gothic* is a popular favorite. More current additions are the reconstructed old Stock Exchange trading room, the Rubloff paperweight collection, and stained glass windows by Marc Chagall. Open daily, Monday, Wednesday, Thursday, and Friday, 10:30 A.M. to 4:30 P.M.; Tuesday to 8:00 P.M.; Saturday, 10:00 A.M. to 5:00 P.M.; Sunday and holidays, noon to 5:00 P.M. Free on Tuesday. Suggested contribution: $5.00 adults, $2.50 seniors and children. Several very special exhibitions are planned for 1988: 100 paintings by Georgia O'Keeffe will be on display March 5–June 19. July 16–September 5 focuses on "Chicago Architecture 1872–1922: The Birth of a Metropolis" with over 250 drawings, furniture, and models. "The Art Of Paul Gauguin" set for September 7–December 10 will feature the artist's greatest masterpieces, including paintings, sculpture, ceramics, prints, and drawings.

**Bradford Museum of Plates.** 9333 N. Milwaukee Ave., Niles, across from Golf Mill Shopping Center. A permanent newly enlarged exhibit of the most actively traded collector's plates. Open Monday through Friday, 9:00 A.M. to 4 P.M.; Saturday and Sunday 10:00 A.M. to 5:00 P.M. (tel. 966–2770). Visitors can also watch the current price quotes as these actively traded plates fluctuate on the exchange. $2 adults, $1 seniors, under 12 free; free Saturdays.

**Cantigny.** 115 Winfield Rd., Wheaton. The generation who grew up listening to Saturday night operettas on WGN in the 30s and 40s will remember Colonel Robert McCormick's endless intermission speeches, usually covering some event during the American Revolution. His fascination with war is reflected on his estate, where the late publisher of the *Chicago Tribune* filled part of the 500 acres with tanks, field artillery, and memories of war. The home is also open to tours. Daily in summer, 10:00 A.M. to 5:00 P.M.; other times, Wednesday through Sunday to 4:00 P.M.; closed January in the mansion. The war museum is open daily 10:00 A.M. to 5:00 P.M. in summer; 10:00 A.M. to 4:00 P.M. the rest of the year; closed Mondays and January (tel. 668–5161). Free. Grounds open 9:00 A.M. to dusk.

**Chicago Academy of Sciences.** 2001 N. Clark. Oldest science museum in the Midwest features exhibits depicting natural history of the area, including a coal forest and swamp. Emphasis is on the Chicago region. Open daily 10:00 A.M.–5:00 P.M. $1.00 adults, 50¢ children and seniors. Phone 549–0606 for information on special exhibits. The South Gallery will feature changing exhibits. There is a winter lecture series each Tuesday and field trips to places like the Indiana Dunes and Starved Rock State Park.

**Du Sable Museum of African American History.** 740 E. 56 Pl. Emphasis is on black history and African art. Many documents pertaining to the history of black Americans, fine African masks, varied sculpture, paintings, a photography collection, and library on the history of midwestern blacks (tel. 947–0600).

**Field Museum of Natural History.** In Grant Park at 12th St. World's largest museum of natural history exhibits. It has a dazzling collection of precious and semiprecious stones. Trace the history of man through lifelike exhibits. Superb exhibits on American Indian culture, China, and Tibet.

New permanent exhibit on plants of the world is considered largest of its kind, with plant models representing 60 yrs. of work. A Pawnee Earth Lodge is an unusual permanent exhibit where visitors sit on buffalo robes in a recon-structed 38-ft. Pawnee lodge and view and handle Pawnee treasures. Maritime Peoples, a newsmaking exhibit in 1983, is now permanent and highlights the Arctic and Northwest Coast. Open daily 9:00 A.M.–5:00 P.M. Admission free Thursdays, other times $2.00 adults, students $1.00, seniors 50¢ and families $4.00. There are facilities for the handicapped (tel. 922–9410). Dazzling new Gem Hall opened as a permanent exhibit in November 1985, with a special Adornment Hall showing how jewelry and adornments have been used in different parts of the world. Display includes the Chalmers Topaz.

**International Museum of Surgical Sciences.** 1524 N. Lake Shore Dr. Traces medicine from prehistoric times to the present. Everything from medicine men's dolls to an old apothecary shop and the history of healing herbs. Located in 2 impressive old mansions, headquarters for the International College of Sur-geons. Open 10:00 A.M.–4:00 P.M., Tuesday–Saturday; 11:00 A.M.–5:00 P.M., Sun-day. No children under 11 admitted (tel. 642–3555). Free.

**Mexican Fine Arts Center Museum.** 1852 W. 19th St. at Harrison Park. Newly opened and only one of its kind in Midwest. Features both permanent and visiting shows of Mexican artists living in U.S. and Mexico. Tuesday–Sunday 10 A.M.–5:00 P.M. (738–1503). Free.

**Museum of Contemporary Art.** 237 E. Ontario St. Offers changing exhibi-tions of one-man, group shows, historical shows. Exceptional museum store and The Site Restaurant featuring Charles Simonds wall-long work, "The Dwell-ing." Free gallery talks Tuesday at noon, Saturday 1 and 3 P.M.; Sunday 2 P.M. No reservations required. Call 280–2660 for details. Hours are 10:00 A.M.–5:00 P.M., Tuesday–Saturday, and Sunday noon–5:00 P.M. Admission varies depend-ing on the show. Usually $3 adults, $2 students and seniors. Tuesday is free. Completely wheelchair accessible.

**Museum of Science and Industry.** In Jackson Park. A 5-star magnet that attracts kids and senior citizens alike with its 14 acres of exhibits in engineering, industrial, and medical progress. Tour a simulated operating coal mine or a captured Nazi submarine. There is an antique car display, Main Street of Yesterday; a must for all ages. You could spend days here. Lots of push-button displays. Building was erected as Palace of Fine Arts for 1893 Columbian Exposition. Open daily 9:30 A.M.–5:30 P.M. in summer. Winter 9:30 A.M.–4:00 P.M., Monday–Friday; Saturday, Sunday, and holidays to 5:30 P.M. Admission and parking free (tel. 684–1414). "Christmas Around the World" begins the

Saturday before Thanksgiving and features elaborate Christmas trees, along with the customs and traditions of many nations. New permanent displays include architecture, petroleum, waste management, and cycling from the 1800s to modern times. The $12-million Henry Crown Space Center is the museum's current celebrity, with 15,000 sq. ft. of space artifact exhibits, including a "Space Shuttle Experience" simulating lift-off and space voyage. Its 334-seat Omnimax Theater presents eye-opening productions which change during the year. Theater admission $4 adults, $2.50 seniors and children 12 and under. Open during regular museum hours, until 9:00 P.M. Tuesday, Friday, Saturday, and Sunday.

**Oriental Institute.** University of Chicago. Has exhibits dating back to 5000 B.C. Scholarly archaeologists from here have been involved in major digs around the world. Artifacts from Egypt, Persia, Anatolia, Syria, Palestine, and Mesopotamia. Call 702–9507 for further information. Admission is free and tours are at 10:00 A.M., 11:30 A.M., 1:00 P.M., and 2:30 P.M., by appointment. Tuesday–Saturday. Sunday hours are noon to 4:00 P.M., with a free film at 2:00 P.M. followed by a 2:30 P.M. tour.

**Peace Museum.** 430 W. Erie St. Tel.: 440–1860. Explores the issues of war and peace by means of visual and performing arts. Open Tuesday, Wednesday, Friday, and Sunday from 12 P.M.–5 P.M., Thursday 12 P.M.–8 P.M. Admission $2.00, 50¢ for seniors and children.

**Polish Museum of America.** 984 N. Milwaukee. Has notable stained glass, Polish and American art, sculptures, Paderewski and Kosciuszko rooms. Source of great pride to the city's Polish population, 2nd only in size to that of Warsaw. Open 12:00 P.M.–5:00 P.M. daily (tel. 384–3352). Free. No children under 12.

**Ripley's Believe It Or Not Museum.** 1500 N. Wells. Shows fabulous exhibits of often bizarre oddities collected by Robert L. Ripley during his foreign travels. Daily. Summer hours noon–9:00 P.M. daily, Friday and Saturday to midnight. Call 337–6077 for winter hours. $4.75 adults, $2.50 children under 12.

**John Shedd Aquarium.** Across Lake Shore Dr. from Field Museum. So many species on display here that you will be an ancient mariner before you are able to remember them all. Seasonal special exhibits. 7,000 fish of over 700 species are highlighted by a 90,000-gallon Coral Reef where divers hand-feed fish daily at 11:00 A.M. and 2:00 P.M. Open 9:00 A.M.–5:00 P.M., March through October; 10:00 A.M.–5:00 P.M. other times. 939–2438. Adults $2.00, children $1.00, seniors 50¢. Thursday free. New fresh-water otter prairie display is a spellbinder.

**Spertus Museum of Judaica.** 618 S. Michigan. One of the world's largest private collections of Jewish artifacts, manuscripts, and ceremonial objects. Fridays are free. Admission $1.00 for seniors and students, $2.00 adults. Wednesday, Thursday, Sunday 10:00 A.M.–5:00 P.M.; Tuesday to 8:00 P.M., Friday to 3:00 P.M.; and Sunday to 4:00 P.M. (tel. 922–9012).

**Telephony Museum.** 225 W. Randolph. Traces the history of the telephone from Alexander Graham Bell's time to the present. A phone used by him in 1892 is here. Open 8:30 A.M.–4:00 P.M. weekdays. Admission free (tel. 727–2994).

**Morton B. Weiss Museum of Judaica.** 1100 E. Hyde Park Blvd. (Isaiah Israel Congregation). Collection of unusually illuminated marriage contracts

# The Art Institute of Chicago

**Lower Floor**

The Art Institute
of Chicago

**First Floor**

# The Art Institute of Chicago

## Second Floor

### Points of Interest

1) Earlier Painting and Sculpture
2) 13th, 14th, 15th century Italian
3) 15th century Flemish
4) 15th, 16th century German
5) 16th, 17th century Italian
6) 17th century Spanish and Italian
7) 17th century Dutch (*Rembrandt*)
8) 17th, 18th century Italian (Baroque)
9) 18th century English Period Rooms
10) 18th century Italian (Neoclassic))
11) Burnham Library of Architecture Gallery
12) Late 18th century British Portraits
13) 19th century English and French (Romantic)
14) Impressionist
15) Late 19th century French
16) Late 19th century Painting and Sculpture
17) 20th century Painting and Sculpture
18) Special Exhibitions

MICHIGAN AVE.

and rare manuscripts in Judeo-Kurdish and Judeo-Persian. Open after worship services and by appointment (tel. 924–1234). Free.

**Terra Museum of American Art.** 664 N. Michigan. Showcases the private art collection of a North Shore industrialist's 19th- and 20th-century treasures. Emphasis spans three centuries of American painting. Monday–Sunday, 10:00 A.M.–5:00 P.M. Admission $4.50 (tel. 664–3939).

**Fox River Trolley Museum.** On Rte. 31 in South Elgin. Has electric street-cars on display and operating. Offers 30-min. ride along the Fox R. via early 1900s trolley cars, along with displays of such vintage vehicles as the oldest interurban rail car in America. Open from 11:00 A.M. to 6:00 P.M. Sunday, May–October. Also Saturdays, 1:00 P.M.–5:00 P.M. in July and August. $1.50 adults, 75¢ children (tel. 697–4676).

**Illinois Railway Museum.** At Union. Features electric railway equipment, locomotives, tours, and a special railroad library. Open daily during summer, 10:00 A.M.–4:00 P.M. During May and September on Saturday and Sunday, 11:00 A.M.–4:00 P.M., and Sunday only in March, April, October, and November. Closed December–February. Adults $4.50, children $2.25 (tel. 262–2266). Also at Union is **Seven Acres Antique Village and Museum,** a pseudo-western town jammed with antiques and a noteworthy phonograph collection. One of the country's largest antique phonograph auctions is held there in June. Youngsters enjoy the weekend gunfights and often insist on staying for several. Occasional weekend antique sales and auctions. Open daily 9:00 A.M.–6:00 P.M. May–September; weekends only April and October; closed November through March. Adults $3.50, seniors $3.00, children 6–12 $1.75 weekdays. $4.50, $3.50 and $2.25 weekends. (tel. 1–815–923–2214).

**Lizzardo Museum of Lapidary Art.** 220 Cottage Hill Ave., in Wilder Park, Elmhurst (tel. 833–1616). This private collection has everything from fossils and petrified wood to exotic carvings on onyx, jade, and agate, plus educational programs and films. Open all year Tuesday–Friday and Sunday, 1:00 P.M.–5:00 P.M.; Saturday from 10:00 A.M. Friday free. $1.00 adults, 50¢ from 13–18, and seniors.

 **MOVIES AND MOVIE PALACES.** In the gilt-edged 1920s, spurred on by the popularity of those newfangled movies, imaginative architects returned from Europe with elaborate ideas for creating standout theaters. The *Chicago Theatre,* 175 N. State Street St., ranked among the nation's most impressive and it still does—a bedazzling, wonderfully baroque, ballroom-like collection of pillars, posts, and statuary, it is part Versailles, with a touch of Roman bath and Greek temple added for good measure. No matter what's playing, it's worth attending a production here to observe the opulent atmosphere. Inquire locally about occasional concerts on the theater's superb organ. Real estate developers would like to tear it down and replace it with some multistory marvel—the battle lines were drawn between preservationists and developers, a battle too often won in Chicago by people with a high-rise mentality. This time the preservationists won, but it has been an uphill battle. Stage performances have included sellout crowds for Red Skelton and Frank Sinatra.

Chicago is a strange city when it comes to films. An award winner may have left outer-Saskatoon long before it ever arrives here, and many classic art films that achieve success elsewhere never come to town. The *Fine Arts*, 418 S. Michigan (tel. 939–3700), along with the well-maintained Art Deco *Biograph*, where John Dillinger attended his last film, before he was ambushed in the alley (tel. 348–1350), tend to feature the unusual in films. *Facets Multimedia* concentrates on the foreign, arty, and offbeat. It is located at 1517 W. Fullerton (tel. 281–9075), in the kind of neighborhood where one likes to park directly in front of the theater. *Chicago Library* in one of the city's architecturally prized settings, 78 E. Washington St. (tel. 744–6630), regularly revives old favorites.

To find out what's playing where, check the entertainment sections of the local newspapers for daily schedules.

 **MUSIC.** From classical to new wave, there's a home in Chicago for every musical taste. Devotees of classical music flock to *Orchestra Hall* at 220 S. Michigan (box office phone is 435–8111), to hear the *Chicago Symphony Orchestra*, acclaimed as one of the world's finest, under the direction of Sir Georg Solti. Chicago's *Civic Opera House*, Madison St. and Wacker Dr., is the home of the *Lyric Opera Company*, which frequently hosts guests performances by opera notables such as Pavarotti (tel. 346–0270). The impressive structure was built by then multimillionaire Samuel Insull. Once Thomas Edison's confidential secretary, Insull rose to power and prestige as president of Chicago Edison Company. At his peak he sat on the board of directors of 85 companies, chairing 65 of them. His overextended empire crashed during the Depression, and when he died in a Paris subway in 1938, he had 85¢ in his pocket.

The fortresslike appearance of the *Auditorium Theater*, 70 E. Congress, gives little indication of the beauty to be found inside. The theater, with its ornately decorated walls and ceilings, has been declared an architectural landmark, but its real beauty (for music lovers, at least) lies in its acoustics, which are said to be almost perfect. It seats close to 4,000, mostly for classical or "conservative" concerts, but occasionally you'll find a pop or rock act scheduled here. The building was designed by Dankmar Adler and Louis Sullivan in 1889, but declined when millionaire Samuel Insull built the Civic Opera House. After years of neglect, millions were spent to restore its gilded beauty—a rare success story in Chicago, where historic buildings are frequently demolished despite protests of preservationists (tel. 922–2110).

For more contemporary musical tastes, indoor concert facilities include *Park West*, 322 West Armitage, on the city's near north side. Since liquor is served, you must be 21 or over. If you meet the age requirement, you'll have a choice of rock, R&B, jazz, soul, new wave, and even folk and country/western acts—and from time to time, you can see big-name acts that don't usually appear in this type of intimate night-club style setting (500-person capacity on the main floor, 250 in the balcony) (tel. 929–5959).

Although the *Chicago Stadium*, 1800 W. Madison, hosts large concerts less frequently than in the past, it sometimes offers concerts by rock, soul, and country/western acts, squeezed in between rodeos, hockey games, and ice shows. The *Arie Crown Theater* in McCormick Place, 23rd St. and the lake, has put a lot of money into improving its acoustics, but it still is used primarily for the road companies of Broadway shows rather than for concerts (tel. 791–6000).

Topline rock, country/western, and contemporary performers appear at *Rosemont Horizon* near O'Hare Airport, Mannheim Rd. and Lunt Ave. (tel. 635–6600), a huge stadium that seats close to 20,000. It's also used for rodeos, circuses, family-style reviews, and home games of DePaul University's basketball team.

Jazz came to Chicago in the early 1920s and went on to become a national preoccupation. After a decline, jazz is staging a great comeback. *Andy's*, 11 E. Hubbard (tel. 642–6805); *Backroom*, 1007 N. Rush St. (tel. 751–2433); *Jazz Showcase* at the Blackstone, 636 S. Michigan (tel. 427–4300); are among headliners. Jazz Institute Hotline is 666–1881.

Summertime is really the best time for Chicago (and out-of-town) music lovers, with an abundance of outdoor concert facilities and plenty of free concerts in parks and downtown plazas. On almost any summer business day (most frequently during the noon hours), you're likely to hear a free outdoor concert at the *First National Bank Plaza* on Monroe between Clark and Dearborn, where you can enjoy the Chagall mosaic while you listen to the concert; the *Daley Center Plaza*, home of the Picasso sculpture; or at the *Chicago Tribune's Pioneer Court*, 435 N. Michigan. The Park District offers 68 concerts at 56 park sites throughout the city. For schedule call 294–2320.

Classical music lovers who enjoy the outdoors are treated in the summer months to outdoor concerts by the *Chicago Chamber Orchestra*, the *Chicago Chamber Brass*, and other small classical groups, mostly at outdoor plazas, as well as at the *Art Institute's* beautiful outdoor garden at Michigan and Adams; the *Museum of Science and Industry*, 57th Street and the lake; and *St. James Cathedral*, Michigan Ave. and Chestnut. Carillon recitals are held at Rockefeller Memorial Chapel, 5850 S. Woodlawn on the University of Chicago campus. The entertainment sections of both major newspapers give complete listings. During colder weather, small-scale classical concerts are also abundant, particularly at the *Cultural Center*, Michigan and Randolph (tel. 744–6630), and at the downtown colleges. Again, check newspaper listings.

*Poplar Creek Music Theater* in suburban Hoffman Estates, highways 59 and 72 at Northwest Tollway (tel. 559–1212), an hour's drive from downtown, is a beautiful outdoor concert facility that offers terrific acoustics and great sight lines for those seated either in the pavilion or on the less-expensive lawn seats farther from the stage. You can bring a picnic dinner to enjoy before the concert at Poplar Creek, or at Highland Park's *Ravinia Music Festival Theater*. Ravinia is an established outdoor concert facility that offers summer concerts by the *Chicago Symphony Orchestra*, dance troupes, and contemporary performers. If you choose a lawn seat at Ravinia, you can hear, but not see, the performers. Ravinia is at the south end of town at Lake Cook and Green Bay roads. For information on the season, which runs from late June through mid-September, call 728–4642. Northwestern University has summer band concerts on their Evanston Campus. For dates and times of these popular events call 491–5441.

*ChicagoFest,* the city's summer festival, has become embroiled in politics, boycotts, and other problems, and was not scheduled for four years, but there is some hope it will be back on a future calendar. A new program of 1-day *Neighborhood Festivals* was introduced in 1981. They are held during June and July and feature ethnic entertainment and food in the city's Jewish, black, Polish, and Mexican neighborhoods. Again, check local papers for schedules.

For discount ticket information, see Note at end of *Theater* section in this chapter.

 **DANCE.** Although Chicago is home to several excellent dance companies, few of them have their own theaters. Maria Tallchief's *Chicago City Ballet* (tel. 943–1315), the *Gus Giordano Dance Company* (tel. 866–9442), and the *Hubbard Street Dance Theater,* 218 S. Wabash, 3rd Floor (tel. 663–0853), perform throughout the city at various locations, as do the many ethnic dance troupes, so it's best to check newspaper listings for times and places. For the most part, the high-powered dance attractions in Chicago are still the touring companies of domestic and foreign dance troupes, and their appearances are generally well advertised. *Mo Ming Dance and Arts Center,* 1034 W. Barry Ave. (tel. 472–9894), hosts dance and musical performances of both local and out-of-town artists and also provides space for art exhibits. Their summer series "Dance for a Dollar Ninety-Eight" showcases talents of local dancers and choreographers and really costs only $1.98.

For discount ticket information, see Note at end of *Theater* section in this chapter. Dance Hot Line is 663–1313. Questions answered live before 5:00 P.M., recorded listing afterwards.

 **THEATER.** Chicagoans choose from Broadway plays and musicals, revivals, original works by established playwrights and newly emerging local talent, avant-garde offerings, and lighthearted revues.

The *Goodman Theatre,* part of the Art Institute cultural complex at 200 S. Columbus Dr., is the home of the city's oldest locally produced theater, and one of the best-known regional theaters in the country. Plays first presented at the Goodman have gone on to Broadway, the Kennedy Center in Washington, D.C., and the National Theatre in England. The Goodman's *Studio Theater* is a very intimate space, seating about 100 and specializing in experimental productions and cabaret. For convenient preshow dining, the theater houses *Ingrid's,* Wednesday–Saturday, open at 6:00 P.M. You pay a set price, then enjoy the freshly prepared gourmet buffet. Reservations advised. Call Goodman Theatre box office (443–3800).

**"Off-Loop" Theaters.** In recent years, Chicago's off-Loop theaters have consistently provided professional legitimate theater offerings at a lower cost and in a more intimate atmosphere than the city's larger facilities. Several plays and musicals that had their beginnings in Chicago, eventually became top Broadway shows, notably *Grease, Mornings at Seven,* and Lily Tomlin's *Appearing Nitely.* If you take advantage of the off-Loop offerings, you may be able to boast one day that you enjoyed a play or musical long before it came to Broadway.

Off-Loop theaters located in the city and accessible by public transportation or cab are the *Wisdom Bridge Theater,* 1559 W. Howard St. (tel. 743–6442); *Victory Gardens Theater* and *The Body Politic Theater,* both at 2261 N. Lincoln (tel. 871–3000); the *Organic Theater,* 3319 N. Clark (tel. 327–5588); the *Apollo Theater,* 2540 N. Lincoln (tel. 935–6100); the *Court Theater* of the University of Chicago, 5706 S. University (tel. 753–4472); *Stage Left Theatre,* 3244 N. Clark St. (tel. 883–8830); *Briar Street Theatre,* 3133 N. Halsted St. (tel. 348–4000); and *Steppenwolf Theatre,* 2851 N. Halsted St. (tel. 472–4141).

**Downtown Theaters.** Chicago companies of Broadway shows most often settle in at the city's downtown theaters, conveniently located in the heart of Chicago's business district. They are a pleasant walk from downtown hotels and only a short cab or bus ride from popular near North Side hotels.

*The Shubert Theater,* 22 W. Monroe (tel. 977–1700), specializes in Broadway musicals; *The Blackstone Theater,* 60 E. Balbo (tel. 977–1700), is most often used for Broadway dramas and comedies. The renovated *Auditorium Theater,* 70 E. Congress Parkway (tel. 922–2110), boasts what many consider to be the city's finest acoustical system, but it is used more frequently for concerts.

Although some Broadway offerings remain at the downtown theaters for as long as 2 years, traveling companies of other shows often choose McCormick Place's *Arie Crown Theater,* Lake Shore Dr. and 23rd St. (tel. 791–6000), because of its size. Since it seats 4,300 people, shows are made available to a larger number of people in a shorter period of time—an important consideration when a road company is scheduled for a short run.

No mention of Chicago theater would be complete without highlighting *Second City* at 1616 N. Wells. The theater's hilarious, frequently outrageous, comedy revues have been the training ground for dozens of nationally known personalities, including Mike Nichols and Elaine May, Alan Arkin, and John Belushi (tel. 337–3992).

*Shear Madness,* a comedy whodunit, holds the city's record for longevity. It opened at the Blackstone Hotel's *Mayfair Theatre* over 5 years ago.

**Note:** The *Hot Tix Booth,* on the west side of State St. between Madison and Monroe, offers half-price, day-of-performance tickets to most of the city's theater, music, and dance offerings. A limited number of tickets are available beginning at 11:00 A.M., and many people are pleasantly surprised to find that seats are occasionally the best in the house. Call Curtain Call, a 24-hour theater information service, to find out what's going on that day (977–1755).

**SHOPPING.** Whether you're looking for a budget bargain or for a designer original, Chicago will come as a very pleasant shopping surprise. As the transportation crossroads of America, merchandise flows in from all directions. Its inland port status and overseas service via nearly a dozen foreign airlines also makes it an unexpected center for imports.

Some of America's most famed merchandising names also got their start in Chicago, sending what became known as their "dream book" catalogs to the most isolated corners of the country. Sears Roebuck and Montgomery Ward are still headquartered here.

Where to begin? Why State Street, that Great Street, of course. Each of the giant department stores that line this shopper's heaven contains floor after floor of everything imaginable. Let's start with 130-year-old *Marshall Field & Company,* a prestige store synonymous with shopping in Chicago. This is such a marvel that the visitor will be tempted to follow the example of locals and spend the whole day there. From its Tiffany-domed ceiling of Favrile iridescent glass to its superb Victorian Antique Jewelery Department, the store is as much a sightseeing attraction as a great emporium.

Field himself set the tone with his motto "Give the lady what she wants." And with 73 acres of floor space, the store has just about everything anybody ever wanted, always displayed in a very special way, whether it's a Russian lynx coat, a find from the bargain basement, or one of the treasures from the famed Antique Furniture Department. Field's makes its own flavorful Frango mints and bakes taste-tempting homemade pastries, and the store restaurants are justifiably popular, fashion shows and all. Right on the premises, the store's fine craftsmen will fix your great grandfather's watch, restring your pearls, reweave your antique tapestry, and restore an ancestral portrait. Everything, whether it be a modest purchase or a designer original from the *28 Shop,* goes out in boxes Chicagoans have labeled "Marshall Field Green." It is still considered fashionable to meet under the massive Field's clock that hangs at State and Washington, where it has been since 1907, replacing an even earlier one. Today, there are 18 stores in the Chicago division, but the State Street Store is the granddaddy of them all. There are guided tours of the store and a staff of interpreters speak over 3 dozen languages. Onetime employee Gordon Selfridge was so impressed he went to London to build one like it. It can be summed up in one sentence: Field's is definitely finer. There is quality here in all price ranges. The bargain basement is actually a store within a store. 111 N. State St. (tel. 781–1000). Open 9:45 A.M.–5:45 P.M., Monday–Saturday and Monday and Thursday evenings to 7:00 P.M. Accept American Express, Master Card, Visa.

Give a Chicagoan a present in a *Peacock* box and it speaks volumes. This is *the* prestige shop for jewelery. The reputation dates back to 1837, when Elijah Peacock opened a small shop making watches and ships' chronometers. Today, the shop at State and Monroe is ultra genteel, with bronze peacock doors opening onto a green marble interior with crystal chandeliers as sparkling as the diamonds they illuminate. The store is also noted for fine English bone china, silver, leather goods, crystal, and other quality gifts. There are now branch shops at Old Orchard, Oak Brook, and other shopping centers. 101 S. State St. (tel. 630–5701). Hours at the State St. store are 10:00 A.M.–5:30 P.M., Monday–Friday and 10:00 A.M.–5:00 P.M. Saturday. Accept American Express, Master Card, Visa.

*Carson, Pirie, Scott & Company* has come a long way since manager Mac-Leish stood on State St. during the Chicago Fire shouting, "50 silver dollars for every wagonload of merchandise you save out of this building." Passing teamsters rescued about 40 percent of the merchandise before the store burned. The company managed to survive. By 1909, the store moved into an elaborate new Louis Sullivan-designed building so famous today that visitors rate it as a sightseeing attraction. Although the company operates over 2 dozen retail stores, this Chicago landmark is still the flagship store. Interpreters can answer questions in nearly 2 dozen languages, and there is a quality selection of fashionable clothes, accessories, and furnishings. Their 7th floor *Kitchentech* is a special housewares attraction, a fully equipped demonstration kitchen featuring cooking classes, famous chef appearances, and product demonstrations Monday through Friday. There are seven different dining areas. *Carson's Eighth-floor Grill* is especially popular for its buffet table. 1 S. State St. (tel. 744–2000). Open at 11:30 A.M., Monday–Saturday, until 3:00 P.M. The store itself is open daily, 9:45 A.M.–5:45 P.M. and until 7:30 P.M. Monday and Thursday. Accept Master Card and Visa.

Nine blocks of State Street from Wacker Drive to Congress is now a landscaped mall closed to regular traffic, and shoppers seem to enjoy the more leisurely mood. Shops of all kinds extend down both sides, ranging from *Charles Stevens,* 25 N. State St. (tel. 630–1500), with a fine reputation for women's clothing, to *Broadstreets,* 123 S. State St. (tel. 726–8902), noted for traditional men's clothes and furnishings and leisure sportswear. Tall women head for *Tall Girls Shop,* 17 N. State (tel. 782-9867) and *Tall Togs,* 105 S. Wabash (tel. 782–2915) where there's a good selection of styles. The fuller-figured shopper does well at *Lane Bryant* on the next block at 9 N. Wabash Ave. (tel. 621–8700), which specializes in larger sizes, half-sizes, and overweight juniors. *Pendleton Woolen Mills* has a shop full of jackets, shirts, robes, blankets, and everything woolen in the Palmer House Arcade, just off State St.—beautiful fabrics in hard-to-resist plaids, 17 E. Monroe St. (tel. 372–1699).

*Sears Roebuck, Montgomery Ward, Wieboldt,* and *Goldblatts* have closed their State St. department stores, and at press time there is talk of establishing a permanent home for the Chicago Library in the Goldblatt building.

## The Magnificent Mile

Head 2 blocks over to Michigan and start north, and the mood definitely changes. Anyone with stamina and sales resistance can spend a glorious morning or afternoon window-shopping his or her way along what is known locally as "The Magnificent Mile." Block after block of ultra-posh shops lining Michigan Ave. are frequented by the city's moneyed class. These range from classic French silk scarfs and purses at *Hermes,* 875 N. Michigan (tel. 787–8175), to status-symbol Italian loafers and luggage at *Gucci,* at 713 (tel. 664–5504). *Lord & Taylor* (tel. 787–7400) and *Marshall Field* (tel. 781–1234) share the limelight at Water Tower Place, 835 N. Michigan Ave., which has over 100 imaginative boutiques all under one roof. For those who can't resist taking home a Chicago-oriented souvenir, *Accent Chicago* (944–1354) there is an unusual specialty shop where all gifts have unique city-oriented themes. Even if you aren't interested in shopping, Water Tower Place is so dramatic and interesting that it deserves a visit.

Next door at John Hancock Center's street level, *Bonwit Teller* (tel. 751–1800) offers chic fashion with a special flair. There's more high style at *Saks Fifth Avenue,* 669 N. Michigan (tel. 944–6500); *I. Magnin,* 830 (tel. 751–0500); *Stanley Korshak,* 940 (tel. 280–0520), all of which cater to the carriage trade. You can buy a conversation-stopping French original or an Americanized adaptation at any of them. *Brittany Ltd.,* at 999 (tel. 642–8560), pleases the classic, tweedy set, while *Guy Le Roche* 835 (tel. 337–0606), is always avant-garde. *Laura Ashley,* 835 (tel. 951–8004), emphasizes classic tradition.

The list is long and very glamorous. For a real "Maine Chance" kind of day or half day, *Elizabeth Arden,* at 717 N. Michigan (tel. 266–5750), offers the whole treatment, pampering customers with facials and the luxury of spa treatments. The store is also noted for its lingerie. *Neiman Marcus* (tel. 642–5900) has opened its largest store outside Texas at the corner of Michigan Ave. and Superior St., occupying 4 floors of the 63-story retail-commercial-residential Olympia center complex. The very luxe store carries everything from designer apparel to prestige furs. Its epicure food complex is one of the most extensive in the Neiman Marcus chain, and there is a Petrossian shop, featuring caviar, smoked salmon, trout, and sturgeon. *Ilona of Hungary,* 45 East Oak (tel. 337–7161), also stands ready to glamorize visitors for a special occasion, as does *Marilyn Miglin Model Makeup,* 112 East Oak (tel. 943–1120). *Georgette Klinger* has a salon in Water Tower Place, 835 N. Michigan (tel. 787–4300), where your travel-tired face can get a facial and mask.

*Spaulding & Company,* 959 N. Michigan (tel. 337–4800), has been selling jewels in the city since 1854. *Tiffany & Company,* 715 (tel. 944–7500), is a more recent addition.

*Jackie Renwick,* 65 E. Oak, (tel. 266–8269), focuses on clothes for the business woman. If the need arises to come up with a fancy costume, *Broadway Costumes* at 932 W. Washington Blvd. can send you off as a queen, a clown, or anything in between (tel. 829–6400). So can *Kaufmann Costumes,* 5065 N. Lincoln (tel. 561–7529).

We're assuming no one is going to sip champagne from your slipper, as visitors once did at Chicago's famous-infamous Everleigh Club—but labels from these shops are definitely fashionable enough, with prices to match. *Joyce Selby Shoes,* 845 N. Michigan (tel. 664–8281), *Charles Jourdan Boutique,* Water Tower Place, 835 N. Michigan (tel. 280–8133), and *Naturalizer* at Water Tower Place (tel. 266–7315). For hard-to-fit sizes, *Nierman's Tall Girl Shoes,* 17 N. State, carries sizes 5 to 14 from quad A to double E (tel. 346–9797). *Chandler's* at 27 N. State (tel. 263–8157) and 650 N. Michigan (tel. 787–6072), and *Bakers,*

133 S. State, carry modestly priced copies of the latest shoe fashions. Incidentally, *Woolworth's,* 18 N. State (tel. 236–9265), has fast repair service in the basement if your favorite walking shoes collapse. *Hanig's Shoes,* 660 N. Michigan (tel. 642–5330), and 1 S. LaSalle (tel. 263–1365), can fit men from sizes 6 - 15 and AAA to EEE.

Almost as many of these specialty shops cater to men and women and there are all kinds of prestige names—*Capper and Capper,* 1 N. Wabash (tel. 236–3800), and *Brooks Brothers,* 74 E. Madison (tel. 263–0100), are only a few. *Jaeger International,* 835 N. Michigan (tel. 642–6665), is typical of many quality establishments that feature both men's and women's things. *M. Hyman and Son* has several stores, all specializing in clothes for unusual sizes. One is at 835 N. Michigan (tel. 266–0060). *Eddie Bauer,* 123 N. Wabash (tel. 263–6005), is an expert at outfitting outdoorsmen, and century-old *Hart, Shaffner, Marx* has a wide selection of quality things sold at *Capper & Capper, Baskins* and *Charles Stevens. Bally Shoe Salon,* 919 N. Michigan Ave., (tel. 787–8110), is noted for its Bally of Switzerland products, including belts, attaché cases, and carry-all bags. *Marks, Ltd.,* 2756 N. Racine Ave. (tel. 883–4477), caters to men under 5'8" in sizes 34–50. Even ties are custom-made for shorter men.

Things have been changing on the shopping scene so fast in the past few years that it is impossible to include all the shops worth a detour. Real estate developers work so fast in Chicago that a building can be torn down and another one on its site by the time a book goes to press. And the turnover percentage in prime locations like Water Tower Place is high enough that it always pays to call before making a special trip to a particular shop. 3 new prestige addresses were recently built along Michigan Ave.—One North Michigan, Olympia, and One Magnificent Mile. Ralph Lauren and Stanley Korshak have shops at the Magnificent Mile location.

People in the know seem sure a Bloomingdale's is also about to appear on the Magnificent Mile. *Beauty and the Beast* is in Water Tower (tel. 337–8002), with a large collection of Snoopy and Peanuts treasures for fans of all ages.

More and more European branch shops have also opened, like *Liberty of London,* 845 N. Michigan (Water Tower) (tel. 280–1134). And of course, for those who like the classic look, *Burberrys* brings their traditional English weatherwear to 633 N. Michigan Ave. (tel 787–2500).

Those who arrive in a winter snow may have a special interest in heading for *Rosenthal Furs,* 940 N. Michigan Ave. (tel 943–1365), and *Evans Furriers,* 36 S. State St. (tel. 855–2000).

*Douglas Kenyon, Inc.,* 1357 N. Wells St. (tel. 642–5300) features art of John James Audubon. *Asian House,* 316 N. Michigan, features treasures from the Orient including lamps and screens (tel. 782–9577).

*Hammacher Schlemmer,* with its unusual range of merchandise, is at 615 N. Michigan (tel. 664–9292).

## Looking for Bargains

Because it has always been America's center for mail-order catalog sales, Chicago has some exceptional bargains at special surplus stores operated by those companies. These feature overstocked merchandise, discontinued items, returns, sometimes scratched, dented, or whatever. *Sears Catalog Supplies* at 5555 S. Archer (tel. 284–3200), offers varies merchandise at 20–80 percent savings.

These warehouse type, no-frill stores in the pipe-rack display tradition usually spell big savings for the shopper, but they're often well-kept secrets, since retail shops normally are not overjoyed by the competition. *Clothing Clearance Center,* 1006 S. Michigan (tel. 663–4170), offers men's designer suits at substantial savings. *Chicago Shoe Outlet,* 3167 N. Lincoln Ave. (tel. 348–0555), has men's shoes at a discount. *Gingiss Formal Wear Warehouse,* 555 W. 14 Place (tel. 829–1188), sells new, used, close-out, and irregular formal clothes at savings of 40 percent and more. *Handmoor,* 70 E. Randolph Ave. (tel. 726–5600), is known for good-quality clothes at good prices, normally 20 percent off, with frequent sales. *Cut Rate Toys,* 2424 W. Devon Ave. (tel. 743–3822), has walls lined with toys and stuffed cardboard boxes marked 3 for $1.00.

*Todd's Factory Outlet* has a no-frills store at 2727 N. Mannheim, Franklin Park (tel. 451–0024). Frye products sold at a discount there are boots, shoes, bags, and briefcases with minor factory defects. *Lands End Outlet* has 2 places on N. Elston, 2317 and 2241 (tel. 384–4170 and 276–2232). Overstocked merchandise, factory seconds, and discontinued items are sold at 10–60 percent off. *Coats, Coats, Coats,* Willow & Phingston, Glenview (tel. 291–0333), features top name designer fashions at 30–50 percent off.

*Spiegel Outlet Store* has nine area locations selling discounted designer fashions. *Entre-Nous Designer Resale Shop,* 21 E. Delaware Place, is one of many in the city selling designer clothes at a fraction of their original cost (tel. 337–2919). Check yellow pages for others handling vintage collectible clothes.

For the ultimate experience, consider Maxwell Street, the old pushcart market where many immigrant merchants got their start. The buyer can still expect high pressure and lots of bargaining.

## Special-Interest Shopping

Book lovers seek out *Abraham Lincoln Bookshop,* 18 E. Chestnut (tel. 944–3085), where Lincoln-expert Ralph Newman has an overwhelming collection of Lincolniana and Civil War history. *Kroch's and Brentano's,* 29 S. Wabash (tel. 332–7500), is one of the giants, a massive operation with 16 branch stores; *B. Dalton* and *Waldenbook's* each has several bookstores scattered across the city and suburbs. For the rare and unusual, collectors will be interested in *Hamill and Barker,* 400 N. Michigan (tel. 644–5933), with first editions and early English classics, and *Kenneth Nebenzahl,* 333 N. Michigan (tel. 641–2711), where the emphasis is on early American works, plus rare prints and maps.

Local museums like the *Art Institute* and *Field Museum* have interesting gift shops that carry colorful prints, books, and items relating to the treasures on display.

If cooking is your thing, *Crate and Barrel* with 7 locations has everything imaginable in the way of gifts. The food section at *Marshall Field* (tel. 781–3668) has an excellent gourmet shop. *Kuhn's Delicatessen,* 3051–53 Lincoln Ave., has an impressive selection of gourmet imports and a remarkable wine selection.

People drive from miles around to browse through *Hubert Hoffmann & Sons Florist,* Ridge (Gross Point) Road at Isabella on the Evanston-Wilmette border across from Lovelace Park. Acclaimed by local food editors for the year-round selection of over 50 different herbs (including specimen-sized bay laurel trees, rosemary bushes, lavender, thyme, and old-fashioned scented geraniums), this large garden center and florist dates from 1908 and specializes in the unusual (tel. AL 1–3300). Closed mid-July to November. Their Memorial Prairie Gardens can be seen from the street throughout the summer.

For antiques, there's *Donrose Galleries,* 751 N. Wells (tel. 337–4052), crammed with French, English, and continental wonders of all sizes and descriptions. And *Sothebys* now has an office at 325 W. Huron (tel. 664–6800). But for the ultimate discovery, read the want ads and locate a genuine house sale, either in the city or on the North Shore, where a lifetime collection of basement-to-attic treasures is often sold at estate sales. So many people turn up looking for bonanzas at these things that numbers are distributed on a first-come basis—but even so, some estates yield rare finds.

 **NIGHTLIFE AND BARS.** Mention Chicago's night life scene and many out-of-towners still have visions of a Capone-era beer truck delivering illicit booze to a back-alley speakeasy. That reputation has been hard to live down. The recent film *The Untouchables* has introduced a whole new generation to images of Elliott Ness raiding mob-associated watering holes. Despite what you may have seen on the silver screen, that image is truly a part of the past. Today Chicago's bar and night life scene is not unlike that in other major American cities. Obviously, the unique midwestern flavor of the city and the traditions of its ethnic neighborhoods continue to create a distinctive personality.

Currently, there are 6,300 liquor licenses in Chicago. These represent establishments as diverse as the city's population, ranging from sophisticated to sleazy. Some are issued to prestigious celebrity hotels, where the mood is subdued, low-key, genteel. Others, frequently changing, cover lively "in" spots considered trendy, fashionable, chic. These often come and go like a flash-in-the-pan performer, lasting only as long as the current craze, then reemerging under another name, with different decor, and a new personality. There are Mom-and-Pop grocery stores selling packaged goods across town from supermarket-sized liquor stores noted for carrying almost every drink produced worldwide.

The latest phenomenon is the sports bar, catering to enthusiastic followers of baseball, football, soccer, basketball, etc. Like-minded visitors would enjoy the camaraderie among fans in some of these; others are located in areas where one would not feel safe, even with Al Capone as a bodyguard! The greatest percentage of licenses is issued to family-operated, neighborhood bars.

A cross section of all these is covered in this section. Emphasis is on establishments in locations both easily accessible to visitors and of some special interest to them. It is particularly difficult to separate nightclubs by category, since one evening pop jazz may be the attraction, with a switch later in the week to punk rock. Some clubs are so diversified they really fit into several categories.

The areas covered include:

*Downtown:* The so-called heart of the city starts at the lakefront and moves west across the Loop. It stretches from the Chicago River on the north (about 400 North) to Congress Street on the south (about 400 South). The action here is often business-oriented, with a good choice of daytime and early evening favorites that quiet down when the after-work set heads back to home.

*Off Downtown:* Just north and west of the main business area, this section starts around the giant Merchandise Mart (housing NBC) and Apparel Center and extends out through the River North area.

*North Michigan Avenue:* This is the elegant side of the city, the "Magnificent Mile" of pricey prestige shops, premiere hotels, and high-fashion lifestyles. It reaches north from the Chicago River (about 400 North) to Oak Street (about 1000 North).

*Rush Street:* In its heyday this was the city's main night life district. Still bustling at night, but by day it looks rather like an old movie theater when the lights go on and patrons can see its shabbiness, with popcorn and gum sticking to the floors.

*Old Town:* Over a decade ago there was considerable renaissance and restoration in this neighborhood—imaginative boutiques, antique shops, popular bars. Now its character seems to ebb and flow like the tide. Although it has lost a lot of its original appeal, there are still some places worth a visit.

*Lincoln Park:* Chicago's trendy town house, condominium, and apartment dwellings set the restored Victorian mood of this area, which takes its name from sprawling, lakefront Lincoln Park. The area west of the park between Armitage Ave. (2000 North) and Diversey (2800 North) is full of popular new-wave establishments in rehabbed buildings.

The category *Potpourri* offers a sample of diverse neighborhoods.

**A word of caution:** Neighborhoods can change quickly in Chicago, as in most major cities. The most fashionable bar or nightclub in a high-rent district may be only one block from the fringes of a seedy, changing district. Walk in the wrong direction and it is not difficult to encounter trouble. It is always a wise precaution to ask your desk clerk or concierge about the safety of the area you intend to visit. They won't be offended, and will appreciate your common-sense approach, and may also have some up-to-the-minute suggestions on the newest "in" places. Be leery of taxi drivers steering you to so-called "hot spots."

There are places where it is safe to stroll day or night, like Michigan Avenue, which is the city's favorite promenade. There are others, like Rush Street's nightclub strip, where one can stroll but might get hustled along the way. Still other neighborhoods of interest to visitors are where it pays to take a cab and keep your eyes open. It is thus the world over. Don't let your common sense take a vacation just because you have.

## NIGHTLIFE

### Blues

**Blue Chicago.** 937 N. State; 642–6261. One of the city's best blues bars, and the only one located in the Rush Street area. Live music seven nights a week with a drink minimum on weekends.

**B. L. U. E. S.** 2519 N. Halsted; 528–1012. Live music seven nights a week in a clubhouse atmosphere. Small but internationally known among fans. Reasonable prices. Limited seating, so suggest arriving early.

**Kingston Mines.** 2548 N. Halsted; 477–4646. A very funky club that alternates live music on dual stages seven nights a week. Like to play until the sun rises. Blues, Lily's, and The Wise Fools are all nearby so blues enthusiasts can circulate between them. Cover, no minimum.

**Lilly's.** 2513 N. Lincoln; 525–2422. The ageless Sunnyland Slim is one of the popular house acts in this cozy club where one can hear some of Chicago's old-time blues artists. Live music Thursdays through Saturdays at 9:30 P.M. Cover on weekends.

**New Checkerboard Lounge.** 423 E. 43d St; 624–3240. Located in one of the city's worst neighborhoods, you'll feel more than welcome once inside the door. Musical regulars include Magic Slim, Johnny Christian and B.B. Odom.

**The Wise Fools Pub.** 2270 N. Lincoln Ave.; 929–1510. A cross between a college hangout and a nightclub. On busy weekends you may have a long wait in the bar before finding space in the modest-sized music room. Music starts at 9:30 every night, featuring blues, big band jazz, and a few pop acts. Cover; minimum on Saturdays.

### Cabaret

**Cabaret Gentry.** 712 N. Rush St.; 664–1033. Back in the 1880s, this was the elegant home of one of Chicago's first society hostesses. Today the old mansion houses a basement bar, main-floor tavern, and an intimate showroom. Attracts a large gay clientele. No cover, no minimum. Often features pop pianists who favor audience requests.

**CrossCurrents.** 3206 N. Wilton (north of Belmont at 950 W.) 472–7884. Locally noted for offering some of Chicago's most innovative bookings. An unusual blend of folk, rock, satire, jazz, and theater. Large lobby bar plus outdoor café and performance room, bakery, and assorted rehearsal rooms. Something offbeat is always happening.

**Miomir's Serbian Café.** 2255 W. Lawrence; 784–2111. Yugoslavian food is served to the accompaniment of Russian, Balkan, and Italian singers. Gypsy orchestra, violinists, and a rare cimbalon lure diners onto the dance floor. No cover or minimum.

The **Raccoon Club.** 812 N. Franklin; 943–1928. Very trendy, new art deco cabaret reminiscent of a classy supper club from a '30s film. Live entertainment seven nights a week includes jazz, comedy, cabaret, and blues. Cover; minimum on weekends.

The **Roxy.** 1505 W. Fullerton; 472–8100. Movie memorabilia in the outer bar complements the live pop, folk, jazz, rock, and comedy entertainment in the main room. Food offerings include the "Hedda Gobbler" (turkey club) and "Chili Chaplin." Cover; minimum on weekends.

**Toledo Restaurant.** 1935 N. Sedgwick; 266–2066. A flamenco nightclub with performers from around the Latin world. Cover and minimum.

## Comedy

The **Clout Club.** 2438 N. Lincoln; 472–2582. Located in the backroom of Nightcaps, in the heart of Lincoln Park's entertainment district, this club's specialty is political humor. Shows Wednesdays through Saturdays. Cover and minimum.

**Second City.** 1616 N. Wells; 337–3992. The list of famous Second City graduates is longer than the credits for "Saturday Night Live" and includes Joan Rivers, Robert Klein, and the late John Belushi. Always innovative, it is a continual source of bright new talent. You can buy a ticket for the main show, then stay for the additional improvisational performance afterwards. Or come at about 10:30 P.M. and just see the improvisations without a ticket. Still a Chicago headliner after 27 years.

**Zanies.** 1548 N. Wells; 337–4027. Zanies is just down the street from famed Second City, their inspiration. A fun place that enjoys being outrageous. Top Chicago comedians are augmented by acts which regularly appear on "The Tonight Show" and "Late Night with David Letterman". Two-drink minimum, plus cover charge.

## Country

The **Lakeview Lounge.** 5110 N. Broadway; 769–0994. A taste of the South in the heart of the North Side's Edgewater neighborhood. Tiny, yet friendly, bands play Wednesdays through Saturdays until 4 A.M. from a tiny stage located behind the bar. No cover or minimum.

**Nashville North.** 101 E. Irving Park Rd., Bensenville; 595–0170. A sprawling and popular nightspot located minutes away from O'Hare Field, complete with a western wear boutique on the premises. Live music Wednesdays through Sundays featuring the house band and occasional national stars. Cover charge.

**R & R Ranch.** 56 W. Randolph; 263–8207. The Sundowners have been performing live country music in this unlikely location for 25 years. Old-time basement-level bar next door to the Woods Theatre is crowded with enough western memorabilia to fill a museum. Reward posters, animal skulls, and Indian rugs line walls along with valuable antique gun collection. Chili heads the menu.

## Disco Dancing

**Baby Doll Polka Club.**l 6102 S. Central; 582–9706. With the largest Polish population outside Warsaw, it seems natural that Chicago should have a first rate polka club. Ed Korosa plays a lively accordion and bouncy music keeps everyone moving. Music starts at 9:30 P.M. Fridays and Saturdays; at 5 P.M. on Sunday. No cover or minimum.

**BBC.** 9 W. Division; 664–7012. There is a big screen for watching sports events and a large dance floor that attracts what is locally known as the Near North singles crowd. Open until 4 A.M.

**Clubland.** 3145 N. Sheffield; 248–7277. A huge entertainment complex featuring a mind-boggling array of 75 TV monitors and five large video screens showing music videos and specially-produced comedy material. The primary clientele is made up of well-dressed young singles, who fill the large dance floor to the sound of classic rock music. Open Wednesdays through Saturdays; cover.

**Exit.** 1653 N. Wells; 440–0535. One of the original video dance clubs. Sunken dance floor backed by a large movie screen mixes vintage films with new wave, heavy metal. Not for the timid.

**Limelight.** 632 N. Dearborn; 337–2985. Chicago's latest conversation-stopper is an eclectic, modernistic disco in the fortress-like former home of the Chicago Historical Society. Don't be surprised if guests and staff have hair colored like the rainbow. One local night-life critic labeled it "art deco gone tutti-frutti." Depending on your mood, you can dance, ogle the colorful crowd from a gallery, or escape to the quiet of the Dome Room. Branch of London and New York Limelights.

**Neo.** 2350 N. Clark; 528–2622. A post-midnight hangout with a large dance floor, plenty of neon, and loud DJ dance music. Cover on weekends.

**Riviera Night Club.** 4746 N. Racine; 769–6300. A beautifully renovated movie palace turned dance club in the somewhat seedy Uptown neighborhood. The huge dance floor accommodates the well-dressed mid-20s to mid-40s crowd to the sound of DJ-spun neo-disco music. Open Fridays and Saturdays until 4 A.M.; cover.

**Snuggery.** 15 W. Division; 337–4349. At the moment the Snuggery is considered one of the more fashionable singles bars. Lots of brass and plants. Dance floors on the first and second levels attract a cosmopolitan crowd.

**Tania's.** 2659 N. Milwaukee; 235–7120. Wednesday through Sunday, this handsome restaurant draws a stylish and diverse Hispanic crowd with good salsa bands. Music starts at 8 P.M., 9:30 P.M. on Friday and Saturday. No cover.

## Folk/Pop/Rock

**Biddy Mulligan's.** 7644 N. Sheridan; 761–6532. This large room in Rogers Park plays so many kinds of music it is hard to categorize. Blues, rock, reggae, and big band jazz. Arrive early for a good seat. Music starts at 9:30 P.M. featuring both local and national names.

**Cabaret Metro.** 3730 N. Clark; 549–3604. Located near Wrigley Field, this is Chicago's top live rock venue, with an emphasis on new wave and underground acts from all over the world. There's plenty of dance floor space, both in the main room and in the downstairs Smart Bar. Open until 4 A.M.; cover.

**FitzGerald's.** 6615 W. Roosevelt Rd., Berwyn; 788–2118. Bill FitzGerald has re-created a big-city salute to old-time roadhouse memorabilia. It's all there, from deer heads on the wall to the down-home neighborliness of staff. Visiting musicians range from Cajun bands and Vanessa Davis to rock, big band jazz, blues, and folk.

**Irish Village.** 6215 W. Diversey; 237–7555. Emphasis is on the ould sod with corned beef and cabbage the Tuesday night special, plus barbecued baby-back ribs, good ale, and folk singers. Live entertainment six nights a week. Showtime Friday and Saturday 9 P.M.

**Orphans.** 2462 N. Lincoln; 929–2677. You can enjoy drinks and conversation in an outer room with a bar, then retire to a music room in the rear where jazz, rock, blues, and folk music alternate. Comfortable and casual. Cover and two-drink minimum.

**Park West.** 322 W. Armitage; 929–5959. A nationally renowned "showcase" club featuring top national pop, rock, R&B and jazz names with state-of-the-art lighting and sound and a classy environment. Expensive.

**The Wild Hare.** 3530 N. Clark; 327–0800. Visitors might be surprised to learn that Chicago has a large Jamaican community. That translates into a number of excellent reggae bands playing at this warm and friendly club not far from Cabaret Metro. Music at 10:30 nightly; cover.

## Hotel Lounges

Some of the city's most glamorous, sophisticated cocktail lounges are found in its prestige hotels. In recent years there has been a decided trend toward establishing traditional English-style hotels here—low-key, understated, very much in London's Knightsbridge tradition. These, added to Chicago's already existing luxury hotels, offer some worthy possibilities for an after-shopping cocktail, pre-dinner drink, or nightcap. It can be an interesting way to experience a hotel even if you aren't staying here. Here are only a few of some interesting possibilities:

**Ambassador East.** 1301 N. State Parkway; 266–0360. *The Pump Room* is the place where coast-to-coast celebrities detrained in the pre-jet age and headed for booth #1. Still elegant and especially popular with singles. *Byfields,* located in the same hotel, features piano music in the English Parlor-styled front bar and occasionally top music and comedy names in the back cabaret. A prestige place.

**The Drake.** 140 E. Walton at Michigan Ave.; 787–2200. There are several fine choices here. Sit around the fountain in the palmy, paneled, Edwardian elegance of the *Palm Court;* try the *Coq d'Or* as Queen Elizabeth did on her visit; or join the thousands who have carved their initials in the much acclaimed *Cape Cod Room*'s lounge. No one can afford to build hotels in this grand baronial style today.

**Hyatt Regency.** 151 E. Wacker Dr.; 565–1234. Dramatic waterfall lobby is focal point for a variety of stylish bars.

**Knickerbocker-Chicago.** 163 E. Walton; 751–8100. *Limehouse Bar* and blond-oak paneled *Prince of Wales* bar are quiet and relaxing retreats.

**Mayfair Regent.** 181 E. Lake Shore Drive; 787–8500. Hand-painted Chinese murals of the large *Lobby Lounge* help make this one of the most attractive rooms in the city. Decor and mood are reminiscent of a town-house mansion.

**Park Hyatt.** 800 N. Michigan on Water Tower Square; 280–2222. This is a totally new concept in Hyatts—smaller, intimate, and quite wonderful. Drinks are served in its intimate lobby to the sounds of piano or guitar music and in *La Tour's* very French restaurant bar.

**Ritz Carlton.** 160 E. Pearson just off Michigan Ave.; 266–1000. Take the elevator to the 12th floor and enter the garden-like *Greenhouse Bar* complete with large fountain, or opt for the plush, more nightclubby atmosphere of *The Bar of the Ritz.*

**Tremont.** 100 E. Chestnut. 751–1900. *Cricket's* is another of those low-key, high-class, club-like settings where celebrities and socialites like to relax.

**The Whitehall.** 105 E. Delaware; 944–6300. Their *Lobby Bar* exudes the quiet, traditional atmosphere so typical of an upper-class London hotel.

**Westin.** 909 N. Michigan; 943–7200. Bookshelves lining the walls of the Lion Bar give it a cozy private den atmosphere. It features live entertainment at 6:30 P.M.

## Jazz

**Andy's.** 11 E. Hubbard; 642–6805. Andy's is an informal, laid-back club that begins its day with jazz at noon Wednesday through Friday, serving food to 4 P.M. No cover for noon shows. Evening performances 5–8 P.M.; Friday until 8:30 and again from 9 to 12; Saturday 9 P.M. to 1 A.M. The Rhythmmakers, Ears with Bobby Lewis, and Eric Schneider are among performers.

**The Backroom.** 1007 N. Rush; 751–2433. Although this is one of the city's smaller jazz rooms, it features first-rate talent. Don't be discouraged by appearances—it was once a horse barn now fancied up. Shows start around 9 P.M. Two-drink minimum.

**Billy's.** 936 N. Rush; 943–7080. The lounge bar of this nouvelle cuisine Italian restaurant has a cozy atmosphere with its own jazz trio. Moderately expensive, like much of Rush St. On the upper level.

**Blondie's.** 936½ N. Rush; 280–0963. A no-frills jazz club on the lower level of Billy's (see above).

**Bulls.** 1916 N. Lincoln Park West; 337–3000. Intimate cave-like cellar level features a number of jazz acts beginning at 9:30 every night. This is an old-timer with emphasis on jazz vocalists.

**Dixie Bar & Grill.** 225 W. Chicago; 642–3336. Hot jazz and food in a Cajun setting Mondays through Saturdays, where diners occasionally overwhelm the music. No cover or minimum.

**The Empire Room.** Palmer House Hotel, State and Monroe; 726–7500. This gilded beauty looks like a transplant from Versailles and is a setting for a pianist during noon lunch. One of the most beautiful rooms in Chicago.

**George's.** 230 W. Kinzie; 644–2290. A supper club with emphasis on northern Italian food. Curving back-lit glass brick bar is a conversation piece, and tiered seating provides good views of the performers. Cover charge with two-drink minimum.

**Gold Star Sardine Bar.** 666 N. Lake Shore Dr.; 664–4215. A Chicago phenomenon, this tiny club has managed to snare such acts as Tony Bennett, Liza Minnelli, and the Count Basie Orchestra. Even on an ordinary evening featuring piano jazz, this is a fun spot on the Magnificent Mile. Music Mondays through Saturdays at 7 P.M. Drink minimum.

**The Green Mill.** 4802 N. Broadway; 878–5552. This Uptown nightspot has a lot of history, dating back to the days when Al Capone was a frequent visitor. These days jazz flows nightly until 4 A.M. in an atmosphere dripping with character. Cover, no minimum.

**Joe Segal's Jazz Showcase.** Blackstone Hotel, 636 S. Michigan; 427–4300. World-class jazz in an elegant setting reminiscent of café society. Attracts a dressy, classy audience every night. Cover charge.

**Moosehead Bar & Grill.** 163 W. Harrison; 922–3640. Large, friendly spot in the south Loop area. Crowded with everything from Mayor Daley posters to Coca Cola bric-a-brac. Noted for its jazz and good hamburgers.

## Piano Bars

**Acorn On Oak.** 116 E. Oak; 944–6835. A Chicago institution, Buddy Charles entertains with a quick wit and a seemingly endless repertoire Mondays through Saturdays.

**Eugene's.** 1255 N. State; 944–1445. English club look complete with wood paneling, leather wing chairs, and whimsical miscellany, such as corporate logos, trucks, and pictures reminiscent of the 21 Club. Across from the classic Ambassador Hotel in the high-rent Gold Coast. Liquor list contains nearly 250 wines and more than 100 cognacs and armagnacs.

**Rendezvous.** 1400 N. Lake Shore Drive; 280–8800. Ask directions at the desk of this residential building. Then settle into plush velvet chairs and sip cognac, cordials, and sherries to the accompaniment of a contemporary pop and light jazz piano. Lots of atmosphere, hard to believe this was once a hotel pharmacy.

**Sage's On State.** 1255 N. State; 944–1557. The ultimate in intimate—a nine-stool bar with two tables, fireplace, Hogarth etchings, dance floor. Classic, very Gold Coast.

**Salvatore's.** 525 W. Arlington Place; 528–1200. The place to go if you like to listen to a pianist with dramatic flair. A special and elegant locale in Lincoln Park.

**Toulouse.** 49 W. Division; 944–2606. This 65-seat restaurant also features a piano bar. Posh with French flair.

**Zebra Lounge.** 1220 N. State; 642–5140. The Zebra motif of this intimate Rush St. area nitery extends to the booths, wallpaper, and scattered Zebra paraphernalia. Lively piano music seven nights a week.

## Sports Bars

Most major cities, particularly those with big-name sports franchises, have loyal sports fans. But Chicago, with professional football, basketball, soccer, hockey and baseball teams, tends to go off the deep end where sports are concerned. The result has been a whole new category of entertainment called the sports bar. These have been springing up not only near ballparks and stadiums, but also in the heart of night-life districts as well. Some are owned by local sports celebrities, others by sports enthusiasts.

**Arno's Place.** 4530 N. Lincoln; 271–4378. Owned by a member of the Chicago Sting soccer team, this friendly bar located in an old German neighborhood on the city's north side is a haven for soccer players and fans.

**Cubby Bear Lounge.** 1059 W. Addison; 327–1662. One could describe this as a neighborhood bar with a split personality. Located directly across from Wrigley Field's front gates, it is packed wall-to-wall with boisterous, cheering, thirsty Chicago Cubs fans on game days. But since the "Cubbies" play only day games at Wrigley, the bar takes on a completely different mood at night. Then bands playing punk, new wave, and next wave rock try to see if they can make as much noise as the sports fans. Prides itself on being "aggresively entertaining." Inexpensive.

**The Bleachers.** Waveland and Sheffield Ave. This is across from the bleachers entrance to Wrigley Field and a gathering spot for more Cubs followers who label themselves "bleacher bums."

**Ditka's/City Lights.** 223 W. Ontario; 280–7660. Chicago Bears' coach Mike Ditka is a part-owner of the glitzy restaurant that (no pun intended) bears his name. Adjacent to it is the equally classy City Lights club, the city's most upscale sports bar.

**McCuddy's.** 35th St. across from Comiskey Park, home of the Chicago White Sox. There are no phones, probably because the noise level on game days is so raucous no one would hear it ring. A down-to-earth Chicago legend, open only on game days.

**Ranalli's off Rush.** 24 W. Elm; 642–9500. Has a three-hole putting green on its second level. Really buzzes on sports nights. Uniforms cover the walls.

**She-Nannigans Irish Pub and Sports Bar.** 16 W. Division; 642–2344. Waitresses dressed as cheerleaders serve a singles crowd surrounded by paraphernalia ranging from Muhammad Ali's framed old workout clothes to a basketball backboard edged by walls of sports stars' autographs. 14 television monitors pick up games from across the country via satellite dish on the roof.

**Ultimate Sports Bar and Grill.** 356 W. Armitage; 477–4630. This was one of the first new-wave sports bars, complete with boxing ring and basketball hoop. Popular with Yuppie singles.

## Other Bars

There are many bars in Chicago that a visitor may want to explore and still stay within the area of his or her hotel. A selection of these, designated by area, follows.

### Downtown

Most of the bars described in this section are the midday/early-evening variety catering to business types, but they are also worth a traveler's attention. Granddaddy of them all and on most lists of all-time favorites is **Berghoff's,** 17 W. Adams, which has been pleasing customers since 1898. This beautifully wood-paneled, traditional Old World restaurant looks like a transplant from Heidelberg or Munich. One of its many unique attractions is its turn-of-the-century stand-up bar serving the gemutlichkeit Berghoff family's own brands of whiskey and beer, plus a varied menu of sandwiches and salads. A tremendously popular spot with Chicagoans and tourists who enjoy the bar, and lunch and dinner in its exceptional dining rooms. This is one of Chicago's finest and a great dollar value.

**Jesse Livermore's Champagne Cognac Bar,** 401 S. LaSalle St., is in the Traders Building, originally built in 1914 as the Fort Dearborn Hotel. The beautifully restored property is now a historic landmark. Plush, green velvet sofas, rich Honduran mahogany, and a fireplace provide great atmosphere for sampling 14 different kinds of cognac, 16 wines by the glass, and 35 champagnes. Various professions tend to congregate at specific sites. **The Sign of the Trader** in the lobby of the Board of Trade, 141 W. Jackson, and **The Broker's Inn,** 323 S. LaSalle, are popular with traders and brokers who begin arriving around 2 or 3 P.M. **Binyon's,** 327 S. Plymouth Court, is a restaurant and bar frequented by U.S. attorneys who work in the nearby Federal Building. Commuters have their after-work gathering spots, too. One is **King Arthur's Pub,** 200 N. LaSalle, an English pub that's also been around for a long time.

Slightly south is **Printers Row** at 550 S. Dearborn. This newly emerging south Loop district was once the city's printshop neighborhood and this restoration of an old printer's building dating to 1897 is typical of the area.

### "Off" Downtown

This area begins just north of the Chicago River, and includes the burgeoning River North area. When the giant Merchandise Mart and Apparel Center empty out at noon and 5 P.M., many occupants head for **Mad Anthony's** on the 15th floor of the Holiday Inn at the Apparel Center, 350 N. Orleans. For an even closer view of the river, there's **The Marina 300** in the bottom floor of Marina Tower, 300 N. State St. Ask to sit near one of its picture windows for a good view of the riverboat traffic and the lowering and raising of those giant bridges. At least once a year *The Medusa Challenger* comes through and works its jinx on bridges that go up and refuse to come down.

Around the corner from the Limelight is the popular **Hard Rock Cafe,** 63 W. Ontario, a veritable rock 'n' roll museum that also boasts excellent hamburgers and a good selection of imported beers. One of the city's lesser-known barroom treasures is the **Green Door Tavern,** 678 N. Orleans. The original bar dates back to before the Chicago Fire, and inside you'll find plenty of old time Chicago memorabilia.

Many bars in this region tend to have an ethnic flavor. **O'Sullivan's Public House** at 495 N. Milwaukee is Chicago-Irish with the kind of turn-of-the-century bar that television fans remember from John Wayne movies. Just across the street is the **Como Inn,** 546 N. Milwaukee, a large, sprawling Italian restaurant decorated in Chicago-Italian baroque. Its bar and **Cafe Pappagallo** serve amaretto coffee and Italian wines to a large repeat business. One of the best deep-dish pizza restaurants in town is **Pizzeria Uno,** 29 E. Ohio, and celebrities who make the Chicago scene sing its praises. **Sogni Dorati** is an expensive nouvelle restaurant at 660 N. Wells, while **Little Joe's,** 1041 W. Taylor St. near the University of Illinois campus, is a folksy reminder of the city's Little Italy district.

One of Greek Town's liveliest restaurants is the **Greek Islands,** 200 S. Halsted, with a bar that favors ouzo, retsina wines, and the subtle aroma of moussaka, oregano, and saganaki. The music may lure you down the block to the **Courtyards of Plaka,** 340 S. Halsted, and **The Parthenon,** 314 S. Halsted. It's almost like bar-hopping in Athens.

Not far from Greek Town is another classic restaurant and bar, **Barney's Market Club,** 741 W. Randolph. Dripping with Chicago history, it's a place where political king-makers used to cut deals while puffing mightily on their requisite cigars. Even if you're not a politician, you'll be greeted at the door with a traditional "Yes sir, Senator!" In a completely different mood, the **Baton Show Lounge,** 436 N. Clark, labels itself "home of the most lavish female impersonator shows in the world." Reservations 644-5269. Open 8 P.M. Wednesdays through Sundays.

### *North Michigan Avenue*

There is a small section of Chicago "underground," just north and south of the Chicago River below Michigan Ave. and Wacker Dr., that actually has two levels, with duplicate streets above and below ground. The out-of-town visitor who stumbles onto it feels he has descended into a mysterious underground maze. Not surprisingly, some of the city's more conversation-stopping bars are located here. **Billy Goat Tavern,** 430 N. Michigan, is one of them, reached by staircase from the upper level of Michigan Ave. It is a favorite haunt with newspaper employees who work only footsteps away (*The Chicago Tribune* is at 435 N. Michigan), and many a column has been hastily typed at one end of its bar. It's also the cheeseburger spot immortalized on *Saturday Night Live.* Also accessible from that lower level (as well as from the upper level) is **Riccardo's,** 437 N. Rush St., which caters to the same news clientele. Young, single professionals gravitate to the **Lower East Side,** 625 N. Michigan (lower level), while **Jerry's Deli & Pub,** 215 E. Grand, specializes in sandwiches and beverages to go. **The Inkwell,** 226 E. Ontario, is across from the Museum of Contemporary Art, near CBS, and attracts the young media crowd.

*Rush Street*

Over the years Rush Street has gained the unenviable reputation as the place conventioneers go to for a night on the town. Their free-spending ways have attracted the expected number of B-girls, muggers, pickpockets, jackrollers, strip joints, porn shops, and other sleaze. Portions of it have, unfortunately, degenerated into something between the Bowery and the Barbary Coast. Other sections have interesting shops, restaurants, and very "in" bars.

Although now surpassed by Lincoln Park's Lincoln Avenue/Halsted Street nexus of restaurants, nightclubs and shops, Rush Street still remains a popular spot with out-of-towners, partly because of its reputation and partly because of its proximity to most of the major hotels.

The blanket term "Rush Street" encompasses neighboring State, Dearborn, Maple, Elm and Division streets, and offers the city's highest concentration of nightspots. Be aware that the Rush Street area is also only a few blocks east of the city's most notorious public housing project, the Cabrini Green Homes. If in doubt about a particular place's location and safety, ask a native.

Among the more popular haunts on Rush Street (the so-called "Street of Dreams") are **Sweetwater**, 1028 N. Rush, and **Harry's Cafe**, at 1035. Both are havens for upscale singles. For a neighborhood bar atmosphere, **Remington's Saloon** at 1007 provides a nice respite. Division Street is filled with singles bars, led by the grandaddy of them all, **Butch McGuire's** at 20 W. Among the others are **P.S. Chicago** at 8 W., **Eddie's Rocket's** at 9 W., **Mother's** (made famous in the film *About Last Night*) at 26 W., and the **Snuggery** at 15 W. A. bit funkier than the rest is **The Lodge** at 21 W., which also features Division Street's best jukebox. If you're looking to sample the area's extremes, **Arnie's Cafe** at 1030 N. State attracts the area's "beautiful people," while the **Hange Uppe** at 14 W. Elm is a rambling, collegiate-style rock 'n' roll bar.

*Lincoln Park*

Located on the Near North side, this area is filled with live music clubs, and trendy restaurants. Places of interest range from the fondue and flamenco music combination at **Geja's Cafe**, at 340 W. Armitage; the relaxing **John Barleycorn**, at the corner of Belden St. and Lincoln Ave., featuring classical music and slides of great works of art; and the Irish bar geniality of the **River Shannon** at 425 W. Armitage.

A bit west is an area of singles bars rivaled only by Rush Street. These tend to be upscale places and include **Glascott's Groggery**, 2158 N. Halsted St., **The Beaumont**, 2020 N. Halsted (which features several rooms and an outdoor garden) and **The Store**, 2002 N. Halsted, which, like the Beaumont, is open until 4 A.M. A bit less predatory is **Nick's**, 1973 N. Halsted, whose chief lure is its jukebox filled with Motown and other baby-boomer oldies.

If you're in a nostalgic mood for the rock 'n' roll music of the '50s and '60s, **Jukebox Saturdy Night**, 2251 N. Lincoln, features a DJ spinning classic "oldies" from the back of a '57 Chevy. Masquerading as a neighborhood corner bar, the *Gaslight Corner*, 2858 N. Halsted, is also a hang-out for actors from the celebrated Steppenwolf Theatre, located across the street.

*Potpourri*

Of the grand total of 6,300 liquor licenses it is hard to pick out all the headliners in this space. As neighborhoods change and evolve, new finds emerge almost overnight. But scattered close to the city, in such diverse locations as Old Town, Lakeview, and ethnic sections of town, are a number of establishments regularly mentioned by Chicagoans.

In Old Town, the **Old Town Ale House,** 219 W. North Ave., is a funky joint which attracts an eclectic mix of artists, actors from the neighboring Second City, and just plain neighborhood folks. A block west at 319 is **O'Rourke's,** a long-time hangout for writers and intellectuals, where you'll find portraits of James Joyce, Sean O'Casey, and George Bernard Shaw on the walls and plenty of Guinness Stout on tap.

**La Canasta,** 3511 N. Clark, features pitchers of sangria and margaritas served on an enclosed patio, along with Mexican beer and exotic frozen drinks. The informal outdoor concept continues to grow in popularity. **Maple Tree Inn,** 10730 S. Western, features Cajun creole cooking and outdoor summer dining. Their bar serves a fiery Cajun martini and Dixie beer in long-neck bottles. **Moody's Pub,** 5910 N. Broadway, also opens a lively outdoor beer garden in summer.

For the artsy crowd with an interest in offbeat and new wave music and fashion, the old ethnic neighborhoods of the Near Northwest side, although off the beaten path, have much to offer. Those worth a look-see are the **Artful Dodger,** 1734 W. Wabansia, **Club Dreamerz,** 1516 N. Milwaukee, the **Rainbo Club,** 1150 N. Damen, **Phyllis' Musical Inn,** 1800 W. Division, and the **Get Me High Lounge,** 1758 N. Honore, the latter probably the strangest jazz club you'll ever encounter.

Those seeking traditional ethnic atmosphere will find it at places like **Zum Deutschen Eck,** 2924 N. Southport, in a large German restaurant reminiscent of a Rhineland inn. Costumed staff serve imported beverages and an oompah band plays on the weekends. **Resi's Bierstube,** 2034 W. Irving Park, has Bavarian flavor, more than 85 beers, and an impressive beer garden with grapes growing on trellises. **Schulien's,** 2100 W. Irving Park, features three generations' accumulation of memorabilia. One of their treasures is a copy of the Volstead Act, which was nailed on the front door by federal marshalls who closed it as a speakeasy back when mob beer trucks were trying to avoid Elliot Ness.

For more "finds," pick up a free copy of the *Reader,* which is distributed all over town and lists the latest entertainment happenings on the local scene.

If none of the above interests you, remember neighboring Evanston was the home of Frances Willard, and the gray board and batten house where she lived is still headquarters of the Women's Christian Temperance Union which she founded. It is open to visitors.

# INDEX

# Index

# FODOR'S TRAVEL GUIDES

Here is a complete list of Fodor's Travel Guides, available in current editions; most are also available in a British edition published by Hodder & Stoughton.

## U.S. GUIDES

Alaska
American Cities (Great Travel Values)
Arizona including the Grand Canyon
Atlantic City & the New Jersey Shore
Boston
California
Cape Cod & the Islands of Martha's Vineyard & Nantucket
Carolinas & the Georgia Coast
Chesapeake
Chicago
Colorado
Dallas/Fort Worth
Disney World & the Orlando Area (Fun in)
Far West
Florida
Fort Worth (see Dallas)
Galveston (see Houston)
Georgia (see Carolinas)
Grand Canyon (see Arizona)
Greater Miami & the Gold Coast
Hawaii
Hawaii (Great Travel Values)
Houston & Galveston
I-10: California to Florida
I-55: Chicago to New Orleans
I-75: Michigan to Florida
I-80: San Francisco to New York
I-95: Maine to Miami
Jamestown (see Williamsburg)
Las Vegas including Reno & Lake Tahoe (Fun in)
Los Angeles & Nearby Attractions
Martha's Vineyard (see Cape Cod)
Maui (Fun in)
Nantucket (see Cape Cod)
New England
New Jersey (see Atlantic City)
New Mexico
New Orleans
New Orleans (Fun in)
New York City
New York City (Fun in)
New York State
Orlando (see Disney World)
Pacific North Coast
Philadelphia
Reno (see Las Vegas)
Rockies
San Diego & Nearby Attractions
San Francisco (Fun in)
San Francisco plus Marin County & the Wine Country
The South
Texas
U.S.A.

Virgin Islands (U.S. & British)
Virginia
Waikiki (Fun in)
Washington, D.C.
Williamsburg, Jamestown & Yorktown

## FOREIGN GUIDES

Acapulco (see Mexico City)
Acapulco (Fun in)
Amsterdam
Australia, New Zealand & the South Pacific
Austria
The Bahamas
The Bahamas (Fun in)
Barbados (Fun in)
Beijing, Guangzhou & Shanghai
Belgium & Luxembourg
Bermuda
Brazil
Britain (Great Travel Values)
Canada
Canada (Great Travel Values)
Canada's Maritime Provinces plus Newfoundland & Labrador
Cancún, Cozumel, Mérida & the Yucatán
Caribbean
Caribbean (Great Travel Values)
Central America
Copenhagen (see Stockholm)
Cozumel (see Cancún)
Eastern Europe
Egypt
Europe
Europe (Budget)
France
France (Great Travel Values)
Germany: East & West
Germany (Great Travel Values)
Great Britain
Greece
Guangzhou (see Beijing)
Helsinki (see Stockholm)
Holland
Hong Kong & Macau
Hungary
India, Nepal & Sri Lanka
Ireland
Israel
Italy
Italy (Great Travel Values)
Jamaica (Fun in)
Japan
Japan (Great Travel Values)
Jordan & the Holy Land
Kenya
Korea
Labrador (see Canada's Maritime Provinces)
Lisbon
Loire Valley

London
London (Fun in)
London (Great Travel Values)
Luxembourg (see Belgium)
Macau (see Hong Kong)
Madrid
Mazatlan (see Mexico's Baja)
Mexico
Mexico (Great Travel Values)
Mexico City & Acapulco
Mexico's Baja & Puerto Vallarta, Mazatlan, Manzanillo, Copper Canyon
Montreal (Fun in)
Munich
Nepal (see India)
New Zealand
Newfoundland (see Canada's Maritime Provinces)
1936 . . . on the Continent
North Africa
Oslo (see Stockholm)
Paris
Paris (Fun in)
People's Republic of China
Portugal
Province of Quebec
Puerto Vallarta (see Mexico's Baja)
Reykjavik (see Stockholm)
Rio (Fun in)
The Riviera (Fun on)
Rome
St. Martin/St. Maarten (Fun in)
Scandinavia
Scotland
Shanghai (see Beijing)
Singapore
South America
South Pacific
Southeast Asia
Soviet Union
Spain
Spain (Great Travel Values)
Sri Lanka (see India)
Stockholm, Copenhagen, Oslo, Helsinki & Reykjavik
Sweden
Switzerland
Sydney
Tokyo
Toronto
Turkey
Vienna
Yucatán (see Cancún)
Yugoslavia

## SPECIAL-INTEREST GUIDES

Bed & Breakfast Guide: North America
Royalty Watching
Selected Hotels of Europe
Selected Resorts and Hotels of the U.S.
Ski Resorts of North America
Views to Dine by around the World

AVAILABLE AT YOUR LOCAL BOOKSTORE OR WRITE TO
FODOR'S TRAVEL PUBLICATIONS, INC., 201 EAST 50th STREET, NEW YORK, NY 10022.